Emerging Theories
of
Human Communication

SUNY Series, Human Communication Processes
Donald P. Cushman and Ted J. Smith III, editors

Emerging Theories
of
Human Communication

EDITED BY

Branislav Kovačić

State University of New York Press

Published by State University of New York Press, Albany
© 1997, State University of New York

For information, address the State University of New York Press,
State University Plaza, Albany, NY 12246

Production by David Ford
Marketing by Dana E. Yanulavich

Library of Congress Cataloging-in-Publication Data

Emerging theories of human communication / edited by Branislav Kovačić
      p.   cm. — (SUNY series in human communication process)
    Includes bibliographical references and index.
    ISBN 0-7914-3451-6 (alk. paper). — ISBN 0-7914-3452-4 (pbk. :
alk. paper)
    1. Communication—Philosophy. I. Kovačić, Branislav, 1957– .
II. Series.
P90. E397   1997
302.2'01—dc20   96–43768
                                       CIP

This book is dedicated to my daughter Sonya and my son Boyan, who frequently distract me but always remind me that the ideal world of books must be tempered by the richness of our shared experiences in the actual world.

Contents

Introduction

Branislav Kovačić

When Donald P. Cushman and I co-edited a previous book on communication theories (1995), we used a template of watershed research tradition consisting of three developed and intertwined components. First, at the philosophical level, each watershed research tradition has explicitly developed assumptions about the nature of communication, its purposes, and its significant domains of reality. Second, at the theoretical level, each watershed research tradition explicitly defines its constructs and specifies a web of relationships between them. This is part of each tradition that generates productive empirical research. Finally, at the practical level, each watershed research tradition articulates communication skills in the form of message strategies, tactics, and activities that need to be performed in order to achieve desired outcomes.

Such a template of a watershed research tradition is a useful backdrop for the present book on *Emerging Theories of Human Communication* for two reasons. First, it helps us to distinguish a received from an emerging theory of communication. Second, it suggests that an emerging theory is a symbolic product that mixes some old and some new components but in creative and significant ways.

It is the intention of this chapter to accomplish three goals. I will first briefly discuss some defining characteristics of an emerging theory. Second, I will critically summarize contributing essays. Finally, I will draw some conclusions.

CLUSTERS OF EMERGING THEORIES

There are three different clusters of emerging theories of human communication in this volume. First, an emergent theory may be formulated from within a homogeneous, well-established tradition. However, conceptual developments, especially at the theoretical level start to overgrow the original framework, and the original formulations become a distant template whose cohesive, integrative force is weakening (see Alexander, 1987). The case in point is new developments in media agenda-suing theory (chapter 5). Second, an emergent theory may be created from within a family of overlapping traditions. Theorists freely borrow constructs and methodological tools in order to establish a new theoretical foothold (see Wagner, 1984). A new theory of relational communication competence (chapter 2), a new theory of conflict communication (chapter 3), and a theory of new rhetoric and new social movements (chapter 6) were minted in such a way. Finally, an emergent theory may be based on a critical importation of relevant constructs from multiple disciplines which are then woven together by a communication framework (see Aldrich, 1988). Examples of such an approach to theory development are an interactional theory of peace (chapter 4), a new theory of communication and culture (chapter 1), and a communication theory of managing government competitiveness (chapter 7).

Let me now turn to a brief, critical summary of individual essays.

SUMMARY OF CHAPTERS

A conception of communication that is located in social scenes and sensitive to cultural variability is developed in chapter 1. Carbaugh, Gibson, and Milburn articulate the relationship between communicative practices in concrete social interaction and culture. The authors first spell out three basic assumptions and two axioms about communication. The first assumption is that communication exhibits some kind of systemic patterns. The second assumption states that systemic patterns of communication implicate social organization/structuring (of interaction, social relations, and institutions) and cultural meaning systems or beliefs and values (regarding persons, social action, and nature). Finally, the authors assume that communication is partly constitutive of sociocultural life. The axiom of particularity states that communication varies from community to community, and the axiom of actuality stresses the actual communication practices.

Carbaugh, Gibson, and Milburn then go on to define three basic concepts of their new theory of communication and culture. The first concept is the communicative scene—the specific place and specific occasion. The second concept is communication practice as a pattern of situated, message endowed actions performed in a scene(s). The third concept is cultural discourse, a system of communication practices that converge topically (discourses of religion, science, and education) and functionally (discourses of identity and action).

The authors conclude that (1) specific communicative scenes demand (2) particular communicative practices that activate (3) cultural discourses of identification/personhood and action. They offer two case studies to illustrate some of the ways social interaction and cultural performances can be integrated into explorations of communication conduct.

Communication competence, as it is manifested in interpersonal relationships, is defined by Wiemann, Takai, Ota, and Wiemann (chapter 2) as the joint creation of a mutually satisfying relationship by constructing appropriate and effective messages. Relational communication competence is a functional process based on an optimal but not necessarily equal distribution of control of messages by the partners for the duration of an encounter and across space and time of encounter.

Wiemann and his colleagues construct a relational model of communication competence that stresses unspecified links between interactional constructs such as goals, relational history, future expectations, and relational satisfaction. The authors' main interest is in the application of the model of relational communication competence to teaching competence skills.

In chapter 3, Cahn outlines and compares three traditional approaches guiding research on interpersonal conflict, then adumbrates an overarching paradigm of conflict communication, and, finally, discusses some implications of the new paradigm. Cahn examines the following three traditional approaches to research on interpersonal conflict: (1) the systems-interactionist approach to couples' conflict, (2) the cognitive-exchange approach to the role of conflict in relationship satisfaction and commitment, and (3) the rules-interventionist approach to disputes between divorcing spouses.

What is theoretically important, however, is that Cahn argues that the three approaches are becoming increasingly intertwined in an emerging, overarching paradigm of conflict communication. The systems-interactionist approach contributes its objective observation of partners' interdependent behaviors in dyads. The cognitive-exchange approach adds subjective self-reports of interdependent cognitions. Finally, the rules-interventionist approach offers objective observation of triads and rules that regulate interaction. Such an integration of theoretical contributions of the three approaches to conflict allows Cahn to articulate three propositions concerning conflict communication theory: First, the new theory specifies escalating versus de-escalating behaviors. Second, the new theory can isolate combinations of peoples' attributions and expectations that lead to negative or positive forms of conflict. Third, the new theory takes advantage of the fact that the agreed-upon rules enforced by mediators make it possible to resolve conflict in a mutually beneficial way.

Peace as a condition of the parties' relationship in interaction is the topic of chapter 4. Donohue proposes an interactionist framework for peace, and then discusses theoretical and empirical issues regarding the framework. Donohue argues that an interactionist framework for peace is based on communication behaviors such as interpersonal aggression and violence, and negotiation and mediation. He implies that peace is also a discourse, a form of talk.

Drawing on multiple theoretic and research traditions such as political science and international relations, psychological, marital communication, and criminal justice and sociology theoretical traditions, Donohue presents an interactionist framework for peace entailing four clusters of peaceful and nonpeaceful behaviors. First, unconditional peace requires high affiliation and high interdependence of actors. Parties are involved with one another in a cooperative manner, consider their relationship as unconditional, and interact in a mostly problem- or task-oriented exchanges. Second, isolationist peace is characterized by low affiliation and low interdependence between actors. Although parties are not fighting, they are not moving forward productively with their substantive agenda. They engage in less frequent and superficial information exchange, and prefer withdrawal. Third, conditional peace is like a courting relationship of high affiliation and low interdependence between actors. In such conditions actors remain friendly and polite, generally as an attempt to escalate the level of interdependence. They test one another to decide whether to expand interdependence and role obligations, and bargain constructively in good faith. Fourth, competition/aggression occurs within a framework of low affiliation and high interdependence between actors. Asserting rights and resisting obligations, especially when key, central, and defining rights have been violated, is the dominant type of interaction. The communication then carries almost a moral imperative and authority with it.

In chapter 5, Zhu and Blood describe emergence of media agenda-setting theory, analyze its relevant extensions, and outline its new frontiers. Media agenda-setting theory is built on three underlying assumptions: First, a content-specific effect (certain issues) is believed to be superior to a content-free effect. Second, theory focuses on an aggregate level effect (creating an agenda for the community as a whole). Third, the ultimate effects of agenda-setting may be that news coverage shapes public concerns about certain issues, which, in turn, act upon the policy-making process, political force and influence of social movements, or actual voting.

The authors articulate new and significant theoretical developments within a media agenda-setting research tradition in terms of five conceptual moves:

1. Issue competition, or whether agenda-setting is a zero-sum process in which the rise of one issue in the public arena is at the expense of another issue.

2. Use of nonlinear models to detect an upper ceiling (saturation point) for any issue salience, time-varying media impacts, and a path the public's attention follows.

3. Psychological mechanisms involved in agenda-setting.

4. Integrating mass and interpersonal communication.

5. This conceptual move is the most ambitious one. It attempts to go beyond the public agenda by specifying (a) the antecedents of media agenda-setting ("media agenda-building"), (b) the consequences of media agenda-setting ("policy agenda-setting"), and (c) the broader democratic context of agenda-setting.

Hauser and Whalen outline (chapter 6) the constitutive nature of the new rhetoric deployed by new social movements. They argue that the constitutive nature of the new rhetoric is based on a radical departure from rhetoric's ancient instrumentalism. Whereas instrumentalist rhetorical theory views the audience as pregiven, its constitutive counterpart posits that autonomous individual and collective identities do not exist free and independent of discourse. This view of rhetoric as a social practice focuses on shared problems, tolerance of interpretative differences in understanding the problems themselves, and a shared world of coordinated social action.

The authors spell out three theoretical postulates or general theory propositions of the rhetorical theory of new social movements:

1. Although anchored in material conditions, the interests of social actors do not predate their formulation and expression through rhetoric. In other words, social actors rhetorically mint new worldviews that then specify a complete set of practices.

2. Movement membership is an individual, extrainstitutional or organizational practice and social movement actors thus must negotiate between unstable individual and collective meanings.

3. Rhetorical situations are the product of choices made by the social actor.

Hauser and Whalen draw four implications for the practical realities of message design strategies. First, audience cannot be addressed in terms of shared interests. Second, the combat involving new social movements is less likely to be orchestrated or waged at the institutional level. Third, vernacular codes are used to express affiliation and personal identity. Fourth, the vernacular codes influence the length of time spent on a question, and the places in which discourse does or does not occur.

A new communication theory of competitive government is presented in chapter 7. Cullen offers a new model of competitive government based on three ingredients. First, the model incorporates trade-offs between three basic modes of management—high production, high autonomy, and high response. Second, the model states that implementation of change in the public sector requires performance management (i.e., that projects lead to operational outputs and real added value) and comfort-zone management (i.e., containing opposition of key groups to key changes). Third, the model stresses the need to manage the timing of change projects more strategically. The author specifies four different transition strategies to move toward the high-response mode:

1. Transitions based on the various Asian development (high production) models.

2. Transitions based on the deregulation of various planned (production-oriented) economies in Eastern Europe.

3. Transitions based on regulated expansion and internal development (the Western European experience).

4. Transitions based on devolution and the empowerment of subunits (the U.S. case).

Such transitions obviously require new concepts of leadership and communication for the public sector.

CONCLUSIONS

Let me now offer three brief observations regarding the formulations of new theories of human communication.

First, they all redefine the constructs of (1) actors, (2) action/practice, (3) order/structure, and (4) change/transformation explicitly in terms of communication.

Second, they borrow freely from the exiting traditions within the field of communication and related disciplines in order to start constructing new theoretical models. As a consequence, they engage in the initial specification of a web of relationships between constructs to the relative exclusion of the philosophical justification of their endeavor. In other words, they tend to ignore foundational debates.

Third, they all strive to have an impact on everyday processes. One result of such an orientation could be a new standard of practical relevance of theorizing about communication.

1

A View of Communication and Culture
Scenes in an Ethnic Cultural Center
and a Private College

Donal Carbaugh, Timothy A. Gibson,
& Trudy Milburn

One of the vexing problems for analysts of contemporary communication is the relationship between concrete social interaction and culture. With attention turned toward social interaction, various sequential structures of conversation and face-to-face interaction are currently being brought into view. Important devices are being unveiled such as the mechanics of turn-taking, person reference, corrections, compliments, openings, and closings. Understanding communicative devices like these, and the ways each is intricately structured in sequence, has helped us unravel the moment-by-moment character of conversation.

With attention turned toward culture, participants' conditions for meaningful social activity are being brought into view. Important premises which participants use to guide social interaction have become pivotal in some inquiries, such as the conception and interactive use of identities, social relations, indigenous sequences of talk, and communication codes. Identifying these cultural premises in conversation has helped us understand the meaningfulness of communication to participants, and the ways these meanings are socially negotiated through the symbolic practices of particular social scenes.

From one angle, social interaction is being subjected to the general interactive devices of face-to-face interaction. From the other, social interaction is being subjected to particular cultural premises for conceiving and conducting communicative action. Can students of communication bring into view both social interactive devices and cultural premises? Can communication theory be developed in a way that integrates social interaction and culture?

Our purposes in this chapter are to introduce and demonstrate one developing view of human communication that seeks to integrate interactive devices and cultural premises. Our basic theoretical goal is the development of a conception of communication that is situated in social scenes and sensitive to cultural variability. Our primary data are the actual communicative practices that people employ in those places. In this chapter, we discuss our general approach and demonstrate it with two ethnographic reports. The demonstrations to follow will apply our basic conception to communicative practices that are extracted from two human institutions, one an alternative, private college, the other an urban Puerto Rican Cultural Center.

HISTORY, BASIC ASSUMPTIONS, AXIOMS

The approach we adopt has diverse and important predecessors. One tradition we build with brings together language and culture, derives from Franz Boas, and has developed—through the works of Edward Sapir and Benjamin Lee Whorf—a view of language as a carrier and creator of views of the world. A tradition in rhetorical theory derives from Kenneth Burke and brings language—and other means of expression—into view as a symbolic activity in its own right. The culture theories of Clifford Geertz and David Schneider help develop the earlier rhetorical theory of I. A. Richards, which together create a view of meaning that is situated not in isolated words, or lexical items, but in systems—in the "interinanimation" as Richards calls it—of symbols, their meanings, and social use. A literature on rules theory formulated by Donald Cushman suggests ways of understanding meanings and uses of communication as legitimated, and standardized patterns of conduct. Each of these traditions of thought are precursors to our approach. Each has influenced our view of communication, and the ways we investigate it, respectively, through uses of language, symbolic activities, cultural practices, and communication rules.

More immediately, our approach is indebted to the ethnography of communication as developed by Dell Hymes (1972), and to cultural communication theory as proposed by Gerry Philipsen (1987, 1989). These approaches have been explicated and reviewed elsewhere (e.g., Carbaugh, 1995). With the former, Hymes draws our attention directly, and radically, to the shaping of communication in contexts and communities. With the latter, Philipsen (1989) guides us to the use of various communicative forms and styles that enact a communal function, or what he calls, a "membering" function of communication. Taken together, communication, in all of its media and meanings, is understood in the cultural contexts where it is lived, and according to the forms, styles, premises, and rules that are locally active, there.

This varied lineage has developed, for us, into three basic guiding assumptions which ground our studies of communication and culture. The three basic *guiding assumptions* about communication from our view are these: When communication occurs, it exhibits, or instantiates, not randomness, but some kind of systemic patterns; Systemic patterns of communication implicate social organization (e.g., the structuring of interaction, social relations, institutions) and cultural meaning systems (e.g., beliefs and values about persons, social action, nature); Communication is thus partly constitutive of sociocultural life (Carbaugh, 1995).

To these assumptions about communication, we add two basic axioms. First is the *axiom of particularity*. Wherever there is communication, and wherever there are technologies of communication, these are conceived, valued, and used in locally distinctive ways (Philipsen, 1992, pp. 10–13). For example, among some Native American peoples such as the Cherokee, if one lives a traditional way, one can (and should) learn by watching and listening to "the world." One need not speak, or participate verbally, in order to learn. However, one should listen aggressively, and do so respectfully, taking in all of the messages in one's environment (Sousa, 1994). "The world" is thus steeped in messages, if one just listens in the properly active ways. Knowledge is available to those who listen. For other people in the United States of America, it is common to require verbal participation as a way of creating, transmitting, negotiating about, and demonstrating knowledge. The examples show how conceptions of communication are particular and distinctive. Each is based upon different, cultural conceptions of the appropriate place and use of orality, indeed, in what is a medium— and media—of communication, what each can (and should be used to) do, how each is conceived and valued. Any possible medium of communication—from trees to talk—and the ways it can be used, and interpreted in social contexts (such as to teach and learn), is deemed particular and distinctive. Consequently, from community to community, or nation to nation, communication varies, and is thus in some degree particular to each.

Second is the *axiom of actuality*. There is already existent in any context, community, or nation, a system of communication practices. People organize their social lives through actual communicative customs that are already coherent and appropriate in their place. While any one system of practices may have limitless potential, or possibility, in any one context, community, or nation—as in the conception and uses of television—this endless potential or possibility can never be exhausted. Contexts for social and cultural action give actual form and meaning to social life, through the actual communication practices that have been and are now being used in those contexts. Focusing upon how actual practices of communication are actually getting done in those contexts, and what it means to those who produce, interpret, and use them, this assumes a central place in our approach, and thus demonstrates our second axiom of actuality.

In stating our assumptions, we seek to highlight how communication is a systemic and formative part of sociocultural lives. In stating our axioms, we wish to draw attention both to communication as locally particular, or distinctive to people and contexts, and to the actual practices that are being used by those people in their contexts of living. Our hope is not to deny the universalities or the possibilities of communication, but to bring knowledge of the particular and actual systems of communication that are already in use, up to parity with the universal and the possible potential in ways of living. One way of doing that, developed below, is to focus upon actual scenes, communication practices, and cultural discourses.

THREE BASIC CONCEPTS:
Scene, Communication Practice, Cultural Discourse

How does an investigator explore cultural features of social interaction? We build our response by implementing *a basic investigative tension*. This tension tacks deliberately between the specific communicative actions being used to construct any one occasion, and the system(s) of expressive practices—or the cultural discursive field—of which that occasioned action is a meaningful part (see Geertz, 1976).[1] For example, in what follows, we explore an occasioned utterance about "time" (e.g., "there's plenty of time and there isn't"), yet do so by collecting other such utterances about "time," and by exploring the larger symbol system (i.e., about "community") in which these utterances of time are being used. This tacking between a single utterance—or image or sound—context, similar utterances, and the system of expression in which each plays a part, helps us understand the role of an utterance, as well as the general shapes and meanings of a community's expressive system.

Within this general investigative process, we use a *descriptive theory* that is well-known to ethnographers of communication. This is the theory of Dell Hymes (1972), summarized with the mnemonic device, SPEAKING. Each letter suggests a question to be asked about communication, with the concepts, together, providing a rather holistic view of any communicative action (i.e., S, setting, scene; P, participants; E, ends, goals, outcomes; A, acts, sequences; K, key, tone; I, channels, media, instruments; N, norms for acting and interpreting actions, G, genre). This descriptive tool helps guide reports and analyses of specific utterances and contexts in which they are used.

In addition to the tension and Hymes's descriptive theory, cultural communication theory has also proposed that we investigate cultural forms of communication such as ritual, myth, and social drama, as well as the codes of belief and value that are active in such forms (Katriel, 1991; Philipsen, 1987, 1992). For example, how does a Puerto Rican coding of "community" create a diffuse geographic scene, but embrace an inclusive social sphere? Or, how does a ritual form of alignment among faculty and students at Hampshire College enact a leveling "communitas" in discussions? The general objective is to hear how potentially diverse people align their actions in mutually intelligible ways through communication practices (Philipsen, 1987).

In what follows, we develop three basic concepts that have helped us hear cultural features in contexts of social interaction. In discussing these constructs, we hope to provide one way of using the Hymesian program, and one way of implementing cultural communication theory, by tacking between descriptions of the pragmatic use of utterances in context and cultural interpretations of those utterances that are based upon the expressive system(s) of which each is a part. For our purposes in this chapter, it is perhaps useful to orient our investigations with these three general theoretical constructs, that is, scene, discourse, and practice.

Communicative Scene

The construct, communicative scene, brings into view both the specific place where communicative practice occurs, and the general "cultural landscape" being presumed in that place, such that the practice of the people takes the shape, and meaning, that it does. The concept of place draws attention to communication on *a specific occasion*, as a situated performance in which particular people are participating, and suggests focusing on the ongoing social practices among those particular people. This draws one's view to the momentary context of utterance (or image use, or sound). This provides a concrete view of context, "a turtle's eye view," keeping vision (or hearing) close to the grounds where people are actually talking. The concept of cultural landscape draws attention to a *system of expressive meaning* that is immanent in communicative occasions, and through them, implicates basic beliefs and values about people, relations, action, nature, and feeling. While this expressive system is implicated in various ways on specific occasions, it runs across other occasions as well. Conceiving expressive meanings in this way, then, provides a "bird's eye view," a scanning of the discursive terrain in order to gain perspective on each of its occasioned parts. Both views, of the turtle and the bird, offer useful insights; together, they draw attention to "discursive places," or occasions, to the particular utterances used there (words, images, sounds, etc.), and to the system of meaning being implicated in those very occasioned utterances (e.g., messages about being, relating, acting, dwelling, and feeling).

Communication Practice

The construct, communication practice, draws attention to a *pattern of situated, message endowed action* that is used in a scene(s). For example, the Puerto Rican Cultural Center schedules an annual dinner, a scene that both supports specific symbolic practices of "community," and plays cultural discourses to the contingencies it sets. Likewise for Hampshire College, classroom "discussions" create scenes in which specific kinds of practices are cultivated, and in which cultural discourses meet the contingencies of an academic life. Any communication practice plays into communicative scenes, and further implicates a part of the cultural landscape when it is in use. Because our construct of communication practice is situated in specific occasions of use, it is closer to the turtle's view, to the actual, concrete, details of social activity. In other words, a communication practice is a pattern of use (and meaning) in identifiable contexts, and requires descriptions of those very uses (and meanings) in those specific contexts in order to understand it. But also, communication practices implicate deeper premises, rules, or meanings about persons, actions, feelings, and nature, with these being creatively activated in the use of the communication practice. In this sense, communication practices are richly radiating as they both shape particular scenes and places, *and* as they also implicate meanings about living that go beyond those very scenes and places. To generate knowledge of a communication practice, then, is to describe a particular situated pattern in use, but it is doing so while being deliberately cognizant of a larger expressive system(s) of which it is a part—including premises about being, acting, feeling, dwelling. As a heavily descriptive and lightly interpretive concept, analyses of communication practices suggest a kind of turtle's eye view, grounded in its concrete place, but a turtle also with a sense of its variable terrain, with an eye toward the bird.

Cultural Discourse

The construct, cultural discourse, is a part of the symbolic culturescape that is significant and important to participants, and is thus "rich" with participant meaning (e.g., Geertz, 1976). Because a cultural discourse is deeply particular, and coheres various practices upon occasions, it requires heavy emphasis upon interpretive inquiry. These interpretations are formulated on the basis of a set of communication practices, which together comprise a cultural discourse. Cultural discourses are, in other words, immanent in communication practices, composed of specific communication practices, and draw attention to a system of symbols, premises, rules, or norms, and meanings that radiate within those practices (Carbaugh, 1991). Any one cultural discourse might imply a system of specific communication practices that converges topically (e.g., discourses of religion, science, education), or functionally (e.g., discourses of identity, action). In this sense, cultural discourses identify rich radiants of meaning within particular discursive practices, and are immanent in, and implicated by the particular communication practices of those places. To generate knowledge of a cultural discourse, then, is to describe actual communication practices, a turtle at a time, and subsequently to interpret systems of symbols, rules, premises, and meanings that radiate through those practices. As a lightly descriptive and heavily interpretive concept, analyses of cultural discourses suggest a kind of bird's eye view of the richly radiating turtles.

Analyses of communicative scenes then tack back and forth between particular occasioned uses and the "culturescape(s)" of which it is a part. The focus on communication practices anchors studies in actual moments of utterance (image, or sound), with a focus on cultural discourses providing the rich and deep web(s) of meanings (e.g., Geertz, 1973) being implicated through those very practices.

The demonstrations that follow show a special attention to two particular *communicative scenes*, some descriptions of specific *communication practices* that are actively used in those scenes, and some interpretive commentary on the *cultural discourses*, the premises, norms, symbols, and meanings, being implicated in those practices. Our analyses, we hope, point the way to a more comprehensive cultural analysis of these institutional communication practices.

COMMUNICATION AND "COMMUNITY":
Constructing Cultural Voice in Puerto Rican Cultural Center

One way to talk about personhood, being, or identity is to investigate it in the everyday talk of people in particular places and times. The particular practices of concern in this section involve activities that are part of the Puerto Rican Cultural Center which is located in Springfield, Massachusetts. The center was founded in 1976. According to its charter, its main purposes are to conduct educational and cultural activities, to facilitate the adjustment of Hispanic people into the mainstream of American society without sacrificing their cultural values, to promote and preserve Puerto Rican cultural heritage, to help develop a better understanding in Springfield of the Puerto Rican community, and to improve the relationship between the Puerto Rican community and other ethnic groups in the city.

The particular focal scene of concern in what follows is the annual dinner held by the center. Each year the Puerto Rican Cultural Center (PRCC) hosts a dinner banquet for its members, business people, and the "city fathers." Approximately 400 people attend. This dinner dance, which is typically held in November, is a celebration of the accomplishments and service that the center has performed through its staff, board members, and volunteers. The 1994 dinner, which is of particular concern to us here, had the theme: "Investing in Our Youth."

As a participant-observer, Milburn took field notes at the center for seven months. Primary data for what follows were generated from observations of the 1994 dinner, and extracts from the yearbook, which is a glossy covered collection of photos, advertisements, and statements about each annual dinner. The 1994 dinner was videotaped and, for the purposes of the following analyses, two, hour-long interviews were also conducted and audio-taped.

The Dinner as a Cultural Scene

The annual dinner dance is an evening affair lasting several hours. It usually begins with a cocktail reception, with a program distributed to each person who attends. The program includes the schedule of speeches to be made during the dinner, as well as the specifics about entertainment (e.g., music, dancing). As a cultural scene, the dinner can be analyzed through some of its key symbols, and their meanings.

Cultural Premises of Time, and Social Tension

The dinner is partly governed by a Puerto Rican conception of time. This sense of time has been suggested by Morris (1981) as fluid and flexible. The boundaries of this kind of time are not fixed by the clock, but are contingent upon the rather spontaneous, ongoing interactions of events. In other words, the particular and ongoing social activities and relations dictate how time is conceived, and events proceed on the basis of this natural, interactional ebb and flow, with little attention to the clock.

During the dinner, however, a tension became apparent between this conception of time and another. According to the dinner program, the activities within the dinner were based on a preset temporal schedule that was to be tightly regulated (i.e., each scheduled event was to begin and end at a prearranged time). The master of ceremonies, who was also the director of the PRCC, oriented to this "clock view" of time when he said, during his introductory remarks, that he did not want the dinner to be governed by "Puerto

Rican time." Also, throughout the dinner, and as keeper of the clock, the master of ceremonies kept referring to "time" as something that was in short supply (e.g., "for the sake of time," "at this time," "kept . . . to two minutes," "we're running behind time," and "there's plenty of time and there isn't").

Tension between these two conceptions of time was made evident during the speaking portion of the dinner. This portion of the dinner event was being governed by, what was to many Puerto Ricans, the less desirable, tight clock schedule. To these participants, this was undesirable on two counts: Time should not be governed by the clock but should be guided by current social activities; and the clock-guided speeches were delaying the more fluid, more highly valued, social time, yet to come. The latter events were known to be guided by "Puerto Rican premises of time."

The tension between these different premises of time increased as those who were scheduled to speak began operating on the basis of Puerto Rican time, yet were asked by the master of ceremonies (MC), to limit the time taken for their speeches. Consider this comment by the MC, made during the introduction of one of the speakers:

> The next speaker I want to come up here and say a few words. I need to say though, that we want to keep him short, sweet, and to the point, 'cuz otherwise we will be here late and I will not be responsible for the actions of the masses.

At another point, between speakers, the master of ceremonies oriented to the tension again by saying:

> We are asking that you stay, not only for the spoken part of our program, but also for the social event, to get to know your neighbor next to you.

Deep symbolic meaning lurks within these remarks. Essentially it says this: The formal business of the evening, that is, the official speeches, the "spoken part," must be and will be governed by clock time; the informal activities of the evening, the social event, may be guided by "Puerto Rican time."

As the events of the evening transpired, participants ably oriented to two standards for their practices: the latter "social," Puerto Rican standard, which is highly valued and deeply felt, and the former officious standard, which is often deemed essential by leaders (MC and others) for operating efficiently. It is precisely this dynamic between cultural premises of time that is a source of tension, at times, among members of this community, in that the tension exudes different and tensely related premises for acting and being in this community.

The continual focus on time in these utterances is thus a deeply symbolic practice. Two contrasting sets of premises for organizing social action are being played against one another through these conceptions of time. One gives priority to the clock, fixedness, efficiency; the other, to ongoing activities, fluidness, and the flow of relations. The former is valued by most of the public, official scenes in Springfield. The latter is valued by many Puerto Ricans and guides their preferred ways of living and doing business. "Time," then, and the tension between these different conceptions of it, expresses deep messages in the dinner event, among members of the PRCC community, and between Puerto Ricans and the larger Springfield community.

The dinner event, like the Springfield community, is not immune from cultural struggles, but is permeated by them, as is evident here. This tension, here exemplified through conceptions of time, is similarly expressed in other of the center's scenes, such as its board meetings, through other contrastive communicative means. Accomplished through these practices in this scene, is a cultural discourse, a discursive tension between times, that results occasionally in fractured social identities (e.g., between Puerto Rican leaders and Puerto Rican community members, and between Puerto Rican community members and others in Springfield) and their relations (e.g., of stress and strain). It is against this kind of tensional activity, and discourse, that elaborations, affirmations, and validations of "community" become especially important.

A Cultural Symbol: "Community"

Within the cultural scene of the annual dinner dance, a key symbol prevails. By exploring communication practices that surround this symbol, we can understand its meaning through its use. Utterances using the symbol, "our community," convey important messages about its members, its size, actions desirable within it, and attributes of its participants. In other words, this symbol is significant partly for describing the kind of person who can claim legitimate membership as a participant in "our community." The question being suggested is this: When reading or hearing phrases such as, "Puerto Rican Community," "service to Latino community," and "crime in our community,"[2] what assumptions need to be intelligible for understanding and acting within this "community"?

The symbol, "community," appears prominently with the pronoun "our" and less so with the definite article "the." This usage defines a primary social site for the center's activities, "our community," and values that social site. In turn, this site is symbolically contrasted with "the community," or "their community." One example of this contrast illustrates these uses of "community." In the 1993 yearbook, the "Chairman's Message" (p. 4) includes this passage:

> There are many issues of concern in our community, but the Puerto Rican Cultural Center can not stand alone when dealing with these issues. The community as a whole must unite with the Center, because it is in the numbers where we have the power.

In this utterance, "the community" should unite with "the Center." Also, "*the* community" is something broader of which "the Center" or "*our* community" is only a part. The utterance presumes, then—echoing the tensional theme of time above—that "*the* community" is not now united behind "*our* community," but needs to be, if "our" current communal lot is going to improve. In other words, "*our* community" is distinct from "*the* community," yet needs the support of "*the* community" to better itself.

Consider this second example in which "the community" is contrasted with "our community." An advertisement describes a local bank as "located throughout *the* community." The sense of "the community" used in this advertisement, contrasts with the sense of "our community" used above. The contrasting meanings suggest again that "our community" is a part of "the community" yet is distinct from it, and needs its support and services. "Our community," as a symbol, is used, then, to identify a prominent and valued social site, to make sense of that site as a distinctive place for "our" productive activities, and as a place that needs "the (larger) community" in order to achieve its goals.

When people at the annual dinner talked about community, they spoke about the Puerto Rican community as "our community." Terms that co-occurred with "our community" point to the boundaries of what this "community" is (and imply what it is not). The symbol community conveys a sense that is not confined to a small geographic area where the Puerto Rican Cultural Center is located. Rather, the sense of "our community" extends beyond this geographic place into a large inclusive social sphere in which all Latinos are members. The following passage by the executive director of the PRCC conveys this sense:

> We are a population that is pretty much spread. When we use the term community, y'know, we want everyone to feel that they're part of the Latino community.[3]

Community is intended and understood, here, in an inclusive, collective sense, in the spirit of "everyone." All "Latino" people, those of this "population," are welcome as a "part" of the community. This sense helps us understand why individual people in the community are not often referred to specifically. When individuals are named, great care is taken to assure the group that the individual is not separate from or outside of "our community." The term community is used to cultivate something that is symbolically holistic and inclusive, of which members are always connected, as a "part." The following excerpt further illustrates this conception of the relationship between persons and community:

> I think that within any community you have those who stand out. You want to make sure that, as part of the whole, that this person can stand out. Not out of the whole, but as part of the whole.

The person can (and should) stand out, but stands (and should stand) not alone, or on one's own, as an individual; she should make her mark within "our community," because she is not only enhanced by it, but is a part of it, and a potential aid for it.

So far, we have described the way "our community," as a symbol, is used in, and helps establish a particular communicative scene. We have heard how this symbol is associated with a tension (through "time") and expresses a cultural distinctiveness (between "our/the community"). When these symbols are used in the communicative practices of this Latino community, cultural discourses are hearable about who these people(s) are, about their conceptions and conduct of appropriate actions, about geographic and sociocultural boundaries, in short, about people being placed symbolically as members of "community."

More specifically, when the "our community" symbol is used, or when Puerto Rican conceptions of time are operative here, people are being cast symbolically as particular communal agents. When "our community" is spoken, implicated is a presumed and valued social group in which one acts, and is thus something, in- evitably, one acts as a part of, within, and for. Culturally, in this sense, one's "self" and one's actions are said to derive from and con- tribute to "our community." As this community model for the agent is used, members speak about actions that people, as such, can (and should) take. For example, the following actions have been dis- cussed as service to "our community": one should "serve," "give back to," "work for," "support," "empower," "organize," and "re- spond to," "our community." The basic potent meaning being acti- vated by these terms for cultural actions can be summarized in the form of a cultural rule: One should act in ways that help "our com- munity." To be deemed of "our community" is to act accordingly.

As that which is inevitably acted upon, "community" assumes a perennial, grammatically "object" position, and thus "our com- munity" becomes an everpresent object of action. As a member in "community," one is thus obliged to adopt a social stance or posi- tion that will improve "our" community, to be a member who acts accordingly, who will value our community, and help address its problems. In the process, as it was put in the 1990 dinner program: "The negative stereotyping and negative economical status of our community will be overcome." In short, our community is valued and could (and will) be better, so please act accordingly.

Because "our community" is valued, but also because it needs to be improved, it is expressed as having certain positive and nega- tive attributes. These attributes become readily interpretable by ex- amining the cluster of adjectives around the term "community." The positive characteristics of "community" include: "education," "strength," "pride," and "spirit." The negative attributes, or imper- fections include: social "needs," "issues," "bad influences," "crime," "problems," and a "poverty cycle." The characteristics of "our community" thus fall along a descriptive dimension of "strong–problem-ridden," with the first terms describing the "strong" side and the latter terms referring to the "problem-ridden" side. Through this usage comes a metaphor, "community" as a con- tainer, as something that contains individuals and their actions, and as something, like "individuals," that "has" needs, issues, and aspirations. While the symbol "community" is something to be ac- tively aided, when it is invoked, it often ignites a kind of "problem talk," a kind of call for constructive, communal action (Carbaugh, 1988). Within the annual dinner, the positive strengths as well as the weaknesses within the community are mentioned in an effort to elicit pride, and help from "everyone" who is interested.

The basic moral impetus for helping "our community" is strong, and is spoken of within a value dimension of blame-responsibility. For instance, before "running out of time," the keynote speaker at the annual dinner invoked this value when he attributed responsibility for acting, and solving community problems to all of the members of "our community" (including himself):

> We, in the final analysis, will be held to blame, for every young member of our community, who doesn't go on to higher education, and is denied the opportunity; for every young member of our community, who wants to work, but can't find a job.

The use of the term "our community" here by the keynote speaker, showed a robust cultural voice, that he was able to speak, he did speak, and was heard to speak in a culturally resourceful way. Here is a cultural discourse woven into his practice: "our community" is a part of "the community"; "the community" will not automatically offer what "our community" needs; "our community" is an inclusive and collective social space; "our community" largely encompasses and seeks to nurture each person; "our community" values "education" and "a job" for "every young member"; in turn, each person can (and should) serve "our community" by productively addressing its problems (i.e., lack of "education," no "jobs"): if not, "we, in the final analysis, will be held to blame." In communicative practices as this one by the keynote speaker, one can hear cultural discourses, models for communal being and acting at work, as cultural utterances and scenes are being symbolically cast.

In the analysis above, we can hear how a scene in the PRCC is set, how it is played through specific symbolic practices, and how those symbolic practices implicate basic beliefs for example, about being and acting. In what follows we explore a second institutional scene, and within it discover normative communication practices that implicate a cultural discourse about being an "active" and egalitarian learner.

BEING AN "ACTIVE" STUDENT:
Normative Communication at Hampshire College

Hampshire College—a small liberal arts college located in Amherst, Massachusetts—was founded in 1970 with the goal of offering a program in the liberal arts that was "something different, something non-traditional." In practical terms, Hampshire's program eschews the traditional "university" system based on credits, majors, and departments, and turns over to students the burden of making most of the relevant decisions about their own education. For example, students must answer for themselves questions like, "What will I study? What classes will I take? What individual projects should I complete to fulfill the requirements for my degree? Whom shall I ask to help me in this process?" By giving this responsibility to the student (rather than to disciplinary academic departments), Hampshire is said to be "completely different" from "mainstream" or "traditional" institutions.

However, with this "freedom" comes "responsibility." As one administrator said, "Sure, you can do what you want [at Hampshire] but you're going to pay for it." Following months of observations and interviews at Hampshire, it became clear that students are expected to "pay" for this "freedom" by adhering to a model of personhood (Carbaugh, 1988/1989) specific to Hampshire. That is, Hampshire students are expected to display that they are "active" and "self-motivated" learners who are "intellectually engaged" in their studies. As one fourth-year student said, "There's this sense that you have to be an intellectual go-getter to make it here." However, while Hampshire clearly expects its students to be "intellectual go-getters," the college has nonetheless established specific institutional scenes within which this "active intellectual engagement" can be learned, performed, and nurtured.

Doing "Active": The Classroom Discussion

At Hampshire, the classroom discussion functions as just such an institutional scene. Specifically, at Hampshire "discussions" serve as a primary symbolic form wherein students can show, both to themselves and to their professors, that they are actively participating in their education. As a central means by which Hampshire-specific meanings are created, shared, displayed, and celebrated, a close analysis of the classroom discussion is therefore in order.[4]

The setting of a discussion usually consists of a classroom with tables or desk arranged in a circle, so the participants—from 10 to 20 students and a professor (sometimes two or three professors)—can face one another. The act sequence of a discussion can vary greatly, but observational and interview data suggests that a discussion typically begins with a statement of general purpose offered by the professor (e.g., "Can theater be used to intervene into gender representation?") and then moves on to a more or less structured sequence of "sharing" individual verbalized thoughts, opinions, or impressions relating to the general topic. Individual student offerings seem to prompt some involvement from the faculty member, who, according to a fourth-year student, usually plays a facilitative role by drawing out student ideas (e.g., "I'm struck by Bernadine's point . . .") and by offering only enough information to "keep the discussion going." The sequence ends with a final probe for last minute participation (e.g., "Does anyone have anything left to say?") and with a concluding statement (e.g., "Next week's reading covers the nitrogen cycle. Any questions?").

Most significantly, however, this sequence is said to be guided by a set of interactional norms that regulate the proper enactment of the form. The foremost category of normative rules concerns student *participation* and the distribution of talk within the discussion. For students, the operative norm is "You should actively participate in discussion." Ideal discussions are said to be comprised mostly of students talking, with the amount of talking equally divided among all student participants.[5] In this sense, talking too much *and* talking too little are considered to be violations of this norm, and both activities are subject to communal sanctions. For example, students who talk too much are said by other students to "dominate" or "monopolize" the conversation, and those who indulge in such "domination" are often the subjects of complaints from other students. Additionally, students who "hardly say a word" are also subject to sanctions. The most dramatic of which is usually employed primarily but not exclusively by facilitators and is called "putting them on the spot." As one professor said, "I'll actually keep track. If you haven't talked yet, I'll insist: 'Now, what were you going to say?'." A more common sanction involves narrative evaluations faculty write for each student in the class at the end of the semester. Lack of consistent participation, according to student consultants, is negatively valued and will appear in your evaluation.

A second set of norms states that Hampshire students, like Boy Scouts, should *"be prepared."* Since students are given the "freedom" to plan their own education, they are expected to "motivate themselves" to complete the course readings. Because students are expected to have this "self-discipline," coming to class prepared to speak carries normative weight for students: it's one important way to prove to yourself and others (especially professors) that you are an active and committed learner. Moreover, unprepared students are said to be more likely to withdraw from discussions, placing the onus of responsibility for sharing and speaking back onto the professor. As one professor said, "the danger of [unprepared students] is that then the discussion really falls back on me—it stops being a discussion and starts being a lecture." This violation—coming to class unprepared—is also subject to sanctions from faculty members. Again, one professor said, "putting them on the spot" during a discussion is useful in that it reminds students of the preparedness norm. "I'm usually very up front with them about it," this professor said. "[I'll] say, 'you didn't do the work. Here's the answer. Write it down.' I get crabby when that happens."

Finally, students should *show respect* for the offerings of their peers during "discussion." As we discovered above, in ideal discussions, faculty and students are said to "take each other seriously" in the egalitarian spirit that "we're all inquirers together." To cultivate this spirit, one professor said, participants should not "belittle" each other's comments, instead, they should act as if "there's no such thing as a dumb question, no such thing as an unacceptable attitude." To Hampshire students and faculty, "respect" is accomplished mostly through inaction—that is, through *not* expressing scorn for a peer's intellect or ideas. This respect is said to be crucial because it creates an "atmosphere where it's safe to take risks, chances with ideas, where nobody's going to jump on you for saying the wrong thing." Therefore, "belittling" or aggressively criticizing a fellow participant's ideas is a clear violation and can wreck the "safe" atmosphere so meticulously cultivated by facilitators and students. Faculty members can remedy this violation in a variety of ways—from pulling the offending student aside after class to "stepping right in" and stating "that's not appropriate."

Taken together, then, these norms—prepare, participate, and show respect—combine to create and regulate a discursive scene conducive to the production of "active" student participation. This communal agreement at the level of form (i.e., we agree to participate, to prepare, and not to belittle each other) rather than at the level of content (i.e., disagreements about course material are, of course, allowed and even encouraged) is reminiscent of the normative structures said by Carbaugh (1990, p. 135) to operate within discourse on the Donohue television program. In both cultural scenes, the norms serve to create a discursive terrain within which "participation" can flourish. In essence, members of the Hampshire community assume that students who are "prepared" and who enter into a supportive and "respectful" environment can legitimately be expected to "participate" actively in discussions. Given the normative power of these rules, it is easy to understand how, as one professor said, Hampshire discussions can be more difficult to end than to begin.

"Discussions," then, at Hampshire, provide an institutional scene within which students can enact (and are expected to enact) a discourse of participation. This prominent feature of Hampshire is supported by a widely held and deeply felt communal belief: Students will be "active" if they "own" their own education. According to one faculty member, "the experiment, at least, or the hope is that if they're really invested in what's going on, they'll be prepared. And that, I think, is one of the underlying motives of using the . . . student-centered education that we do." Therefore, if students are "participating" it is assumed (via this premise) that they are "engaged" and "invested" in their studies. As a result, this premise—the belief that invested students will be "active"—serves as the fundamental rationale for the structure of the Hampshire system of education. It is assumed that with no specific required courses, no predetermined plans of study or majors, students will take control of their intellectual growth because *they*, not the college, will "set the agenda" in their studies. In the end, Hampshire discussions serve as forums where the institution proves to the students that "the agenda is yours" and where the students prove to the institution that this "responsibility" to be "active" is not misplaced.

For all this institutional magic to happen, however, we have seen that Hampshire discussions must provide the "safe atmosphere" most conducive for these institutionalized displays of appropriately "active" studenthood. A second outcome of the particular normative structure of the Hampshire discussion, therefore, is that it functions to create an institutionalized suspension of status roles and attributes—a shared sense that "we (faculty and students) are a community of learners." By temporarily suspending status roles, the Hampshire discussion creates a *communitas*—that is, a mode of human action that de-emphasizes traditional or hierarchical social distinctions and that celebrates the equality of individuals under a shared system of symbols and meanings (Turner, 1974)—wherein students can feel "safe" to "take intellectual risks" in front of their professors and their peers.

For example, consider the discursive roles that students and faculty are respectively encouraged to take in Hampshire discussions.

Students are clearly encouraged to assume the active role within such discussions. The message for students at Hampshire is clear: as one professor said,

> they've asked the questions, they've set the agenda, which is the underlying message. The agenda is yours. I have information, I know where it is, I have experience that will help you . . . but in general, the agenda is yours.

If students are encouraged to take over "the agenda," Hampshire faculty are conversely expected to "get out of the center of the discussion" and "let go of control" over what parts of the reading are covered and the speed at which students progress. By releasing this status-based authority, at least during discussions, faculty at Hampshire believe this will open up the space necessary for students to "take risks," to "take responsibility," and to become active learners.

What results in discussions, then, is an eclipse of traditional status differences and an openly expressed premise that, at least in the context of a first-year "discussion" event, "we're inquirers together." A distinctively Hampshiresque *communitas* is therefore created where participants, both students and faculty, are bound not by the structural ties of hierarchy but by sharing a scene for and enactment of communal action, a common set of symbols, meanings, goals, and egalitarian norms for communication conduct. In the end, this liminal state of *communitas* serves to make "discussions" fertile ground for maximum participation from students and allows students to show that they are the "active" learners so prized by the institutional discourse of Hampshire College.

CULTURAL DISCOURSE

In these two brief ethnographic reports, we hope to have shown how specific communicative scenes are enacted through particular communicative practices, and further how each scene and set of practices implicates cultural discourses. The scene of the annual dinner was conducted, partly, through the enactment of Puerto Rican "time" and integrative symbols of "our community," with each implicating premises about being and acting in a Latino way. The scene of a Hampshire College classroom was conducted, partly, through the "discussion" event and norms, with these implicating premises about being and acting as an egalitarian "learner" at

Hampshire. Both studies show how institutional scenes, through very particular communication practices, implicate cultural discourses of symbols, symbolic forms of action, normative rules, and their meanings.[6]

Of special concern in both studies are cultural discourses of identification, or personhood, as these are active in situated social scenes. In other words, both studies have described communication practices that implicate deeply held beliefs about acting, relating, and being. In the Puerto Rican Cultural Center's annual dinner, these are immanent in patterned usage concerning the organization of "time" and expressions of "community." Both of these patterns convey deeper messages, to members, about how to be actors and active agents in this community. Similarly, at Hampshire College, through normative communication, and its use to guide and evaluate student activities, is hearable deeper meanings about being a participant learner, about egalitarian relations, about the communicative structuring of a "liminal institution" (Gibson, 1995). Both studies thus suggest how scenes are sites of highly particular communication practices, each with its own meanings, and each with its own preferred ways of modeling, and identifying persons, actions, and social relations.

Also, through the communication practices of the Puerto Rican Cultural Center, we find contested symbols and premises, and thus contested premises about being and acting. This of course is a complex enactment, and our treatment of that feature of the practice, here, is more suggestive than comprehensive. Nonetheless, we hope to have shown how different cultural standards for organizing activities, and affiliating those so organized, can be immanent in specific scenes of social interaction. For example, through communication practices, the same symbol, "time," is differently conceived and evaluated in the dinner program, in the master's of ceremonies comments, in different speakers' remarks, and elsewhere in other scenes. Within this "community," different cultural discourses are being implicated. Suggested are contrasting and competing discourses, with the Puerto Rican practices at times being supplanted by an Anglo practice, and with each vying through verbalizations for social efficacy. That these dynamics provide richly radiating sites of cultural and communicative activity can hardly be denied. That this kind of process needs to be understood, here and elsewhere, can hardly be disputed.

Our investigations have attempted, therefore, to be attentive at once to concrete social interactions *and* cultural meaning systems.

Our specific way of integrating these has involved explicit use of the concepts of communicative scene, communicative practice, and cultural discourses. With the concept, scene, we have drawn attention to specific places, situated communicative activities, and the broader meanings those made relevant; with practice, we have focused upon specific patterns of message endowed action; and with cultural discourse, we have interpreted meanings about persons, actions, and feelings, and so on, that are implicated through specific communicative practices in scenes. Cultural dynamics are heard, then, as deriving from and dwelling within concrete communication scenes and practices.

In concluding, we want to draw special attention to the construct of cultural discourse, and the ways it has been used and developed in our inquiries. While our general argument addresses the relationship between social interaction and cultural meanings, we have used the construct, cultural discourse, as a way of understanding how cultural meanings are immanent in situated communication practices. Our specific analytic procedure for doing so has followed, and suggests these four basic propositions (and two corollaries):

1. Wherever there are communication practices, there are cultural discourses immanent in those practices.

    1a. Cultural discourse(s) may be explicitly or implicitly invoked, contested or presumed in those practices.

2. Cultural discourses consist of systems of symbols, symbolic acts, sequential forms, rules, and their meanings.

3. The meanings of cultural discourses—of the symbols, acts, forms, rules—consist in basic premises about being (identity), doing (action), relating (social relations), feeling (emoting), and dwelling (living in place).

    3a. Not all premises are always relevant, nor equally salient in all scenes.

4. The deep meanings of communication practices consist in the creative and contingent use of cultural discourses in particular scenes.

Following this procedure has enabled us to identify communication practices in particular scenes, and to interpret some of the meanings that are active in those practices. In short, then, this summarizes some of our emerging efforts to construct a view of communication that integrates social interaction and cultural meanings.

Along the way, we hope to have introduced our developing approach to the study of communication and culture, as well as demonstrated what it yields when guiding these two ethnographic studies. We hope that readers will find the approach suggestive and interesting, and invite future investigations which pay careful attention to particular and actual scenes of communication, communication practices employed in them, and cultural discourses implicated through them. Of special interest are studies of the ways messages about being, acting, relating, feeling, and dwelling are implicated through communication practices, for we suspect that some of these messages richly radiate, in particular and telling ways, from all communication practices that people create in social scenes. There is much work to be done, and we hope to have suggested some of the ways social interaction and cultural meanings can be integrated into explorations of situated communication practices.

NOTES

1. The distinction draws upon Malinowski's discussion of "context of situation" and "context of culture." The former draws attention to actual social settings and psychological dimensions of those, while the latter draws attention to the wider cultural premises and rules that go into the production of those very settings (see Malinowski, 1935/1965).

2. The keynote speaker used the word "community" 25 times during his address. The yearbooks for the last five years have the word printed a total of 118 times.

3. Furthermore, O'Flannery (1968) states that "the newest migrants to New York City, the Puerto Ricans, seem to be deprived of the opportunity to form a community based upon geographical proximity" (p. 212). This statement could explain, in part, why the term "community" extends beyond specific geographic boundaries.

4. Note that we are treating the Hampshire term "discussion" as a cultural term for talk, which itself identifies a prominent communicative event. Communicative enactments of that event convey messages about communication norms, models for persons, and the appropriate arrangement of social relations. For a discussion of the model of "terms for talk" in

use here, see Carbaugh (1989). For additional examples of its use, see Baxter (1993), Baxter and Goldsmith (1990), and Hall (1995). For uses of the interpretive dimensions, see Fitch (1994) and Philipsen (1992).

5. This preferred distribution of talk in a Hampshire discussion—with the lion's share of talk produced by students—is often contrasted with "lectures," pedagogical activities that are said to have just the opposite distribution of talk. Lectures place faculty members in the "active" role and therefore transform students into passive note-takers or, at most, periodic question-askers. Since lectures are said to encourage "passivity" in students, they are more highly associated with "mainstream" institutions and are said to be less common at Hampshire.

6. The conceptual framework summarized here is applied and further discussed in several related essays (e.g., Carbaugh, 1988; 1991; 1993, p. 182ff.; 1996).

2

A Relational Model of Communication Competence

John M. Wiemann, Jiro Takai,
Hiroshi Ota, & Mary O. Wiemann

Communication competence is a concept that clearly has as many definitions as there are researchers. One such definition is, "the ability of an interactant to choose among available communicative behaviors in order that he may successfully accomplish his own interpersonal goals during an encounter while maintaining the face and line of his fellow interactants within the constraints of the situation" (Wiemann, 1977, p. 198). Under the guise of such concepts as interpersonal competence, social competence, rhetorical sensitivity, relational competence, and social skills, among others, it has been a central issue in interpersonal and intercultural communication research (e.g., Spitzberg & Cupach, 1984; Koester, Wiseman, & Sanders, 1993; Hammer, 1989; Martin, 1993; Wiemann, 1977), and in their application (Hammer, 1984; Hammer, Gudykunst, & Wiseman, 1978). Competence has garnered much attention in the education field, as well (Rubin, Graham, & Mignerey, 1990; Wiemann & Backlund, 1980). The tradition of communication competence owes much to early linguists, such as Chomsky (1965) and Hymes (1972), who attempted to define effective aspects of language. The history of communication competence could even be traced to ancient Greece, where speech oratory and eloquence were the main educational themes. Aristotle's five canons of rhetoric is probably the earliest model of *competent communication*.

Competence continues to be one of the core areas of research in communication. Research seeks to define how people need to communicate effectively in order to build, develop, and maintain good relationships (e.g., Canary & Stafford, 1994), and how they influence others to achieve their goals (e.g., Kellermann, 1992). Spitzberg (1994) even argues that social incompetence is socially and relationally damaging, based on studies by House, Landis, and Umberson (1988), and Spitzberg and Cupach (1989). He maintains that, "there is little question that the successful accomplishment and management of relationships is integral to one's well-being" (p. 28). Hence, it is important to clearly understand the processes toward competence, as it is applied to the maintenance of healthy social life in various situations.

Communication competence as an area of study has long had a tradition of theoretical absence. Spitzberg and Cupach (1989) argue that "competence research has tended to explore 'tributaries' rather than theoretical 'well-springs.' Most of the research ignores the big picture by creating thematic or contextual models of competence, to the exclusion of investigating the fundamental processes and mechanisms involved in competent social interaction" (p. 217). Typical research in the area has placed a focus on the skills or dispositions of the individual, a reductionist approach which cannot take into account the individual's dynamic interaction with contextual factors.

One trend in competence research that has attempted to acknowledge the importance of contextual factors is the relational approach (Cupach & Imahori, 1993; Imahori & Lanigan, 1989; Spitzberg & Hecht, 1984; Wiemann & Bradac, 1989). With this approach, the focus is placed on dynamic relational processes of communication. The rationale behind this approach is well illustrated in Wiemann and Kelly's (1981) assertion, "Interpersonal competence is intimately bound to the maintenance of mutually satisfying, effective relational systems. . . . In fact, from an interactional perspective, it makes no sense to talk about a person being competent apart from a specific relationship or set of relationships" (pp. 289–90). The relational perspective can be considered to be an emergent one, as it is still in its conceptualization stages, and little empirical work has been done on it. However, we believe that it is the most promising of all approaches, in that it gives a more complete view of communication competence as a dynamic process, and in that there is more of a potential for a theoretical explanation of competence. In this chapter, our goal is to elaborate on an original model of communication competence, based on a system theoretical, relational perspective, and one which integrates existing interpersonal communication theories. In order to fully understand the position in which this relational model stands amongst other competence models, it will be necessary to first review some of the more common models. We will then propose our model of communication competence, outlining its system components in a later section.

MODELS OF
COMMUNICATION COMPETENCE

One way in which competence models can be categorized is by their focus. Based on prime focus, four categories of competence models emerge: (1) the dispositional model, (2) the process oriented model, (3) the relational system model, and (4) message focus model. Examples of these models will be discussed along five dimensions of: (1) definition of competence, (2) locus of competence, (3) contextual variables, (4) outcomes, and (5) cultural implications. *Definition* of competence includes the components of competence, and its nature (e.g., trait versus state). *Locus* of competence refers to where competence resides, that is, within individuals or outside individuals. *Contextual variables* refer to the situations in which the competence of the individual is tested, within a relationship which is constantly facing the challenges of the environment. The *outcome* of competent communication refers to indices of success in interaction. Finally, *cultural implications* refer to differences in the conception of competence depending on culture (e.g., Miyahara, 1994; Takai & Ota, 1994). Hence, a good model of communicative competence should account for cultural variability in some ways to avoid a possible cultural bias.

Dispositional Models

The first, and perhaps most common category is the dispositional model, which looks at competence as a trait that individuals possess. They do not necessarily look at interaction itself, but assume that the possession of certain skills and traits by the individual leads to success in interaction. These skills and traits help the individual manage the contextual challenges imposed by social interaction.

Interaction Involvement. Cegala (1981) and Cegala, Savage, Brunner, and Conrad (1982) focus on a cognitive dimension of communicative competence, which they call *interactional involvement*. They rely heavily on Goffman's (1959) notion of face. From a behavioral perspective, they define communication competence as the *knowledge* of appropriate language use in social context, so that one does not cause loss of his/her face, or the face of others. Three components can be separated: perceptiveness; responsiveness; and attentiveness. Perceptiveness refers to the ability to attach appropriate meaning to others' behaviors, i.e., attribution. Responsiveness, on the other hand, refers to the ability to respond appropriately (e.g., when and how) to social circumstances. Finally, attentiveness refers to the cognizance or awareness of others' behaviors.

Obviously, competence, according to this perspective, is a cognitive ability which individuals possess. Cegala and colleagues (1982) seem to use a relational perspective, but their discussion seems to be limited to the level of the individual. The outcome of one's competence is appropriate verbal and nonverbal behaviors in interaction. Contextual variables are not attended, and no elaboration of cultural variability has been made by this model.

Adaptability. Adaptability is a cognitive construct and is conceptualized as, "the ability to perceive socio-interpersonal relationships and adapt one's behaviors and goal accordingly" (Duran, 1992, p. 255). Adaptability is a component of competence which resides in individuals as a disposition. It facilitates effective (e.g., goal achievement) and appropriate (e.g., avoiding violating rules) interaction. Adaptability is composed of six dimensions: social experience, social confirmation, social composure, appropriate disclosure, articulation, and wit.

Adaptability helps individuals meet the requirements of various situations, and has been linked to social attractiveness, communication satisfaction, and loneliness. However, not much connection can be made to a relational process, and some components of adaptability are not relevant in some cultures (e.g., wit). Discussions have not been made in the literature about the influence of contexts where communication takes place.

Intercultural Competence. From a systems-theoretic perspective, Y. Y. Kim (1992) argues that individuals are open systems. Intercultural communication competence (ICC) resides in individuals in their ability to facilitate communication with members of other cultures. Adaptability is equated with competence in her view, and she refers to it as a "capability of an individual's internal psychic system to alter its existing attributes and structures to accommodate the demands of the environment" (p. 268). Three dimensions of ICC are isolated: cognitive, affective, and behavioral components. These three dimensions help individuals to manage the challenges from the environment, and adapt to novel situations.

Kim (1992) strongly argues that ICC is located in an individual's internal capacity, not in the consequence of interaction. Individuals with high levels of ICC are self-organized, and are able to manage environmental challenges. Cultural environments are treated as a data field where individuals take in information to enrich their competence. Kim's discussion, though, is aimed primarily at an intercultural level, thus its scope is rather limited.

Communicative Competence. Wiemann (1977) developed a model of communicative competence from a behavioral/social skills perspective. Competence is defined as the ability to execute communicative behaviors in order to achieve one's goals, while maintaining anothers' face. Five dimensions are identified: interaction management, affiliation/support, empathy, behavioral flexibility, and social relaxation. He argues that other-orientedness is an alternative expression of competence, and is an abstract, composite construct that includes the above five interrelated dimensions.

Competence lies in an individual as traits, according to this model, which discusses it at an interpersonal level. Attention is not given to a context where communication takes place, and no account for possible cultural variability is given. The outcome of the demonstration of competence is a smooth interaction, and the establishment of oneself as a social being.

Process-Oriented Models

The second category of models is the process-oriented models, which elaborate on the processes by which competence emerges. Central constructs (e.g., uncertainty, anxiety, identity, face) are used to define competent communication. These models indicate that individuals' dispositions and skills affect the relational process.

Gudykunst's Anxiety/Uncertainty/Management (AUM) Model. Gudykunst (1993) uses the term *effectiveness* in communication rather than competence. Effectiveness is demonstrated by minimizing possible miscommunication between interlocutors. People perform effective communication by managing cognitive uncertainty and affective anxiety. The uncertainty and anxiety management process is mediated by *mindfulness* (Langer, 1979). In Gudykunst's (1993) model, three components (i.e., motivation, knowledge, and skills) are isolated for competence based on Spitzberg and Cupach's (1984) model. Accordingly, competence is located within the dyad, and culture is treated as a variable in the model. Gudykunst incorporates cultural variability (Hofstede, 1980) within his model to make it accountable for cultural differences, but he does not encompass contextual variables.

Communicative Resourcefulness. Ting-Toomey (1993) views communication competence as a process of effective identity negotiation. Individuals manage security/vulnerability and inclusion/exclusion dialectics in order to perform identity coordination smoothly. Four types of *communicative resourcefulness* that individuals possess facilitate effective identity negotiation processes are cognitive, affective, behavioral, and ethical.

In this perspective, competence is located in the dyad as conjoined perceptions of each individual's competence. In this sense, it is more relational-oriented than individual-centered, although dispositional traits and skills at the individual level are considered important building blocks for the ultimate perceptions of competence. Goal maximization, mutual understanding, and development of relationships are examples of the competent interactions.

Cultural variability of individualism and collectivism (Hofstede, 1980; Triandis, 1990) affects the locus of identity. People from individualistic cultures emphasize *independent* construal of self, and hence have an "I" identity, while their collectivistic counterparts emphasize *interdependent* construal of self, which leads to an emphasis on *we* (Markus & Kitayama, 1991; Ting-Toomey, 1989).

Identity Management. Cupach and Imahori (1993) developed a relational model of communication competence by incorporating facework (Goffman, 1967; Brown & Levinson, 1987). They define communication competence as the ability to negotiate mutually satisfying identities in interaction through the management of three dialectical tensions: (1) autonomy face versus fellowship face; (2) competence face versus autonomy face; and (3) autonomy face versus fellowship/competence face. The outcome of competent dyadic interaction is defined as the development of relational intimacy. Three stages are isolated for the relationship development: trial; enmeshment; and renegotiation. In brief, individuals negotiate a symbolically interdependent relationship where identity support, and integration of mutual identities are achieved.

According to this perspective, then, competence basically lies in each individual as skills for negotiating face. On the other hand, the processual and relational nature of communication is well accounted for, as evidenced by the attention paid toward the developmental course, and by the requirement for managing dialectic tensions, salient at each given stage. Cupach and Imahori (1993) are more interested in the process of competent relationships than competence in each individual. In this theoretical model, culture is an important variable, as it provides the knowledge necessary for facilitating effective identity management. Contextual variables are not incorporated in this model.

Relational Systems Models

The third group of models, the relational systems models, focus their attention on the dyad as a system. They are interested in how the variables associated with individuals in the dyad affect their relational interaction.

Spitzberg and Cupach's Relational Model. Spitzberg and Cupach (1984) proposed a model of interpersonal competence from a relational perspective. According to them, relational competence is a functional goal achievement through a cooperative and appropriate execution of communication. Competence has two dimensions: *effectiveness* and *appropriateness* (see Wiemann, 1977). Effectiveness is pertinent to goal attainment, such as satisfaction, desired change, or creativity. The importance of appropriateness indicates the contextuality, or relation/context specificity. One's knowledge, motivation, and skills affect the perceived effectiveness and appropriateness, and ultimately influences other's judgment of competence.

Spitzberg and Cupach's (1984) model of relational competence assumes that competence, in principle, resides in the dyad. Both state and trait perspectives are taken, since emphasis is placed on both contextuality and importance of individuals' skills and knowledge. Neither cultural variables, nor contextual variables are specified in the model.

Relational Model of ICC Competence. Imahori and Lanigan (1989) developed a relational model of communication competence specifically applied to the sojourner/host interaction context. They presented four axioms of their model: (1) ICC competence is composed of motivation, knowledge, and skills; (2) competence of the two individuals in the dyad should be measured; (3) competence should approximate an interpersonal relation; and (4) appropriateness and effectiveness are the two dimensions of competence. Based on the four axioms, competence is defined as "the appropriate level of motivation, knowledge, and skills of both the sojourner and the host-national in regards to their relationship, leading to an effective relational outcome" (p. 277).

According to this model, competence resides both within each individual as motivation, knowledge, and skills, and in the dyad as a relational outcome (e.g., development of intimate relationships). They are aware of the importance of the processual nature of communication. The model applies mostly at an interpersonal/dyadic level. Contextual influences are not noted in the model, while culture is accounted for at the knowledge level.

A Message Focus Model

The last type of model, the message focus model, places its focus on the kind of messages individuals deliver. In other words, it seeks to explain and predict what kind of messages should be used, and how they should be delivered, in order for communication to be deemed competent.

Interactive Constraints Model. The conversational constraints model, devised by M. S. Kim (1993), looks specifically at conversational strategies. Competence refers to one's appropriate and effective use of various languages within interaction aimed toward goal attainment. There are two constraints that individuals must be concerned with during interaction: face support and message clarity. Face support is indispensable for maintenance of relational harmony. Clarity of message represents how clearly and explicitly one's intentions are verbally expressed.

Competence, from this perspective, resides in one's use of language in a particular situation, and how it is perceived by others. In other words, competence is in the eyes of the beholder. Culture affects both interactive constraints, in that, individualists tend to be concerned more with message clarity, while collectivists tend to emphasize face support in their message delivery. Contextual variables are not incorporated in the model.

Multidimensionality of Competence

We examined the various models of communication competence above, and it can be noted that each type of model (i.e., dispositional, process, relational systems, and message focus) places an emphasis on one dimension of competence only. For instance, dispositional models emphasize traits and skills of the individual, but overlook the interactive, process nature of communication. Process-oriented models do attend to the processes of human interaction, but put relatively light emphasis on the messages. Relational systems models avoid the reductionistic approach to competence, but do not illustrate how the relational process is managed, nor do they tell much about the exchange of generated messages. Finally, the message focus models do emphasize the message, but they overlook the relational process and internal capacities of the individual. In view of the limitations of each type of model, it is apparent that a model of communication competence which encompasses all of the dimensions mentioned above is desired.

A RELATIONAL MODEL OF COMPETENCE

The vast majority of communication competence models discussed deal with competence within individuals (Canary & Spitzberg, 1989; Cegala, 1981; Cupach & Spitzberg, 1983; Duran, 1983; Pavitt & Haight, 1985). These models view competence as a concept that lies within the individual, and normally consist of operationalizations in the form of trait or state. Other models focus on the relational system, while not explaining individual or cultural variance. Our approach, however, centers on the relationship between individuals, as well as on the individuals themselves. It encompasses traits and states, and looks at the dynamics of interaction between individuals in relationships.

Rather than identifying the locus of competence in the individual, we take an interactional and pragmatic perspective. Wiemann and Kelly (1981) asserted that judgments of competence should be made in terms of systemic effectiveness, appropriateness and satisfaction. Our position is that competence is something that is created within a relationship. Communication competence is "the ability of two or more persons to jointly create and maintain a mutually satisfying relationship by constructing appropriate and effective messages" (O'Hair, Friedrich, Wiemann & Wiemann, 1994,

p. 32). With this definition, individuals who would be deemed incompetent through traditional definitions can be attributed competence. In other words, even a person severely lacking in social skills can be considered competent, so as long as he/she is engaged in a mutually satisfying relationship with a significant other.

Unlike the trait approach, dispositions of individuals do not take precedence, and unlike the state approach, the focus is not on specific situations, but rather on an ongoing, dynamic process of relationship development. This is consistent with Wiemann and Kelly (1981), who noted that "competence is manifest in the endless developings and workings-out" (p. 289). We shall hereon make reference to *competent relationships*, rather than competent individuals, as our focus is on the well-being of a relationship as a result of communication competence within interactions between relationship partners.

Assumptions of the Model

Our model of interpersonal competence is basically a reconception of the pragmatic perspective of competence developed in Wiemann (1977) and Wiemann and Kelly (1981). In particular, Wiemann and Kelly's model of competence was based on relational control as its core, as is our present model. The new model differs from existing relational models, such as Spitzberg and Hecht's (1984), in that it centers on the communication process within a relationship, not on individuals within a relationship situation. The following is an explanation of the assumptions on which this competence model is based.

1. Competent communication produces optimal distribution of control, expressed affiliation, and orientation to goal.

The primary functions of communication in the relational model consist of control, affiliation and goal achievement. In all functions, communication serves as a medium for negotiation between relationship partners to attain optimum levels of control and affiliation expression, and for negotiation of task orientation for goal achievement.

Control refers to the constraints interactants place on each other which limit behavioral options appropriately available to each relational partner, and to the relationship system as a whole (Wiemann & Kelly, 1981). In other words, it is the ability of an individual to influence the other individual(s) in a relationship, and to influence the manner in which their relationship is conducted. Communication serves to negotiate for the distribution of control. Equal distribution is not a necessary condition in competent relationships, as the *appropriate* distribution and exercise of control within the relationship context are more important. For example, in a supervisor-subordinate relationship, the former would be allotted more control without resentment from the latter to that fact. Furthermore, this distribution need not be temporally stable throughout a relationship, as relational partners can change (e.g., become an adult) or relationship structures can change (e.g., one partner gets promoted).

Affiliation is the affect held by the individual toward the other(s) in a relationship. It can be positive or negative. Through communication, the *expression* of affiliation is negotiated. An optimum amount of affiliation expression at a given stage in a particular relationship constitutes competence. Too much expression, or too little of it, at particular phases of a relationship could entail relational dissatisfaction. This is congruent with self-disclosure theories (Jourard, 1968; Altman & Taylor, 1973; Gilbert, 1976; Bochner, 1981), which posit that relational satisfaction is dependent upon an appropriate amount of self-disclosure.

Goal achievement refers to the focus of attention on the task at hand in order to achieve one's goal. Relationship partners may have common, relational goals, and they may have individual goals. Partners must negotiate the allocation of time and effort placed on each of their goals, so that mutual goal achievement, and thus, relationship satisfaction can be realized. There is some overlap here with Bochner and Kelly's (1974) competence criteria of the ability to collaborate effectively with others. Partners must be sensitive to the needs of others, as well to their own needs and the relational needs of the unit.

Relational competence is, thus, dependent upon the amount of control relational partners have over each other, the appropriateness of their expression of affiliation, and the degree to which they can accommodate to each other's goals. Although these are the primary features of competent communication within the relationship, there are also some secondary functions which are instrumental to relational competence. First, the communication of empathy is an important feature, which mediates each of the three primary functions. Sensitivity to the needs of the partner is important in achieving control of him/her, as it is in judging appropriate affiliation expression and his/her goal achievement needs. Wiemann and Kelly (1981) assert that feeling empathic is not enough, but one

must be able to communicate empathy to his/her relational partner. Second, display of social relaxation is crucial to reducing apprehension within a relationship (Wiemann, 1977). Competent relationships allow for a safe environment for communication, and
relationship partners are free of any debilitating communication
apprehension. "Positive" or "successful" conflict is possible because
of the nature of the competent relationship. Finally, the involvement of relationship partners must be communicated by their responsiveness to each other. Communication of involvement can be
done by nonverbal expressive behavior, including those listed by
Wiemann (1977) as being characteristic of empathy, such as other-
directed gaze, active listening cues, and physical proximity, as well
as through verbal means.

2. Competent communication is process-oriented.

Communication competence has been widely observed through
personal outcomes, addressing variables such as loneliness
(Spitzberg & Canary, 1985), mental disorder (Zigler & Phillips,
1960), relational quality (Canary & Spitzberg, 1989), state of feeling
good (Cupach & Spitzberg, 1983), and intercultural effectiveness
(Nishida, 1985). These studies concentrate on the effects on the individual. Wiemann and Kelly (1981), on the other hand, contend
that from a relational perspective, "judgments of competence can
only be validly made in terms of systemic effectiveness, appropriateness and satisfaction" (p. 289). Our model, with a locus of competence in the relationship, places a greater emphasis on the communication *process* than on outcome.

Competence is created or processed through interaction between relational partners. What is important, then, is not the end,
but the means to the end. That is, how relational partners arrive at
goal accomplishment is of more interest than whether they accomplish it or not. Our focus is on the communication process by
which partners interact to negotiate how they will achieve their
common goals and their respective personal goals.

3. Competent communication is generally appropriate and effec-
tive for a given relationship.

As already mentioned, our relational model views effectiveness
and appropriateness from a systemic perspective. According to
Spitzberg and Cupach (1989), effectiveness "derives from control

and is defined as successful goal achievement or task accomplishment" (p. 7), while appropriateness "reflects tact or politeness and is defined as the avoidance of violating social or interpersonal norms, rules, or expectations" (p. 7). In the context of our model, effective communication is reflective of the extent that each partner is able to successfully achieve his/her goals within the relationship. Furthermore, communication is appropriate when it meets the expectations of (1) one's specific communication partner, (2) other people in one's immediate presence, and (3) the demands of the situation. What is appropriate behavior is negotiated and agreed upon within the relationship through communication between partners. Effectiveness and appropriateness in a relationship is achieved when the communication process optimizes outcomes for all relational partners, thus leading to a state of mutual satisfaction.

Components of the Model

Whereas most existing models feature as their components individual dispositions and outcome variables, our model looks at the relationship and those features related to it. The individual is not slighted, however, as he/she assumes an important position within the relationship. Our model consists of context, the individual, interactional goals, relational history, future expectations, process reflexivity, and process complexity as its components (see figure 2.1).

Context refers to the social environment in which the relationship is formed. We propose three types of contexts: (1) cultural, (2) physical, and (3) relational. With regard to cultural context, partners share relatively similar values, beliefs, attitudes, and behavioral rules within an intracultural context, while they must interact with different cultural assumptions within an intercultural context. Takai and Ota (1994) assert that culture has an impact on the appropriateness dimension, implying that differing conceptions of interpersonal norms and rules may complicate communication in the latter situation. Next, physical context refers to the surroundings of relational partners in interaction. Proximal distance, privacy, physical surroundings, and other spatiotemporal factors affect the communication between partners. Finally, relational context refers to the nature of the relationship. The same communication behaviors would convey much different messages depending on relational factors such as intimacy, status differences, gender, goal-orientation, and age differences.

The individual is the second component, and of importance are

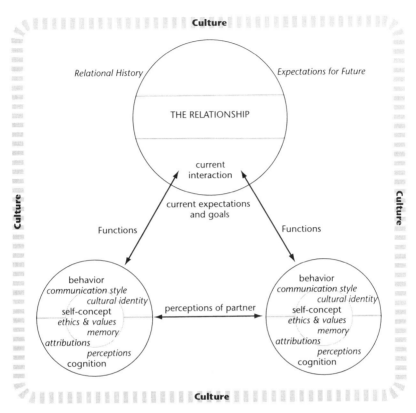

Figure 2.1.
Model of Communicative Competence
Source: Wiemann & Wiemann (1992).

his/her dispositions. In particular, self-concept, cognitive skills, and behavioral skills are important. The self-concept influences the manner in which communication will be conducted with the partner, and is the basis by which he/she decides with whom relationships will be sought (Gudykunst & Hall, 1994). It can be restructured within a relationship as relational partners affect each other, and the boundary between the self and relationship become less defined (O'Hair et al., 1994). Cognitive skills play a crucial role in the developmental stages of a relationship, where uncertainty between partners is high (Berger & Calabrese, 1975). Relationships are more competent when the effect of perceptual and attribution biases (Kelley, 1973) are minimal, so cognitive skills are required for perceptual precision in the interpretation of messages. Behavioral skills run in conjunction with cognitive skills, in that once a situation has been assessed, an appropriate response is warranted. These skills are often called *social skills*. Much of the trait conceptions of competence constitute a social skills view, which assumes that competence consists of specific behavioral routines that people possess (Wiemann & Kelly, 1981).

The third component, interactional goals, refers to individual and relational goals within the relationship. The congruence of the relational partners' goals in terms of control, affiliation expression, and goal achievement is the center of attention. When the control distribution is perceived as being unjust, or when affiliative expressions exceed or do not meet expected levels, or when goals are not being achieved, the relationship is not competent, and partners may opt to direct their communication toward rectification of the situation, or they may decide to terminate the relationship.

The fourth component, relational history, is the sum of objective events and shared experiences of the relational partners. History serves to inform current expectations and interpretations in on-going interactions. Communication in long-term relationships does not normally need to be elaborated as much as "shallow-history" relationships. Codes unique to the relationship usually develop that give partners a type of relational "shorthand." Overlap with Bernstein's (1971) restricted and elaborate code distinction, as well as with Hall's (1976) high and low context communication distinction can be seen. Long-history relationships can be characterized by a relatively restricted, low-context style of communication, as partners share much common experience. In other words, partners sufficiently understand each other, so they need not explain every intent and purpose through verbal channels of communication. Of course, at crisis times in long-term relationships, the "shorthand" language is replaced by more specific and intensive verbal communication.

The fifth component, expectations for the future, encompasses long-term individual and relational goals. Communication behaviors are highly dependent on the partner's expectations, which reflects the direction in which a relationship is headed. Relationships which promise positive outcomes for the future are more likely to be treated with importance than those which are viewed as only temporary.

The sixth component, process reflexivity, refers to the accommodative process within the relationship. Partners reflect on the relationship, their behavior and the behavior of their partner. Adjustments are made to accommodate for the partner or for changes in situation; thus, the communication serves an important relational maintenance function.

The seventh and final component, process complexity, implies the need for cross-situational generalizability of experience. Communication episodes vary along dimensions of formality, audience size, and familiarity of situation. Individuals accumulate experience in various communication situations, characterized by varying levels of these dimensions, and they learn to generalize what would be appropriate communication behavior in similar situations. Therefore, an individual would be prepared to face new situations by virtue of his/her experience, and the ability to generalize across situations.

Taking these components systematically, interpersonal competence boils down to the perceived quality of communication that occurs within the relationship, as relational partners realize their individual and relational goals. The outcome of the model, then, could be defined as relational satisfaction. Goal achievement attained within a facilitative and collaborative interpersonal setting brings about feelings of satisfaction of being in the relationship, and its continuation is desired. Incompetent relationships, however, induce feelings of discontent. Inappropriateness in control distribution, expression affiliation, and/or goal orientation could bring about dissatisfaction.

Implications of the Model

Our relational model of competence places an emphasis on the communication process, not on relational outcomes. This pragmatic view of interpersonal competence, unlike other competence models, employs the relationship as the unit of analysis, not the individual. Although it is still in the developmental stages, we foresee great utility and advantages over existing models.

One area in which we see an advantage over individual-centered models is that of attention to the cultural context. Because interpersonal norms and rules are culturally defined, models that specify certain skills may suffer from validity problems across cultures. The conceptualization of competence, then, is culturally specific from the perspective of a trait approach. What is deemed competent in one culture may not be so in another. Gudykunst, Gao, Schmidt, Nishida, Bond, Leung, Wang, and Barraclough (1989) examined the validity of the self-monitoring scale across cultures and discovered conceptual problems were inherent in the scale when administered to people of a culture other than the one in which it was developed. Takai and Ota (1994) contend that the appropriateness dimension of competence is particularly sensitive to culture, and criticized the use of translated measurements of competence. Our relational model averts cultural complications by accounting for culture in its contextual component. Moreover, a focus on the relationship allots greater emphasis to the process by which individuals work out differences than to cultural dispositions brought into the relationship by them.

Because of the relational nature of our model, there is little constraint on the number of relational partners within a competent relationship. Our model does not assume the relationship to be dyadic, as Imahori and Lanigan (1989) do in their relational model. Rather, relationships of any size, so as to allow for the elements of competence to exist, are possible. For example, a work unit, or possibly even a school class can constitute competent relationships. We do not assume a one-on-one relationship in our definition of relationship.

Whereas individual-centered models are based on a static conceptualization of competence, that is, possession or lack of skills, our model accounts for dynamics within relationships. Our focus is on interaction, which is ongoing. Relationships are undergoing constant change with each new interaction between relational partners.

The theoretical nature of our model lies in its system theory perspective, in its treatment of communication competence as something arising from an interactional system: the relationship. Hall and Fagen (1956) define a system as, "a set of objects together with relationships between the objects, and between their attributes" (p. 18). Our model proposes that the components of relational competence are interrelated to form a whole, allowing competence to be seen from a holistic perspective. According to Watzlavick, Beavin and Jackson (1967), interactional systems are, "two or more communicants in the process of, or at the level of, defining the nature of their relationship" (p. 121). We believe our model adequately accounts for not only the individuals within a relationship, but for the contextual factors as well, giving it a much wider perspective than the mainstream, reductionist, dispositional approaches.

Furthermore, our relational model can be seen to incorporate tenets of several existing interpersonal theories. First, at the relationship development stage, relational partners can be conceived of wishing to reduce uncertainty within the relationship (Berger & Calabrese, 1975). Competent relationships would be characterized by effectively reducing uncertainty in appropriate manners. What is deemed appropriate in this case would be determined through transaction and negotiation between partners. Depending on the traits of the individuals and the context in which they lie, relationships would differ in the rate that they develop. For example, one partner may feel a need to rush into a relationship, thus use intense self-disclosure to coax his/her partner for reciprocation of the self-disclosure (Altman & Taylor, 1973), but the partner may not respond favorably. In this case, the former would have to adjust his/her disclosure level to that which is comfortable for his/her partner, or in Giles, Mulac, Bradac and Johnson's (1987) terms, resort to convergent tactics, while the partner would show divergent behavior to express the inappropriateness of the former's behavior.

Second, tenets of relational maintenance theories can also be integrated into the relational model. For example, the relational partners' input into the relationship can be weighed against the outcome, according to equity theory (Walster, Walster, & Berscheid, 1978). Partners can negotiate equity, so that a mutually satisfying equity level can be reached, or they can evaluate the relationship against the prospective outcomes of alternative relationships (Thibaut & Kelley, 1959), possibly terminating the relationship. According to our model, the dissolution of the relationship may even constitute competence so as long as both individuals are satisfied with such a consequence, and they do so in an appropriate fashion, that is, no hard feelings are left.

The relational processes occurring within our model can be generally explained by communication accommodation theory (Giles et al., 1987). In a relationship, individuals must make adjustments in their behavior in order to accommodate to his/her partner's goals. Depending on the partner and the situation, convergence or divergence is required to bring control to an appropriate distribution, to adjust affiliative expressiveness, and to facilitate mutual goal achievement.

TEACHING COMMUNICATION COMPETENCE

A model is only as good as its application. A model of a house or a rocketship only proves itself when the real thing is built and we observe its performance. Observing and reacting to behavior is the test of the Communication Competence Model. Professors who teach communication behavior, understanding and skills, see the application of communication models and thus test their strength.

There are five challenges that communication professors must meet in helping their students to understand the complexity of communication competence.

The first challenge is addressing the prescriptive/adaptive dialectic. In teaching communication skills, we often teach students certain skills (i.e., paraphrasing, perception-checking, specific conflict resolution techniques). It is a challenge to teach those skills in an adaptive way, because the "formulae" for behaving are almost inherent in the skill-building. Knowing a range of skills enables students to be more adaptive, so prescriptive/adaptive dialectic becomes obvious. Earlier in this paper, we acknowledged that an unskilled person interacting with another unskilled person might still create a competent relationship. In reality, that is probably quite rare. More satisfactory relationships are more common in adaptive relationships.

The second challenge in teaching competence involves two myths that are common to students. The first is the common sense myth. Here individuals believe that competence is inborn, that it is almost a survival skill, that everyone has "common sense" communication behavior. That is clearly a myth when we consider the failures of communication among so many people in so many contexts. Effective and appropriate communication is clearly more than just common sense. The second myth involves the widespread belief that individuals have the power to change others. While this is partially true, especially if we consider our ability to influence others, the notion that we can "correct" or "form" communication relationships so that we can cause another's behavior to be the way we want it to be, is clearly problematic. Freeing people from the responsibility of "causing" others' behavior is a primary challenge of communication professors.

The third challenge involves teaching people to self-monitor. Individuals need to be able to recognize their own behaviors, to see the effective and ineffective aspects of their behavior, and to recognize the adaptive capacities needed in each communication situation, in order to create effective and appropriate communication behaviors.

"I tried it once and it didn't work" encapsulates the spirit of the fourth challenge to communication educators. We may try a food for the first time and, since we haven't developed a taste for it, we think it is distasteful. In much the same way, we may try a new communication behavior for the first time and find ourselves awkward or find a partner unwilling to cooperate, and thus we decide not to try it again (in a different way, with different partners, in a different context). Adapting our behaviors within the communication competence model is important when we realize that the same behavior may be much more effective in one relationships than in another.

The final challenge for communication educators lies in the increasingly complex intercultural classroom. We know that different cultures evaluate competence differently, that different behaviors are judged as more or less effective depending on the culture or co-culture, and that within cultures perceptions of competence can vary widely. Today's classrooms are filled with students from different cultures and co-cultures, and from different international cultures. This is complicated by the second- and third-generation communicators who are unique blends of national cultures and adaptive cultures—individuals who embody 'both worlds" and thus represent even more potentially complex communication competence situations.

CONCLUSION

The relational model of communication competence we have presented is a comprehensive model, based on theoretical principles of relationships, and integrating the important components of communication as a dynamic process. Unlike existing models, our focus is on the relationship between individuals, and not on the individuals themselves. The pragmatic, systemic perspective with which we view competence gives our model many advantages over existing models. At the same time, because our model incorporates a vast amount of variables surrounding the communication situation, a challenge is posed toward probing into the means by which competence within the relationship can be measured. As a future directive, we plan to devise some method of empirical assessment of relational competence.

3

Conflict Communication

An Emerging Communication Theory
of Interpersonal Conflict

Dudley D. Cahn

One school of thought views communication as multidisciplinary in nature. Because communication is a multifaceted and complex subject, some communication scholars incorporate the theory and research methods that exist in different disciplines and create where possible an overarching paradigm that governs their research in communications (Cahn & Hanford, 1984). For a number of years, some communication researchers who are social scientists have studied interpersonal conflict from within such a broad encompassing research program that incorporates many theories and research methods used in other disciplines.

Some might argue, however, that conflict is not an appropriate topic for communication research. Some aspects of conflict certainly appear to be miscommunication or noncommunication in nature. For example, during a conflict a communicator's message may be thought by the message receiver to be arbitrary, gratuitous, or incomprehensible. To this observation, I have three responses. First, expressions of conflict often take the form of verbal and nonverbal messages as when one insults, threatens, swears at others, engages in putdowns or name calling, and stonewalls or neglects the other. Second, even a violent conflict often includes verbal and nonverbal messages that (a) contribute to escalation, (b) occur along with the violent behaviors, and (c) are produced (as a response to the violence) to repair an interpersonal relationship after the abuse. Third, some conflicts share features with other communication acts known as compliance gaining attempts in which the one person desires compliance by another. Thus, researchers are finding that interpersonal conflicts are embedded on broader interaction patterns (Cahn 1992, 1996).

Today more researchers are including interaction patterns in their study of interpersonal conflict. Many of these communication studies are part of an explanation that falls on the "dark side" of interpersonal communication (Cupach & Spitzberg, 1994), and have explored sexual intimacy, deception, marital dissatisfaction, extramarital affairs, divorce, parent-child relationships following parents' divorce, coercion, sexual harassment, as well as negative emotional communication involved in expressions of anger, jealousy, and power over others. However, the dark side of interpersonal communication is as important as the study of the positive and constructive side (such as openness, altruism, trust, love, empathy, etc.) because of the equally important roles both sides play in the growth, maintenance, and destruction of interpersonal relationships.

This chapter examines developments in interpersonal conflict theory and research by describing the philosophical, theoretical, and practical dimensions of three traditional approaches guiding research on conflict and by identifying the distinguishing features of an emerging overarching paradigm for the study of conflict communication.

THREE TRADITIONAL APPROACHES
Guiding Research on Interpersonal Conflict

In the past, different disciplines in the social sciences studied interpersonal conflict by using three perspectives on research: the systems-interaction approach to couples' conflicts, the cognitive-exchange approach to the role of conflict in relationship satisfaction and commitment, and the rules-interventionist approach to divorce mediation. Merely introduced here, each of these approaches receives more detailed treatment in Cahn (1992).

Systems-Interaction Approach to Couples' Conflicts

Philosophical Underpinnings

The system-interaction approach was heavily influenced by theoretical developments in cybernetics toward the end of World

War II. At that time it was realized from the study of machine and animal behavior that feedback enabled adaptation to environmental changes. In addition, cybernetics proposed that feedback may result in circular relations between an individual and her/his environment as well as change that occurs when one gets feedback and responds by adjusting accordingly.

The development of cybernetics coalesced in time with the development of information theory, which is credited with viewing processes as stochastic. In a stochastic process, the data for research take the form of a series of events that occur in a sequential pattern governed by probabilities of occurrence. Because of their interest in stochastic processes, information researchers theorized about the role redundancy. In real life, communication encounters noise (error, misunderstanding, or distortion). In communication generally, redundancy functions to overcome noise.

Cybernetics and information theory were later subsumed by general systems theory. A common definition for system is a set of interrelated components acting together as a unit. According to general systems theory, a system has some purpose—it is goal-directed and adaptable. The system need not be aware or conscious that it has a goal, but the goal functions to direct activity toward its attainment. Able to adapt or reorganize itself on the basis of feedback about environmental changes, a system is controlled by its aims, a type of self-maintenance or self-regulation. To restore homeostasis, changes in the environment fed back to the system create imbalances to which the system responds. Thus, the system maintains itself in pursuit of a goal.

Theoretical Developments in Couple's Conflicts

The application of general systems theory to conflict and intimacy emphasizes the whole, the overlap, or area of commonality shared by communicators as partners or as a couple. This holistic perspective views components of a system as a unit acting in concert. Since a couple's interrelationship consists of the mutual exchange of messages, systems-interaction researchers view the couple as a communication system. They compare a couple's communication to a game where the move of one partner constrains the alternatives available to the other, thereby reducing uncertainty in predicting subsequent moves or plays.

The systems-interaction perspective views conflict as a form of dyadic communication that is classified as positive or negative by referring to its effects on the intimate nature of a couple's relationship.

Conflict that has a negative effect on relationships consists of negative affect, coercive/controlling, escalating, and rigid message.

Negative Affect. As suggested earlier, the systems-interaction paradigm views behavioral patterns and interpersonal relationships rather that particular behaviors or individuals in isolation. Partners' behaviors are understandable only when viewed in a behavioral context—in terms of an overall pattern or interpersonal relationship. Gottman (1979) has observed that dissatisfied couples are more likely than satisfied couples to use cross-complaining and counter-complaints and less likely to engage in validation sequences (Gottman, Markman, & Notarius, 1977). Ting-Toomey (1983) has discovered that, compared to satisfied couples, dissatisfied couples are more likely to begin a conflict by directly attacking one another with criticism and negatively loaded statements, followed by attempts to justify oneself and blame the other.

Coercive/Controlling Behaviors. As argued above, systems-interactionists have learned from general systems theory to view couples and families as whole systems rather than mere collections of individuals. Researchers have revealed that coercive and controlling behavior during interaction (as well as at other times) is associated with dissatisfying marital relationships. Partners who engaged in controlling behavior when resolving conflicts were more dissatisfied with their relationship than spouses who did not (Billings, 1979).

Escalation: Negative Reciprocity. The concepts of feedback and stochastic process add to an understanding of how conflict escalates in intimate relationships. Because of the interdependent nature of behaviors during the conflict process (where antecedent behaviors influence the probabilities of subsequent behaviors), the systems-interaction approach emphasizes behaviors that are linked to one another in an escalating, stochastic process. The general systems concepts of feedback and control have led systems-interaction researchers to examine conflict behaviors that are linked to one another in an escalating process. Pike and Sillars (1985) found a strong reciprocity tendency in couples' interaction in that avoidance behaviors were typically followed by other avoidance behaviors. Once hostility is expressed by either partner, Gaelick, Bodenhausen, and Wyer (1985) show that it is likely to escalate in frequency over the course of the interaction. In both dissatisfied and satisfied couples, negative communication behavior is more likely to be reciprocated than positive, but there is greater negative reciprocity for dissatisfied couples than for happy ones (Gottman et al., 1977; Gottman, 1982a, 1982b; Margolin & Wampold, 1981; Pike & Sillars, 1985; Wills, Weiss, & Patterson, 1974).

Rigidity. As discussed above, information is thought to flow from one person to another when a move by one partner constrains the alternatives available to the other, thereby reducing uncertainty in predicting subsequent moves or plays. Research shows that interactions of dissatisfied couples show a higher degree of structure and more predictability of one spouse's behaviors from those of the other than is found in the interactions of satisfied couples. Gottman (1979) reviews evidence of greater temporal predictability in the interactions of dissatisfied couples.

Practical Implications

The behavior of individuals is to be understood within a relationship or interpersonal system (defined as the way partners interact with one another). If change is to occur, it must be brought about in the system as a whole or the way partners interact with each other.

From a systems-interaction perspective, once people begin to use negative conflict behavior, they frequently discover that the conflict escalates. Some behaviors lead to more positive outcomes than others—that is, some behaviors de-escalate emotional outbursts. To prevent the escalation of conflict and to restore homeostasis, de-escalation behaviors need to be identified and encouraged. For example, discussion that focuses on resolving a problem is less emotionally upsetting than name calling and partner blame. It is very important to de-escalate the conflict in its early stages. To accomplish this goal, systems-interaction proponents have developed behavioral modification and communication skills training to reinforce positive and constructive behaviors but not negative and destructive behaviors.

Essentially, conflict training based on the systems-interaction approach shifts from an emphasis on the individual to a view of the couple or family as a system in which the individual is only a part. To enhance couples' abilities, education and training are needed to help them develop constructive attitudes and conflict management skills. In many systems-interaction oriented programs, the teaching of effective conflict management skills is directed toward enhancing intimacy within the marital relationship. Common problems of conflict which are targeted for treatment by skills training exist at two levels: the concrete verbal and nonverbal behaviors making up an interaction and meta-communication level behaviors that structure the interaction and provide for adaptation and change of that structure. Research has shown that training in conflict management skills enhances the effectiveness of couples' training.

Cognitive-Exchange Approach to the Role of Conflict in Relationship Satisfaction and Commitment

Philosophical Underpinnings

Those researcher of interpersonal conflict who take a cognitive-exchange approach have identified at least two important characteristics of relationship development: satisfaction (positive affect or attraction to the relationship) and commitment (the tendency to maintain the relationship and to feel psychologically "attached" to it). A key idea behind the cognitive-exchange approach is that relational partners engage in social exchange in ways that lead to either relationship satisfaction and commitment or to dissatisfaction and lack of commitment. From this perspective, interpersonal behaviors are viewed in terms of their utility and are associated with perceived rewards and costs. A satisfying or attractive relationship is derived from a perceived reward-cost ratio that exceeds one's expectations. In addition, relationship development is influenced by other social exchange variables, namely perceived alternative attractions, perceived investments in the relationship, and perceived social pressure from others who comprise a social network in which partners are embedded.

Theoretical Developments

Regarding the role of interpersonal conflict in the development of romantic relationships, Braiker and Kelley (1979) argue that relationship satisfaction and commitment depends on the following four dimensions: Love, conflict/negativity, ambivalence, and maintenance behavior. These dimensions of relationship satisfaction reflect "both the nature of the interdependence and the kinds of conflicts occurring in the relationship's course" (pp. 147–48). The degree of interdependence is reflected in the love category by references to caring, needing, and attachment (e.g., doing things for each other, spending time together, acting like a couple). The conflict-negative affect category indicates interpersonal conflict (arguments, disagreements), and the ambivalence category reflects internal conflict within the individual (e.g., confusion about partners' feelings toward one another). The maintenance category is represented by references to self-disclosure, efforts to change, and efforts to solve problems (e.g., spending time trying to work out problems, telling partner what each needs or wants from the relationship). Ambivalence, conflict/negativity, inability to solve problems and talk things out, and lack of love lead to relationship dissatisfaction and lack of commitment.

Perceived Imbalance in Resources of Social Exchange

Building on a system that Foa and Foa (1974) originally devised and based on a review of the research literature, Rettig and Bubolz (1983) hypothesized that marital satisfaction depends on feelings about seven resources available for exchange in the following order of importance: (1) love—nonverbal expressions of positive regard, warmth, or comfort, (2) status—verbal expressions of high or low prestige or esteem, (3) service—labor of love for one another, (4) information—advice, opinions, instructions, or enlightenment, (5) goods—contributions of material goods, (6) money—financial contributions, and (7) shared time—time spent together. In their study, Rettig and Bobolz observed that husbands and wives experienced marriage differently. Husbands tended to value more highly the instrumental dimension of the relationship (e.g. cooked meals, household repairs), while wives emphasized the affectional dimension of the relationship (e.g., acceptance, affection, and approval). The worst kind of marriage seemed to be one in which partners felt that they did not get what they deserved.

Perceived Inequity. Perceived inequity that refers to unfairness or a perceived imbalance in the resources of exchange may be viewed as a major source of conflict in intimate relationships. Equity theory (Hatfield, Utne, & Traupmann, 1979; Walster, Walster, & Bercheid, 1978) predicts that when individuals find themselves in inequitable relationships, they become distressed, which will motivate them to restore equity (Hatfield et al., 1979). Conversely, equity theory predicts that men and women in equitable relationships are more content than those in relationships where there is inequity in four different areas: personal concerns (how attractive spouses are, how sociable, and how intelligent), emotional concerns (how much spouses like and love each other, understand each other, sex, commitment), day-to-day concerns (how much money both bring in, house maintenance, being easy to live with, fitting in socially), opportunities gained or lost (opportunity to be married or married to someone else, to have children). Accordingly, people are classified into three groups:

1. *The Overbenefited:* those men and women who are receiving more than they feel they deserve from their marriages.

2. *The Equitably Treated:* those who are receiving just what they think they deserve from their marriages.

3. *The Underbenefited:* those who are receiving less than they feel they deserve from their marriages.

Research results showed that spouses who felt equitably treated were more content in their marriage and perceived the marriage as more stable than men and women in unequal marriages. Neither women nor men appeared to be differentially concerned with equity. Moreover, Sabatelli and Cecil-Pigo (1985) found that perceived equity in the distribution of outcomes within a relationship was the variable found to account most for commitment for both husbands and wives.

Perceived Unequal Distribution of Power

Perceived unequal distribution of power in a relationship often results in conflict between intimates. In unequal relationships, one partner dominates the other. However, dissatisfied couples report that their partners are more coercive and less cognitive in their conflict discussions (Billings, 1979). Researcher findings show that husband dominance is a common problem because many wives indicate that they would prefer less controlling behavior from their husbands (Hawkins, Weisberg, & Ray, 1980). According to a detailed study by Ting-Toomey (1984), couples who share power equally rank highest in marital satisfaction, husband-dominant couples rank medium, and wife-dominant couples rank lowest in marital satisfaction.

Moreover, intimate partners who perceive a balance of power in their relationships are likely to prefer strategies that confront issues, whereas power imbalances tend to produce a preference for avoidance strategies. In imbalanced relationships, powerful partners may be expected to confront, while powerless partners are expected to chose avoidance strategies. One form of confrontation avoidance is the "chilling effect" as a sign of "powerlessness" (Roloff & Cloven, 1990). Power is viewed here as the chance to influence the behavior of others in accord with one's own wishes.

Hocker and Wilmot (1985) suggest that some partners downgrade their requests prior to making them simply because they anticipate negative reactions from their more powerful counterparts. Further, they may be inhibited from even initiating influence attempts, the essence of the chilling effect. As such they meet the following conditions: they focus on interests that have a negative impact on their partners, they withhold comments on these interests from their partners, and they are afraid that confrontation would damage the relationship.

While "powerlessness" may influence the extent to which one is likely to confront a partner, interestingly, it may also be seen as an outcome of uncommitted relationships. Clearly, the chilling effect is most likely to occur when a relationship is perceived to be unstable (or lacking in commitment), an important condition that specifies when differences in power have the greatest effect.

While scholars theorize about the role of conflict in relationship satisfaction and commitment, Rusbult and Zembrodt (1983) examine responses to sources of conflict and have developed the following typology that is related to social exchange theory:

- *Exit.* Divorce, breakup, and separate.

- *Voice.* Attempts to change the relationship, discuss problems, compromise, work things out, and adopt a problem-solving orientation.

- *Loyalty.* Accepting of minor problems, highly committed to maintaining the relationship, and assuming that conditions will improve.

- *Neglect.* Ignore the partner, not care about the relationship, and allow conditions to worsen.

As so often happens when researchers attempt to devise a typology, there are mixed cases in which partners preferred strategies typical of more than one category.

Alternative responses to conflict relate to social exchange theory in the following ways. Where partners are satisfied with their relationship (rewards outweigh costs), perceive no superior alternatives to their primary relationship, make high investments in a relationship, partners prefer to be *loyal* (nonconfrontational) or *give voice* (confrontational in a constructive way) as alternative cognitive responses to perceived sources of conflict. The greater

the satisfaction, investments, and social pressures to remain together, and the more inferior the alternatives, the more the partners are committed to the relationship, and the more likely they
will respond with voice rather than loyalty.

However, where partners are not satisfied with their relationship (costs outweigh rewards), perceive superior alternatives to
their primary relationship, have not made investments in a relationship, and perceive no social pressures to remain in the relationship, partners prefer destructive nonconfrontational ways (e.g., prefer to *neglect* or *exit* from the relationship) as cognitive responses to
conflict. The lesser the satisfaction, investments, social pressures to
remain together, and the more superior the alternatives, the less
the partners are committed to the relationship, and the more likely
they will prefer to exit rather than neglect.

Building on Rusbult's typology of reponses to conflict, Healy
and Bell (1990) argue that partners may progress through different
types of cognition as dissatisfaction grows. At first, they might prefer loyalty as a strategy, hoping that things will get better soon.
They may turn to the strategy of giving voice when the situation
does not improve, then decide to neglect the partner when that
fails, and eventually choose to exit the relationship. By combining
Healey and Bell's notion of progression with social exchange theory, it might be argued that newly formed couples would prefer loyalty because they fear losing their partner who is not fully committed to the relationship. Research shows that those who are not yet
committed to a relationship prefer more conflict avoidance than
partners at later stages in their romantic relationships (Fitzpatrick &
Winke, 1979). However, after commitment takes place, they prefer
to give voice to their dissatisfaction, but if conditions only worsen,
then they prefer neglect. Finally, when superior alternatives appear,
they prefer to exit. Thus, taken as a whole, cognitive responses to
perceived sources of conflict may be viewed as a dynamic process.

The roles played by conflict in relationship satisfaction and
commitment is mediated by attributions and efficacy expectations.
According to Sillars (1980), the simple choice of confronting or
avoiding a conflict hinges on attributions like those revealed by the
following questions: Were the abrasive actions of the partner inten-
tional or not (causal judgment)? Is the person "reasonable" and ap-
proachable about the conflict (social inferences)? Is the person
likely to continue with similar actions in the future (predicted outcomes)? In addition to such attributions, Fincham, Bradbury, and
Grych (1990) call attention to the role of efficacy expectations

which represent the individual's "belief that constructive problem-solving behavior can be executed" (pp. 171–72). Given low-efficacy expectations, a partner is unlikely to engage in efforts to resolve a conflict and will choose to avoid it or withdraw from it. Given high-efficacy expectations, however, the person is likely to undertake such efforts and confront the problem. This may partially explain why romantic partners who perceive a balance of power in their relationship are likely to prefer strategies that confront issues, whereas power imbalances tend to produce a preference for avoidance strategies by low-power partners (Roloff & Cloven, 1990).

Attributions and efficacy expectations are mentalistic concepts that presumably influence the way communicators view their own and one another's actions and respond to them. Because cognition cannot be observed by others directly, cognitive exchange researchers rely on self-report measures as means of "observing" subjective cognition.

Practical Implications

According to the cognitive-exchange approach, some of the sources of conflict result from faulty perceptions or inferences. Without intervening to alter faulty perceptions, unrealistic expectations, and faulty inferences, training intimate partners is unlikely to have much impact. Before partners can engage in effective problem solving, faulty cognition needs correction. Of particular interest are perceptions of undesirable behavior and inferences made from them. The most sweeping changes in treatment of marital problems include not only communication training, but also cognitive restructuring, which is a means of increasing relationship satisfaction and commitment by relabeling "faulty" cognition such as misperceptions and unwarranted inferences.

Cognitive restructuring may be useful in the following ways:

- It may be used to align partners' feelings about each other. Many partners need to realize that their feelings about one another depend on their behavior toward each other. Once partners see the connection between their positive feelings and the other's behavior, they may see the necessity for acting more in ways that appear loving to the partner.

- It is useful as a means for converting unrealistic into realistic expectations and for adopting more positive expectations.

- It may be used as a method to help spouses understand "where the partner is coming from."

- Cognitive restructuring may help partners see the value of adopting a mutual orientation or a collaborative set, enacted in the form of cooperative behaviors.

- It may also be used to produce strategies of accommodation where appropriate or necessary.

Rules-Interventionist Approach to Disputes between Divorcing Spouses

Philosophical Underpinnings

Understandings that define a relationship (friends, romantic partners, spouses, parent-child) and govern interaction may be created by people over time, but during some disputes these understandings may no longer hold resulting in a breakdown in communication. The addition of an interventionist to the conflict process provides an opportunity for the mediator to fill the vacuum with rules that redefine the disputants' relationship and create new patterns of communication. Moreover, compared to private conflicts that tend to occur in the privacy of one's home or involve only the relationship partners themselves, mediated conflict in the case of divorcing spouses is more of a social, public, and cultural event.

Rules-interventionists define conflict as mediation in which a neutral third party assists parties in the process of resolving their dispute. Mediators are trained to create and enforce rules to give the mediator greater control over the outcome of the interaction. In theory, rules define social relationships and regulate social interaction. Rules are defining because they affect the way people view their relationship. Members of a culture share a common set of rules or expectations regarding friendship, courtship, marriage, or other interpersonal relationships.

In addition, as guides to action, rules may also regulate interaction when they function as criteria for choice among alternative messages (Cushman & Whiting, 1972). Analytically, regulative rules take the form of practical reasoning. X intends to bring about Z; X considers that in order to bring about Z, she or he must do Y; and therefore, X sets out to do Y. It is argued that there exists a class of human behaviors governed by a particular set of rules and that persons have some degree of choice among alternative behaviors and rule sets, monitor and critique their performance, and act in response to normative forces. Although rules are social conventions which can be violated or changed by individuals or groups, it is argued that, when people know the rules, they tend to conform to them.

By including choices, rules, and normative forces, rules-interventionists view divorce mediation as a structured social activity guided and defined by rules designed to convert competitive orientations and actions into cooperative ones. It is probably no accident that even early practice in divorce mediation was based on a rules approach.

Theoretical Developments in Divorce Mediation

Donohue, Allen, and Burrell (1988) found that successful mediators were more likely than unsuccessful ones to use more intense structuring and reframing interventions in response to attacks. The more successful mediators were also more likely to rephrase negative comments into more positive ones. Donohue and Weider-Hatfield (1988) coded twenty custody-visitation sessions (ten reaching agreement, ten not reaching agreement). They found that more successful mediators were more in control of the mediation, used more interventions to involve the divorcing partners in finding the information necessary for agreement, and distributed more of these interventions fairly and consistently between disputants.

Slaiku, Culler, Pearson, and Thoennes (1985) discovered the following patterns of actions implying that other rules are also operating:

- Speaker time was fairly evenly divided among three parties: the two spouses and the mediator.

- While mediators tended to address both spouses, husbands and wives generally directed their remarks to the mediator.

- Mediators tended to be responsible for most of the questioning in a mediatation session.

- Mediators expressed statements on procedural issues three times more than did disputants. Mediators conveyed information on what mediation is (25% of utterances) and made statements regarding the process itself (13%).

- Mediators tended to offer more statements summarizing the spouses' comments than did either party.

- Spouses emitted more emotionally toned statements than did the mediator.

- Mediators engaged in only about half as many attribution statements as did spouses. More than 35% of the statements made by both spouses were self-disclosures. Another 20% were attributions about the attitudes, motives, and actions of others, usually the other spouse.

- Perhaps in an effort to establish rapport and encourage the spouses to share their feelings, mediators' statements showed more empathy than did those uttered by the spouses.

- Mediators attempted to balance proposals by specifying how both parties could be involved, while each spouse tended to specify what he or she could do.

- Fewer than 3% of the statements were classified as interruptions (where the thought was not resumed).

Practical Implications in Divorce Mediation

By gaining control of the interaction between spouses to build a structure that is productive for creating cooperation, mediators create and enforce rules in the form of structured interventions. It is necessary to create rules that define the situation as cooperative in order to produce more cooperative action and to help the parties to understand how to integrate their own and the other's messages into a final agreement that satisfies both parties and their concerns. To do this the competent mediator functions as a translator who re-labels and redefines concepts or creates new ones in an attempt to create a common language for mediating disputes. By rewording emotionally laden statements, by stating negative comments in a more positive manner, and by explaining the value of a proposal, the mediator uses language effectively to provide an insight that can facilitate cooperative outcomes. Mediators should explain the positive and negative consequences of various proposals, restate comments as proposals, identify areas of agreement and offer their own proposals to stimulate discussion and consensus.

Divorce mediators should discourage competitive behavior where disputants present their positions and attack the other's position and encourage cooperative behavior where they discuss mutual interests, goals, or desires. First, mediators are encouraged to enforce discussion rules regarding turn-taking, interruptions, who speaks first, and who talks to whom. They should make it clear that they have the right to keep the discussion on track and to intervene when necessary. Second, because of the adversarial relationship between the parties initially and the need for the mediator to establish credibility with them, the mediator must work to create trust by laying down a few ground rules. One of these rules is to put the adversarial process, including attorneys, on hold. This rule helps create trust by eliminating the worry about being taken to court. Another ground rule is to fully and accurately disclose information regarding children, property, finances, and the parties' needs. To ensure confidentially, the parties must agree not to call the mediator to testify in court nor to introduce in court information obtained during settlement negotiations.

Mediators also need to help the parties redefine themselves and their relationship which will necessitate that they relate to one another in new ways. To do this, mediators should define the roles of all participants in the mediation session. Moreover, redefining may be accomplished through reframing intervention which attempts to revise or create spouses' understanding of their relationship.

AN OVERARCHING PARADIGM
OF CONFLICT COMMUNICATION

Presently, the three approaches to researching conflict are becoming increasingly intertwined as researchers utilize two or all three in combination (see, e.g., Weiss & Dehle, 1994). This interdependence among research approaches has resulted in the term *conflict communication*. Although conflict is a subject that has interested researchers in several different disciplines, "conflict communication" is a relatively new term that cuts across recent interdisciplinary developments by social science researchers in psychology, social psychology, communication, and family studies regarding the study of interpersonal conflict (Cahn, 1994). Conflict now refers to the general concept of any difference or incompatibility that exists between people. Although it has intuitive appeal, conflict may not be observable, but rather inferred from observed and self-reported conflict communication.

The brief description of three traditional approaches that guided research in interpersonal conflict suggests that systems-interaction includes a subject matter (partners' behaviors that are interdependent) and a method (objective observation of dyads), cognitive-exchange includes a subject matter (cognition that are interdependent) and a method (subjective self-reports), and rules-interventionist includes a subject matter (rules that regulate inter-action) and a method (objective observation of triads). An overarching paradigm would fuse (1) research on communication-related be-havior, cognition, and rules, and (2) research using a variety of methods, qualitative and quantitative.

An overarching paradigm suggests at least three propositions concerning conflict communication:

1. From the systems-interaction perspective comes the proposition that some behaviors are interdependent such that they may esca-late while others may de-escalate a conflict.

2. From the cognitive-exchange perspective comes the proposition that cognitions are interdependent such that some combinations of people's attributions and expectations lead to negative forms of conflict, exacerbate them, and make them difficult to resolve while other combinations of cognition lead to successful preven-tion or resolution of harmful conflicts.

3. From the rules-interventionist perspective comes the proposition that conflicts are influenced by communication rules that govern behavior and define cognition such that the lack of agreed upon rules makes it impossible to resolve conflict in a mutually benefi-cial way, while the creation and enforcement of shared rules make it possible for disputants to cooperate, communicate, and reach agreement.

Thus, as the term has broadened from conflict to conflict commu-nication, the different research approaches have become increas-ingly subsumed under an overarching research paradigm. By care-fully considering the relation among conflict communication behavior, cognition, and rules, an overarching paradigm offers a broader perspective on interpersonal conflict than any one of the traditional approaches.

Conflict communication theory has distinguishing features that reflect multidisciplinary developments in theory and research. First, conflict communication theory encompasses certain interpersonal behaviors and self-reported cognitive processes that reveal when a conflict exists between people. By combining behaviors and cogni-tion, researchers define conflict more broadly. As interpersonal behavior, conflict may be observed as interaction between persons expressing opposing interests, views, or opinions (Bell & Blakeney, 1977). This behavioral definition not only identifies conflict as a form of human communication but also restricts it to certain interpersonal behaviors. As self-reported cognitive processes, conflict refers to conflict management strategies involving self and other perceptions and intentions that range from a preference for direct confrontation to avoidance (Cahn, 1992). According to this cognitive definition, conflict may exist even when people are not engaged in overt disagreement. In such cases, people are said to be in conflict when they report perceived sources of conflict and select a conflict management strategy for dealing with it.

Second, conflict communication theory includes interpersonal behaviors and cognitive processes that are negative and destructive as well as those that are positive and constructive. Including both types of interpersonal behaviors and cognitive processes further broadens the concept of conflict. Researchers used to focus more on negative and destructive patterns of conflict. One reason for this is because people typically react to their differences by planning and engaging in negative behavior that becomes increasingly destructive to their relationship. Conflicts often heat up, get out of hand, and make matters worse (Rands. Levinger, & Mellinger, 1981; Gaelick et al. 1985). The self-reported cognitive processes that tend to be negative and destructive consist of conflict management strategies or preferences for dealing with conflict by avoiding (lose-lose), accommodating (obliging, lose-win), and competing (dominating, win-lose).

Conflict communication does not have to be negative, however. The interpersonal behaviors that make up positive/constructive conflict communication are supportive, equalitarian, tentative, listening, empathic, trusting, respectful, honest, problem-solving, co-operative, and nondefensive. The self-reported cognitive processes that are considered positive and constructive consist of compromising (win-some, lose-some) or, better still, collaborating (win-win). Thus, whereas many researchers used to view conflict as negative and destructive, currently conflict communication encompasses positive and constructive behaviors and cognition.

Third, conflict communication theory deals with both confrontational and nonconfrontational (avoidant) behavior and cognition. Traditionally, research on conflict is biased in favor of conflict resolution and in turn favors direct confrontation (e.g., communication) rather than avoidance. This view is embodied in the belief that the only good conflict is a resolved conflict (Hawes & Smith, 1973). Rather than favor the absolutely necessary resolution of conflict through direct confrontation, some scholars are advocating nonconfrontation (Alberts, 1990; Fitzpatrick, 1988; Pike & Sillars, 1985). Because some issues cannot productively be resolved and some relationships are not sufficiently stable, committed, or involved to handle conflict resolution, knowledge about conflict management strategies is necessary for the functioning of long-term relationships. Thus, whereas most researchers used to view conflict as a confrontational activity, more researchers are including avoidance behaviors and strategies as part of conflict communication.

Fourth, conflict communication theory covers three different situations:

1. *A Specific Disagreement.* A specific communication act or interaction, namely, an argument over a particular issue. Sometimes this disagreement is referred to as a difference of opinion or view, a complaint, criticism, hostile/coercive response, defensive behavior, or unpleasant action. In any case, people overtly disagree on some issue.

2. *A Problem-Solving Discussion.* A more extended communication act known as a negotiation or bargaining session or problem-solving discussion.

3. *An Unhappy/Dissolving Relationship.* A general pattern of communication characteristic of dysfunctional couples, stormy marriages, and partners who report that they are unhappy, dissatisfied, maladjusted, or seeking counseling.

Whereas some researchers limited themselves to one of the three conflict communication situations, others have found that the three types (specific disagreements, problem-solving discussions, and unhappy relationships) are intertwined and interrelated (Cahn, 1987). Raush, Barry, Hertel, and Swain (1974) observed husbands in unhappy marriages and determined that they used more coercive strategies and fewer reconciling acts in response to coercive strategies. Unhappy couples were found to be more coercive and less cognitive in their conflict discussions (Billings, 1979). Moreover, dissatisfied couples appear to engage in particular destructive communication behaviors when engaging in specific disagreements. Studying satisfied and dissatisfied couples, Gottman (1979) found that unhappy couples were more likely to engage in cross-complaining sequences and less likely to engage in validation sequences. Similarly, Menaghan (1982) linked the level of problems to the choice of coping efforts suggesting a worsening spiral. She concluded that as problems mount, typical coping choices may actually exacerbate distress and relationship problems. According to Ting-Toomey (1983), marital partners typically begin a conflict in a manner directly attacking one another with criticism and negatively loaded statements, followed by attempts to justify oneself and blame the other. Thus, it might be argued that partners may start out with specific disagreements that may lead to problem-solving discussions and may soon end in unhappy relationships.

Fifth, conflict communication theory attempts to explain both the interaction behaviors and cognition of the parties involved in the conflict and those of neutral third parties who intervene in an effort to help the parties resolve the conflict. Not all conflicts are alike. They vary in intensity, degree of interdependence, importance of outcomes, power imbalances, and number of parties involved. While some conflicts may be resolved by the parties themselves, other conflicts reach a point where the parties are unable to resolve the issues on their own due to a breakdown in communication, and normal relations are unlikely until the dispute is resolved. Because mediators are neutral third parties who are trained in ways to restore communication and normalize relations, they may play a positive and constructive role in resolving interpersonal conflicts.

Sixth, conflict communication theory is applicable to a broad range of interpersonal relationships. Whereas twenty years ago interpersonal conflict researchers dealt primarily with marital conflict including marital assessment, marital satisfaction, marital therapy, and divorce (e.g., Gottman, 1979), today conflict communication researchers study interpersonal conflict in dating/courtship (e.g. Lloyd, 1987), friendship (e.g., Healey & Bell, 1990), classmates at school/college (e.g., Burrell & Cahn, 1994), intercultural relationships (e.g., Fontaine, 1990; Ting-Toomey, 1994), gay/lesbian relationships (e.g., Patterson & Schwartz, 1994), violent relationships (e.g., Lloyd & Emery, 1994), parent-child relationships (e.g., Osborne & Fincham, 1994), adult children and their aging parents (e.g., Halpern, 1994), and neighbors (Danielsson, 1994).

CONCLUSION

An overarching paradigm for researching conflict communication holds the system-interaction, cognitive-exchange, and rules-interventionist approaches simultaneously in tension. A critical perspective on assumptions underlying research on interpersonal conflict, the communication paradigm allows diversity of theory and methods and maximizes perspective to render more meaningful judgments than any one of the traditional approaches. Hence, conflict communication has become a useful concept and may be defined as verbal statements and/or nonverbal cues that indicate (directly or indirectly) that a disagreement, difference, or incompatibility is perceived to exist. Because the emerging overarching paradigm is broad enough to deal with the subject of conflict communication, yet flexible and diverse without losing objectivity and rigor, it has significant potential for studying interpersonal conflict.

4

An Interactionist Framework for Peace

William A. Donohue

Scholars from any number of fields continue to search for a more refined understanding of the concept of peace. Kelman's (1981, 1991) reflections on these efforts explore the various academic disciplines that conduct research and training on the subjects of war and peace. Research in communication focuses on interpersonal aggression and violence, and such methods as negotiation and mediation to constructively manage conflict.

But, what is most interesting about Kelman's (1981, 1991) work is his reflection on the eternal struggle to define what is meant by the construct *peace*. Kelman is, of course, correct in struggling with this weighty issue because peace is probably viewed by most citizens and scholars as the optimal outcome of conflict and a necessary condition of civilization. Peace is what well-motivated citizens and dispute professionals typically work to achieve. So, it only stands to reason that we need something other than a primitive understanding of this construct. Certainly, many academic disciplines and contributors to the peace movement referenced in Kelman's articles have tried to understand the dimensions and characteristics of peace (and war) with perhaps the political scientists in international relations taking the lead in these discussions.

Yet, despite the length and intensity of these efforts, a functional, theoretically grounded understanding of the construct of peace remains elusive. Many definitions of peace are not well developed theoretically. Still others fail to offer any heuristic or pragmatic value. Nearly all conceptualize peace as a static, unidimensional phenomenon thereby glossing its subtle, complex features. I

want a better definition of peace that I can describe to students, justify to practitioners, and use in my research.

This chapter seeks to extend the dialog on this issue by first
bringing together many disciplines left unconnected in this debate,
and secondly, offering some conceptual underpinnings that might
once again infuse it with the energy it once enjoyed. I will begin
with a review of peace definitions across a variety of disciplines.
These reviews are not meant as comprehensive, but as representa-
tive of the diverse approaches available across these disciplines.

DEFINING PEACE: A REVIEW OF TRADITIONS

Political Science and International Relations

By far, the most explicit definitions of peace have grown from
the area of international relations within the field of political science. This field appears to have taken ownership of this phenomenon and has made several attempts to explicity define peace as a
concept. The other social science disciplines reviewed here have
failed to explicity define peace, but use several implicit definitions
in the conduct of their research. In political science, Kelman (1981,
1991) does an excellent job of tracking the historical foundations of
the peace science and research movement. Based on this review and
several other sources, I will approach this review organically to reveal how the definition of peace has grown into its current position.

As a leader in the peace movement, Galtung (1971, 1985) has
worked extensively to create an explicit definition of peace that has
become widely cited. In his view, peace is the absence of direct and
structural violence. Direct violence threatens personal needs for security, survival, and freedom. Structural violence threatens needs
for welfare and identity. Galtung believes that peace evolves from
societal development in which the citizens' survival, freedom, welfare, and identity needs are satisfied.

Sorensen (1992) finds this definition excessively utopian since
he believes it is impossible to point to developed (or any, for that
matter) societies where violence, repression and alienation are absent. Development is a two edged sword that brings material
wealth, but many forms of oppression. Instead, Sorensen (1992) re-
treats to the more simple concept of viewing peace as the *absence of
violence*. To conceptualize peace in terms of a set of positive human

conditions requires establishing unrealistic, utopian prescriptions. Sorensen expands this approach by describing what he calls developmental violence. A little violence administered in the short term to prevent escalated violence later is developmental violence. Sorensen views this developmental violence as an act of peace. This position has been criticized extensively, generally because peace is not really distinguished from war and its consequences (Kelley, 1991). Nevertheless, the Sorensen argument represents an important, controversial position in the peace movement.

Rapoport (1972) provides an additional, explicit definition of peace. His vision of peace certainly mirrors Galtung's (1971), while simultaneously rejecting the Sorensen's (1992) utopian critique. Rapoport, with Kelman's (1981) endorsement, defines two types of peace: positive and negative. Positive peace is the unification of humanity into cooperative enterprise. This state of human interaction creates conditions that prevent violence from occuring, and provides the context for arms control, crisis manipulation, and deterrence. In contrast, negative peace is the absence of systematic, large-scale, collective violence. The spirit of cooperation is not present. People are simply not fighting. Sorensen would probably support the concept of negative peace and dismiss the utopian vision of a positive peace. Kelman (1981) moves a step beyond the rather fuzzy Galtung model of peace as development, and defines positive peace in terms of a public health model. He lays out a set of assumptions that explicity defines peace as the establishment of good public health policy. A peaceful society is a livable (not perfect), socially desirable (not conflict free), and healthy (not disease free) place.

This brief summary of very detailed positions on peace represents some of the most well-developed, *explicit* thinking on peace. However, there is an extensive body of work on war and violence in political science that yields many *implicit* definitions of peace. Or, at least these works make certain assumptions about what peace is or is not, or what conditions constitute peace. In fact, each of these positions seeks to fulfill Galtung's, Rapoport's, and Kelman's need to say what peace is while implicitly rejecting Sorensen's position that this is a futile task. Thus, it seems prudent not to ignore these works simply because they fail to provide explicit definitions of peace. These works should be discussed because they round out our understanding of what a peaceful or nonpeaceful society looks like.

For example, several major lines of research seem to make the implicit claim that *prolonged affect or irrationality* is not peace. Singer's (1990) concept of the "invisible hand" comes to mind as an example of this position. Singer claims, drawing on Adam Smith, that the invisible hand of rationality, in which nations or individuals function in their own best self-interests, is an important precondition for avoiding war. Unfortunately, he concludes that nations are not prone to act with this invisible hand as evidenced by a wide variety of wars and conflicts that are self-devastating for nations. Nevertheless, the rational hand possesses the logical capability of bringing about peace.

Carmet's (1993) investigation of the effects of prolonged affect on ethnic violence represents an empirical extension of Singer's hand. Prolonged, affective, and presumably irrational interactions among ethnic groups contribute extensively to increased violence. Affect blinds parties to their own interests, and certainly to the interests of the other parties in any integrative sense. Herek, Janis, and Huth's (1987) often-cited paper on decision making in international conflict demonstrates how affect and irrationality impede productive decision making in crises. When parties fail to use careful (or vigilant) decision-making processes, they also fail to create and enact policies in their own best interests.

These positions seem to converge around the implicit definition of peace as an *interaction condition that mixes rationality and irrationality with more of the former and less of the latter*. At least two features of this position are important. First, peace appears to rest not just in the psychological constructs of citizens, elites, ethnic groups, or any other populations. Rather, this position fixes peace within the domain of an interaction structure between people that is dominated by systematic exchange patterns. This position certainly does not claim that peace is absent from the mind. People have affect, values, beliefs, and attitudes. In fact, Morrow's (1989) work shows very clearly that actors who value risk are more likely to go to war. However, this position implicitly claims that peace also exists in, and is negotiated through interaction. Therefore, it is subjected to the myriad constraints on human interaction. So, we must know about interaction to know about peace. Second, this focus on rationality and affect does not claim that only rational discourse is peaceful. The position only calls for a balance between affective, irrational interaction, and systematic, rational interaction.

Three other research programs in political science also locate peace within the context of interaction, but focus more on negotiation and dispute resolution rather than on decision making. For example, Greffenius and Gill's (1992) interesting examination of approaches to implementing foreign policy directives finds that carrot-and-stick offers secure compliance more readily than straight coercion. Negotiation works better than force. This finding is interesting in light of the U.S.–North Korea crisis in which coercion had little impact on the North Koreans, but the offer of a nonmilitary nuclear power plant seemed to turn the North Koreans toward negotiation.

Along a parallel track, Suedfeld and Bluck (1988) focus on governmental communications between nations involved in surprise attacks with one another. They note that just before surprise attacks, the integrative complexity of the communication decreases significantly. An integratively complex message recognizes the existence of alternative perspectives, arguments, and positions on issues. As attackers move closer to their surprise invasions, they keep talking, but they start sending significantly less complex messages about two to four weeks before the actual attack.

Focusing more broadly on dispute resolution in peacekeeping efforts, Evans (1993) lays out the conditions under which the U.S. military involvement is needed. He begins by defining peacekeeping as the variety of measures taken to prevent and control violent conflict. He includes arbitration, mediation, and election supervision as examples of such measures. Evans then describes the value of using the military to facilitate these peaceful measures. Thus, both the Evans' and the Suedfeld and Bluck's (1988) programs emphasize communication aimed at understanding the subtlety and diversity of opposing positions in a secure environment.

These three orientations assume the position that *peace is integratively complex, incentive-based (noncoercive) communication aimed at a good-faith effort to negotiate differences*. Again, the emphasis is on interaction that tries to remain rational and problem centered. Rationality appears in the incentive-based approach to peace, and integratively complex messages signal good faith communication efforts. Thus, peace is cooperative, mostly systematic discourse.

Finally, it is important to discuss the power issue and its role in war and peace. Two research programs are worth noting here. Houweling and Siccama's (1988, 1991) research seeks to address the role of power balance transitions among major military powers in causing war. Indeed, these authors find historical support for the hypothesis that big power swings among major military powers encourage war making. Power instability sufficiently disrupts relations and emboldens militaries. In another research program focusing on power and affiliation, Winter (1993) searches for a psychological explanation for war. In an analysis of messages across several international conflict situations, he learned that war generally follows messages that communicate domination and disaffiliation.

These research programs are significant for this chapter because they demonstrate the importance of maintaining power stability and communicating in a manner that reifies that power stability in achieving peace. When parties seek to dominate one another either communicatively or militarily, they sow the seeds for war.

Based on these research programs, derived largely on an international relations, political science approach to understanding peace, we can glean a summary definition of peace: *Peace is mostly rational, integrative, and cooperative, incentive-based interaction between risk-averse actors who like one another and function within balanced and stable power relations.* Peace is not simply the absence of war or hostile, destructive conflict. Peace is a behavioral (generally interstate communication behavior) condition among interdependent actors. This last point is important because none of the papers reported here discuss peace as a state of affairs among nations that are exclusively independent with one another. The assumption that these studies appear to make is that two nations that have never communicated, traded, or exchanged contact of any kind cannot be at peace with one another. These nations are simply irrelevant to one another. "Being at peace" only makes sense when the parties have chosen to develop some kind of relationship with one another, and have chosen the path identified in this definition.

Finally, it is important to note that I have concentrated on defining peace in its conceptual domain. I am not concerned with how peace is operationalized through international peace keeping efforts, for example. Peacekeeping is an entirely different subject. This chapter deals with the core conceptual issues regarding how people view peace.

Psychology

Like political science, the discipline of psychology continues a strong tradition of searching for knowledge about destructive conflict, violence, and aggression. An extensive review of studies in this area moves beyond the scope of this paper. Felson and Tedeschi's (1993) recent volume on aggression and violence does an excellent job of reviewing these traditions. However, several major research programs stick out as instructional regarding their views of peace. But, like the majority of peace perspectives reviewed in political science, those offered in psychology remain an implicit product of their theoretical orientations.

For example, Deutsch's (1973, 1994) work on cooperation and competition must be viewed as a very pivotal research program that promotes very explicit ideas about peace, although Deutsch never explicitly labels them as peace initiatives. However, in a recent article on this issue, Deutsch (1994) outlines a very detailed program aimed at preventing destructive conflict. He prescribes specific communication and negotiation strategies that people in government, education, the media, and so on, can use to build a more cooperative (and peaceful) society. Again, peace is viewed as a set of prosocial interaction conditions.

Blake and Mouton's (1964) and Rahim's (1983) pioneering works on conflict and managerial styles propose similar orientations about peace and conflict. These research programs describe the productivity gains associated with individuals pursuing more collaborative approaches to the management of conflict. They also talk about the dangers of relying exclusively on such strategies as avoiding conflict, capitulating to others' demands, or encouraging prolonged periods of competition. Again, peace is a particular form of constructive interaction that promotes positive outcomes.

Finally, Berkowitz's (1989) view of peace contrasts a bit with his fellow psychologists because he (not explicitly) takes Sorensen's (1985) position of defining peace in terms of what it is not. Berkowitz's research on aggression seeks to explain its driving forces. By settling on his famous frustration explanation and avoiding the pursuit of Deutsch-like strategies to reduce aggression, Berkowitz implicitly defines peace as simply *the absence of aggression*. When frustration dominates behavior, the potential for aggression looms large.

Combining these orientations, it seems reasonable to assume that the psychologists reviewed here define peace as *integrative, collaborative interaction, conducted in the context of nonfrustrating circumstances, that does not avoid conflict, or capitulate to the other's demands*. The trend observed in political science continues in psychology. Peace exhibits a variety of positive interaction qualities that humanity must strive to maximize. And, more significantly, the psychologists steadfastly stick to this position despite its vulnerability to the utopian critique.

Marital Communication

The marital communication literature is vast and growing. In recent years, several texts have appeared that seek to provide couples and their therapists/facilitators with insights aimed at strengthening marriages. The consensus among the most prolific authors contributing to this area is that the key to understanding long-term marital satisfaction lies in understanding how couples communicate, or exchange information (Notarious & Markman, 1993; Gottman, 1994). More specifically, these authors make the rather bald claim that they can predict, with over 90 percent accuracy, whether or not couples will divorce based *only* on an analysis of their conflict management interaction behaviors. They need no other information about personality compatibility, attitude similarity, religious orientation, etc. to predict marital satisfaction.

The apparent goal of this literature is to identify how married couples keep the peace, or interact in a way that strengthens their relationship. Basically, this research has discovered that marital peace is, once again, an interaction condition. Peace is *reciprocally supportive communication that avoids excessive criticism, contempt, defensiveness, or stonewalling (avoidance).* Perhaps this position provides tactical fiber to the psychologist's call for more integrative, collaborative interaction. Parties interact collaboratively when they, at a minimum, display verbal and nonverbal signals of respect for one another. These signals become a necessary condition for peace.

Other research in the communication area refines this position a bit. Sillars, Weisberg, Burggraf, and Wilson (1987), Putnam (1990), and Donohue (1991), report work from their research programs that seeks to unearth plausible explanations for the fairly powerful findings in the marital area. Their work focuses on the fundamental qualities of language in the formation and development of interpersonal relationships. In sum, these programs center largely on the issue of relational control. When parties try to dominate one another using a broad range of linguistic markers, they compromise their ability to resolve conflicts productively (Sillars et al., 1987), negotiate integratively (Putnam, 1990), or reach mediated child-custody arrangements (Donohue, 1991). Their take on peace seems to fall in line with previous positions by again implicitly defining peace as *relationally constructive interaction that avoids oneupsmanship, or an exclusive focus on relational, nonsubstantive issues, and personality-based attributions of responsibility that lead to conflict avoidance.* Clearly, these research trends parallel one another and give fairly detailed prescriptions about what qualities lead toward productive conflict management.

Criminal Justice and Sociology

Research in sociology and criminal justice displays a long history of working to address various conflict and violence issues. For example, in criminal justice, Felson and Tedeschi (1993) review many decades of research, much of which is their own, that seeks to understand the theoretical and empirical foundations of violence and aggression. Unlike the psychologists, they take a symbolic interactionist view on these issues and provide considerable evidence to support the claim that aggression and violence are used to protect individual identity. They describe specific interaction sequences individuals use to escalate identity reproaches into physical violence. Similarly, Gittler's (1989) sociological take on conflict presses this same emphasis on identity in a series of invited papers dealing with families, gender, ethnicity, race, and related topics. For example, Kim's (1989) chapter, seeking to explain inter ethnic conflict, drives home the point that ethnic conflicts develop around the protection of identity needs. Other chapters dealing with gender and families make similar points.

Collectively, then, both the criminal justice and sociological orientations toward conflict make the implicit claim that peace is *controlled, non-identity-threatening interaction that avoids escalation to aggression.* Once again, these traditions focus on peace as a quality of interaction supporting the focus on this behavior, or the assumption that interdependence is required for a condition of peace to exist. When individuals interact in a way that refrains from reproaching the other's identity, they reduce the potential of escalating to aggression. However, these research traditions do not claim that avoiding conflict also leads to peace. To the contrary, they maintain that avoiding divisive identity issues often breeds aggressive interaction. These underlying tensions surface in the guise of some other issue. So, peace does not involve hiding from anything.

Of course, many other disciplines, and research programs within these disciplines, provide insights about the concept of peace. These brief reviews seek only to highlight what appear to be the major themes running through various scholars' understanding of peace. This brief review demonstrates that there lies a great deal of consistency across positions, and more importantly, provides for the possibility of creating a new definition of peace that is more conceptually secure and pragmatically useful. Perhaps the best place to begin this quest is to identify some criteria for defining peace based on these research traditions. Following these criteria, a model and definition of peace will be offered.

CRITERIA FOR A MODEL OF PEACE

A Balanced, Nonprescriptive Perspective

Nearly all the traditions and programs reviewed here choose to view peace in terms of what it is as opposed to what it is not. This positive presentation casts peace as a set of conditions that facilitate "peaceful" behavior. I do not share Sorensen's (1992) concern that this positive cast completely undermines the concept because of the difficulty of achieving these conditions. Indeed, most of the perspectives reviewed here do not argue for the presence of these conditions in their extreme. For example, Deutsch's (1994) most recent comment on this issue fully recognizes that peace is really a balance between cooperative and competitive behavior (but, with admittedly more of the former and less of the latter). So, to some extent, Deutsch falls into the same utopian trap as the others who choose to specify ideal behaviors capable of fostering a better society. Yet, Deutsch moves a step further by maintaining that peace is essentially a balance between opposing forces. This step moves in the right direction of trying to avoid being excessively utopian, so it seems reasonable to require that any model of peace reflect this notion of balance between opposing forces.

However, if we take the position that peace is really a balance between opposing forces, then we must also be less prescriptive about what people must do to achieve peace. As Sorensen (1992) points out in his position about developmental violence, sometimes circumstances require promoting aggressive behavior in the short term to avoid prolonged aggressive behavior in the long term. This position suggests that it is quite difficult to build a model of peace that prescribes the specific path parties must pursue to achieve peace. Parties have available a full range of behaviors they can use to achieve the kind of peace they find very functional. Outsiders may choose to call that form of peace dysfunctional and they are certainly free to voice those concerns and work with the parties to alter those behaviors. Nevertheless, it seems reasonable to build a model of peace that is more descriptive of the balance parties achieve between opposing forces.

Focused on Interdependence

The second criterion reflected in these research traditions is that peace is a condition of nations, groups, and people who share some history of interdependence. They have some linkage that yields some kind of interaction history. This relational criterion can be very weak, of course, in the sense that two developing nations that have never directly exchanged anything find themselves involved in alliances that oppose one another. This indirect linkage forms the basis of at least some kind of relationship. For groups the concept of independence is a bit easier to understand because it is more likely that groups can exist independently from one another while it is difficult to envision that possibility about nations. Nevertheless, it makes no sense to view two nations or groups at peace if they have no history of interdependence. In this case, they are independent and not at peace. Peace is a quality of a relationship, not of a nonrelationship.

Relationally Centered

Third, and related to this quality of interdependence, the various disciplines reviewed here seem to view peace (or war and violence) as primarily a relational concept. They seem to argue that because a relationship is necessary to say that entities are at peace, we should probably study peace from this relational perspective. What we know about relationships and how they develop should be brought forward into this discussion.

For example, Winter's (1993) paper makes the most explicit claim about the dimensions that ought to be used to understand peace. He (implicitly) makes a pitch for conceptualizing peace using two prominent relational clusters: domination/power/ interdependence and affiliation/trust/respect. The first cluster focuses on the extent to which parties can influence, or control one another. The traditional view of power looks at compelling adversaries to do one's will. However, a more contemporary view of power seeks to understand how parties can influence or control one another. Boulding (1990) argues convincingly that power associated with threat, exchange, or love only makes sense in the context of the relationship between parties. Power is an interdependence issue. Coming from an interaction perspective then, *interdependence is defined as the extent to which individuals can demand rights and impose obligations on one another.* This notion of power as interdependence is suggested in Houweling and Siccama's (1991) analysis of power transitions. Consistent with Boulding, their position assumes that power is really a balance issue and is only meaningfully understood, at a minimum, as a dyadic, relational phenomenon.

The second relational cluster, affiliation, pulls together research in psychology and other fields cited above that focuses on expressions of warmth, friendliness, intimacy, respect, trust, and cooperation (see Winter, 1993, for a review). Parties typically draw from a long list of well-practiced messages that have the effect of building affiliation with one another (see Donohue & Roberto, 1993, for a review). *Affiliation is defined as the extent to which individuals communicate attraction, liking, acceptance, and trust.* Parties can exchange these messages of affiliation directly through overt expressions of liking, or they can indirectly frame their messages with expressions of approval, liking, and trust. In his research, Winter codes affiliation messages by focusing on expressions of friendship, intimacy, negative feelings, and nurturing acts.

Interactively Accomplished

Fourth, the research programs reviewed here make a fairly strong claim, generally implicitly, that peace is a condition of parties' interactions. States exchange messages through many media that range from letters to missiles, and individuals choose a similar range of communication tools to accomplish their goals. This position does not claim that peace is not also a state of mind and that message exchanges are simply a reflection of those thoughts. Rather, peace is witnessed through sequences of behaviors that achieve that label. When those sequences are demonstrated, then parties can claim that they have accomplished peace. Parties may actually hate one another, but interact in a peaceful manner. So, it is probably most productive to stick with observables and consider peace as something that parties do, together, as opposed to primarily something they think about.

Dynamically Managed

The final criterion for creating a more functional definition of peace addresses the problem of change. Winter's work (1993) is instructional here. In his study of power and affiliation message shifts during the Cuban Missile Crisis of 1962, Winter discovered that government leaders frequently altered their power and affiliation orientations toward one another, often in the same day. It would make no sense to look at that crisis and declare that one kind of peace prevailed throughout. Different orientations toward peace fluctuated dramatically as they typically do in crisis (Donohue & Roberto, 1993). Peace is always in the act of becoming something different, while also redefining what came before. Any attempt to understand peace must capitalize on this insight about relationships. The framework ought to provide language capable of tracking the way in which nations, organizations, groups, and dyads move between various kinds of peaceful orientations.

These criteria identify some principles we might use to build an appropriate framework for thinking about peace. Clearly, any discussion of this topic ought to reflect a range of peaceful and nonpeaceful behaviors and not function prescriptively to specify what counts in some absolute sense as peaceful interaction. And, it should also claim that peace is achieved only when parties are interdependent. In addition, the framework should approach peace as a relational process that is accomplished through, and observed within interaction. Finally, the framework ought to capture the way in which parties transition in and out of various peace conditions. With these criteria in mind, the framework can be presented.

AN INTERACTIONIST
FRAMEWORK FOR PEACE

Overview

This framework seeks to position interdependence and affiliation in relation to one another. There is some empirical precedence for this approach. For example, Winter (1993) discovered that expressions of high power (dominance) and low affiliation (unfriendliness and disdain) typically preceded war. Similarly, Donohue and Roberto (1993) found in hostage negotiations that messages of high interdependence (parties seeking to dominate one another) combined with low affiliation (parties seeking to psychologically distance themselves from one another) often preceded periods of high physical threat. Conversely, when parties expressed high interdependence and high affiliation, they were more likely to problem-solve. These precedents suggest that examining these two relational clusters as functions of one another can yield significant bounty. For this chapter, the labels of affiliation and interdependence will be used, as defined above. With these two dimensions, the following framework is offered:

	Low Interdependence	High Interdependence
High Affiliation	Conditional Peace	Unconditional Peace
Low Affiliation	Isolationist Peace	Competition/Aggression

Unconditional Peace. Unconditional peace is typical of a utopian view of peace. When parties communicate using expressions of high affiliation and interdependence, they are proposing to become more involved with one another in a cooperative manner. This combination challenges parties to create a relational context that honors role obligations over individual rights. The focus on obligations invests parties in the needs of the relationship over the needs of the individuals. In this sense, the relationship is unconditional. Parties express mutual liking, so they accept their obligations for the sake of solidifying the relationship while paying little attention to their individual rights that might upset the relationship. Since the relationship or other related issues like identity or trust are not the focus of the interaction, parties are free to concentrate on exchanging information, pressing proposals, offering concessions, and so forth to create a mostly problem or task-focused exchange.

Isolationist Peace. However, when parties communicate with low levels of both affiliation and interdependence, they send isolationist messages. Parties seek to reduce their ties, push away from one another and isolate themselves from the relationship. It is an isolationist peace in the sense that parties are not fighting, but they are not moving forward productively with their substantive agenda. Perhaps they might need time to recover from some incident with the other party. Or they might need to isolate themselves for a while. Nevertheless, the goal in this condition is to create distance from role obligations, and perhaps create new role frameworks to restructure or terminate the relationship. Interaction in this condition might consist of less frequent, and superficial information exchange simply to keep up appearances of adhering to old role prescriptions. Or parties might try to distribute messages supporting their own face to maintain their credibility while they are trying to withdraw from the relationship. Under Sorensen's (1992) perspective, this kind of peace would not be different from unconditional peace because, in both conditions, parties are not aggressing upon one another. However, unconditional peace emphasizes constructive processes while isolationist peace emphasizes withdrawal.

Conditional Peace. In this condition of low interdependence and high affiliation, parties exchange messages that seek to retain their role autonomy, yet demonstrate approval and positive affect for one another. They assert few rights because they are not sufficiently interdependent to demand much. Yet they remain friendly and polite, generally as an attempt to escalate the level of interdependence. This is conditional peace because parties are typically testing one another to decide whether to expand interdependence and role obligations. A courting relationship might be a useful metaphor here. They send increasing signals toward a desire to encumber the role obligations associated with increased interdependence, but their commitment is conditional. This conditional acceptance is stripped away in unconditional peace. In unconditional peace, parties have made the commitment to remain highly involved with one another and encumber those role expectations. However, in both conditional and unconditional peace, the relationship is generally secondary to substantive agenda. Under both conditions, parties could be expected to bargain constructively in good faith.

Competition/Aggression. In this final condition, parties send unaffiliative and disapproving messages in the context of relational dependence. The focus moves away from group, or dyadic priorities and toward parties asserting their rights aimed at achieving their own goals while also resisting their group/alliance obligations. Since the focus is on asserting rights and resisting obligations, the communication carries almost a moral imperative and authority with it. Parties must resist with all their resources because key, central, and defining rights have been violated. This is the kind of communication Winter (1993) observed during the Cuban Missile Crisis of 1962. The United States certainly asserted its right to enforce the Monroe Doctrine that seeks to prevent non–Western Hemisphere countries from establishing military dominance in the Western Hemisphere. Yet, as letters from Khrushchev became more conciliatory, the United States altered its focus away from rights more toward specific substantive issues. The parties moved away from aggression temporarily by trying to increase affiliation.

These four cells constitute an alternative way of conceptualizing peace in its various forms. It contrasts with other positions because it offers more refined ways of thinking about peace. To provide a sense of the value of this framework and how it might work, it is necessary to specify how it functions both theoretically and empirically.

FRAMEWORK FUNCTIONING

Theoretical Issues

Interactionism. Understanding and using this framework requires addressing certain key theoretical and empirical issues. Let's begin with the theoretical issues. The first issue that needs development is the issue of locating peace in interaction as opposed to locating it in the psychological constructs of actors. This is the heart of an interactionist perspective on this problem. Interactionists believe that interaction-based research perspectives (like the peace definition and framework offered here) should focus on the joint accomplishment of the communicators and not only on the communicators as individuals (see Donohue, 1990, for a review of interactionism). The rationale surrounding this perspective stems from symbolic interactionism as articulated most recently by Blumer (1969). Specifically, individuals form their essential social awareness as persons through the interaction process. Through role-taking, individuals develop self-concepts, or identities, by aligning their social actions with one another and then assessing the confirming or disconfirming nature of that social interaction. This process forges the link between interaction and identity. An individual's, group's, organization's, or nation's identity is a product of the way in which these parties align their actions with other individuals, groups, and so on. For example, through various official communications, a national government can send dominating communications to another government that acquiesces to those dominating moves. Overtime, the persistence of this pattern forms identities about strength and national, political will for both nations. And, just like people, nations interact with many other nations so their identities are complex and ever changing.

The point of raising this issue is to identify the conceptual home for this framework. The home is symbolic interactionism and its ability to tease out the key qualities of relationships. Since relationships are the essence of this peace framework, it is important to be very candid about its conceptual roots.

Transitions. The second conceptual issue that warrants exposure surrounds the dynamic quality of the framework. Specifically, the framework is not meant to simply expand the number of ways we think about peace from one to three. The important point of the framework is that peace means understanding the transitions between the various conditions. This dynamic way of thinking is fairly foreign to disciplines caught in static, Aristotelian perspectives. As a communication scholar, the conceptual apparatus I use must mirror the ephemeral quality of the communication phenomenon I study or it has no chance of revealing its essential features. Peace, if viewed as an interaction condition, must then be approached from a similarly ephemeral perspective. That is, it is not particularly important to say that a nation, or group is communicating in a manner that signals unconditional peace right at this moment. We must strive to understand how patterns stabilize into a constructive or destructive contexts. Patterns will be different for different relationships. Functional patterns for some will be dysfunctional for others. We must honor this reality and adjust our thinking about peace accordingly.

Peace as Subtextual Negotiation. The final conceptual issue that bears upon this framework deals with the problem of identifying a theoretical perspective that explains how peace gets accomplished between parties. First is the problem of where peace is located interactionally. That is, I have argued that peace is a condition of parties' relationships and is enacted and revealed through their interaction. But is it generally an overt condition that lies on the surface as a formal topic of interaction? Or is peace subtextual, lying beneath the surface of other substantive topics? In their review of relationships in conflict, Donohue and Ramesh (1993) make a case for viewing relationships as subtextual phenomena. Parties infrequently discuss issues of respect, control, trust, and the like. Rather, disputants are more likely to raise other topics relevant to the substance of the conflict. For example, in divorce mediation, Donohue (1991) found that divorcing parties use custody and visitation issues to work through their relational problems. They cloak these problems in more superficial issues that were really unsolvable unless the relational issues are brought to the surface and addressed. How parties use language to frame topics provides the data about the relationship.

Second is the problem of how more or less peaceful contexts are constructed by parties. Perhaps the best current explanation of this process lies in Strauss's (1978) Negotiated Order Theory. Strauss contends that social order is negotiated subtextually as parties interact about their substantive issues. Individuals establish a wide range of social limits through this tacit negotiation process. One party tacitly proposes a relational limit, for example, and if the other party reciprocates that parameter, then Strauss argues that one parameter of the social order has been negotiated. The limit stays in effect until it is tacitly raised again by one or both parties.

For example, parties always negotiate relational limits when they interact. Messages about control are always present in communication (Watzlawick, Beavin & Jackson, 1967), for instance. One party may send a message using very formal language that, in effect, seeks to create or verify a formal communication context. The other may reject that formality by using profanity or other informal messages. Parties may continue with this lack of consensus for some time, or they may converge on limits they find useful for their purposes. Strauss's (1978) theory is useful because it defines the process by which individuals negotiate peace and move from condition to condition within the framework.

The pragmatic value of taking this position is evident in both Suedfeld and Bluck's (1988) and Winter's (1993) communication studies. These studies examined characteristics of individual messages and then tied them into war events. In both research programs, the communicative displays examined were subtextual features of the messages. However, in both studies, the authors explored message features from only one party's perspective. The model offered in this chapter would look at message exchange, and the joint negotiation of peace parameters. It would look for tacit peace proposals and acceptance and rejection of those proposals, and the establishment of peace limits. It would then explore the development of peace patterns over time and determine which patterns lead to and away from war.

Empirical Issues

Message Exchange. The first empirical issue stems from the conceptual move to examine message exchange in contrast to features of single messages in isolation. To accomplish this task empirically, it is necessary to tie messages to one another and provide evidence that the messages respond to one another in a sequential manner. This task is fairly straightforward in ordinary interpersonal, face-to-face exchanges in which the researcher assumes that each message is linked to its prior and subsequent message. This assumption is more difficult in analyzing official messages between governments. Who is to say that one message was delivered in response to a prior message? The point here is that meeting this empirical standard is necessary when using the peace framework offered here.

Operationalizing Peace Parameters. Certainly, the empirical strength of this framework is found in the parameters used to analyze the message exchanges. Most studies have used language analyses because they have obvious advantages. The data are present, observable, and any number of ways are available to tease relational information from the language. Donohue and Roberto's (1993) study of relational patterns in hostage negotiations examined verbal immediacy. This study looked for cues that the parties were seeking to expand or reduce psychological distance from one another, and trying to dominate one another. This framework demands that researchers identify relational parameters that provide good estimates of affiliation and interdependence. This task may be difficult if nonlanguage-based messages are the focus of the study.

Data Analysis. Traditional time series analyses are difficult to use when conducting this kind of research. One technique that is valuable in understanding the negotiation of subtextual peace parameters is phase mapping (Holmes & Poole, 1991). In this technique communication messages are coded into some small number of categories, generally from 4 to 8. The procedure then groups the messages sequentially by consistent codes. For example, in a recent study of hostage negotiation, Donohue and Roberto (1993) categorized hostage-taker, police-negotiator interaction into the four peace-related categories presented in this chapter based on an analysis of disputant's verbal immediacy. The results are listed in table 4.1 for the first twenty relational contexts developed in one hostage negotiation case.

Without going into extensive detail about the coding scheme, the study, these data provide an example of how disputants negotiate peace conditions as they interact. The first three contexts reveal how the system works. In the first context, over 70 percent (the cut-off criterion) of utterances 1 through 20 sought to establish a condition of isolationist peace, as indicated by the verbal immediacy markers described previously. The hostage-taker and hostage negotiator reciprocated these same relational orientations for

TABLE 4.1
Peace Contexts for a Criminal Hostage Negotiation

Context Number	Peace Condition	Start Number	Stop Number
1.	Isolationist Peace	1	20
2.	Null	21	23
3.	Isolationist Peace	24	39
4.	Aggression	40	70
5.	Null	71	74
6.	Isolationist Peace	75	80
7.	Isolationist Peace/Aggression	81	89
8.	Aggression	90	95
9.	Isolationist Peace	96	118
10.	Aggression	119	124
11.	Null	125	132
12.	Aggression/Isolationist Peace	133	141
13.	Isolationist Peace	142	146
14.	Null	147	156
15.	Aggression	157	166
16.	Isolationist Peace	167	170
17.	Null	171	173
18.	Isolationist Peace	174	178
19.	Null	179	181
20.	Isolationist Peace	182	194

The start and stop numbers indicate the utterance number at which the phase started and stopped.
Do the patterns afford more or less productive intervention points?

twenty utterances. Then, at utterances 21 through 23, there was no agreement on a relational condition between the disputants, which is called a "Null" condition. Then, at utterance 24 the parties transitioned back into an isolationist peace condition for the next several utterances. When two conditions are specified as in context 7, then parties alternate between the two contexts. Looking at all twenty contexts it appears that the disputants alternated between isolationist peace and aggression in developing their relational contexts.

This same kind of approach could be used to analyze any kind of message exchange process to determine how parties negotiate peace between themselves. Statistics from each negotiation can be calculated and tied to outcomes. For example, in the Donohue and

Roberto (1993) article, several independent variables were calculated including the number of phases across each of the five (including the null) main relational conditions. These variables estimate the amount of talk time the disputants spent in any one given phase. Then, the number of mixed phases were tallied. The mean length of the phases was also calculated to determine if phase stability is important. Also, a ratio of null phases to the non null phases was calculated to determine the level of relational consensus in the conflict. In another study using this same approach in a divorce mediation context, we are currently tying these independent variables to various outcome variables.

CONCLUSIONS

Meeting the Criteria

This new framework for peace works to meet the five criteria for what an alternative approach should look like. For example, the framework is not prescriptive in the same tradition as Kelman's (1981) bold notion of positive peace. Nor does it impose behavioral objectives on parties. It seeks to understand, in a more refined sense, how parties transition through various relational states and balance, or fail to balance, opposing forces. The issue then becomes learning how to support the constructive patterns and redirect unconstructive ones *for those parties.* It does not assume that "one size fits all," and that everyone should work toward unconditional peace. Parties may find other constructive patterns that work for them, and these should be respected. In a sense, this framework extends Deutsch's (1994) idea that peace is a balance between competition and cooperation. Parties find their own balance points.

The framework also tries to meet the other criteria head on. For example, the framework stresses *interdependence.* Peace is only an issue for people exchanging messages and building relationships. Also, the framework is *relationally centered* and *interactively focused.* The framework sits directly on the point that peace is a relational issue, and that relationships are accomplishments of interaction, and thus, best centered there. Finally, the framework assumes that peace is managed *dynamically.* Parties create more or less constructive relational contexts that are continuously in the process of being redefined. The framework offers the theoretical and empirical tools to gain access to these two characteristics of peace.

A Third Alternative

Redefining peace is a tradition in political science and other fields that work so persistently to uncover something that will make a difference. Scholars like Sorensen (1992) seem to have given up on specifying what peace is by preferring to identify what it is not. More scholars prefer to make the utopian plunge into more constructive waters and see if it is possible to create a sense of peace that serves as a set of prescriptive, behavioral objectives for humanity. Rapoport (1972) and Kelman (1981) are notable examples of this prescriptive, utopian approach.

This chapter takes a third approach. It looks at peace not as a set of behavioral objectives for civilization, but as a set of relational conditions that scholars, practitioners, politicians, and the like, can use empirically and pragmatically to understand patterns that lead toward and away from aggression. It is important to emphasize that this chapter does not claim that all interaction must occur within the cell labeled "Unconditional Peace" since this condition may lead to Janis's (1972) famous phenomenon of groupthink. Members of the group are afraid to disagree or demonstrate any negative affiliation since that might risk group cohesiveness.

Rather, this chapter claims that nations, organizations, groups, or individuals may develop peaceful relational patterns that they find quite constructive for their needs. They may develop a pattern that begins at conditional peace, and moves quickly to unconditional peace and stays in that context briefly until it moves to competition/aggression briefly, and then back to unconditional peace. This pattern may stabilize and become quite functional for the parties involved.

This third position may address many of the strengths and weaknesses evident in the opposing positions of Rapoport (1972) and Kelman (1981), who advocate a utopian position on peace, and Sorensen (1992), who advocates the not-war view of peace. In contrast to the Sorensen position, the third alternative pressed in this chapter claims that peace must be viewed as something other than not war. It must consist of some relational conditions. And, in contrast to the utopian positions prescribing what we should be working toward (unconditional peace), this third alternative makes no claims about what kind of peace will work for everyone. The more prudent approach is to provide a refined understanding of what peace is, and then understand how people create it dynamically to suit their own purposes. This backs away considerably from the stronger prescriptive approach, but makes the concept more useful than the not-war approach.

I have been conducting research and outreach in conflict long enough to know that peace is not a simple phenomenon. It is not possible to provide a set of prescriptions that people should live by. Yet it is also not something that we should back away from understanding because of its complexity. Accomplishing peace among nations, organizations, groups, and individuals means understanding those parties and how they negotiate their complex social order. Only by tapping into that social order can we begin to help parties build something constructive for themselves. Every mediator lives by this rule. As scholars, we should live by it as well. Unfortunately, we have not had the conceptual tools to do so. Hopefully, this third approach provides some of those tools.

5

Media Agenda-Setting Theory
Telling the Public What to Think About

Jian-Hua Zhu & Deborah Blood

EMERGENCE OF A RESEARCH TRADITION

In 1972, two journalism professors at University of North Carolina-Chapel Hill, Maxwell McCombs and Donald Shaw, published an article in *Public Opinion Quarterly* that proved to be the genesis of a new research tradition in mass communications. Known as the Chapel Hill study, McCombs and Shaw demonstrated that the mass media could influence audiences in ways only previously speculated. Using a simple but innovative methodology, they first conducted a content analysis of both the press and television newscasts in order to identify what issues the media were emphasizing during the 1968 presidential election, and then surveyed 100 undecided voters in the Chapel Hill area to find out what issues they felt to be the most important. By performing a simple rank-order correlation, the authors found some stunning results: an almost perfect correlation (as high as .97) between the two sets of issue salience (figure 5.1). It appeared that issue salience, or what the public considered to be the most important issues of the day, was being shaped by the mass media. McCombs and Shaw labeled this phenomenon "agenda-setting," observing that "the mass media set the agenda for each political campaign, influencing the salience of attitudes toward the political issues" (1972, p. 177).

While the term "agenda-setting" and its branch of research can be traced to the McCombs and Shaw article of 1972, the notion of a media capable of determining what the public deems important

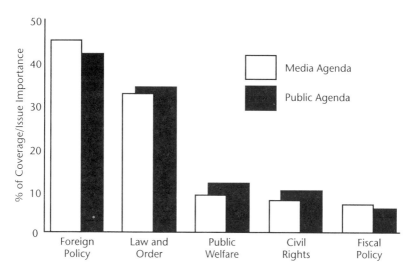

Figure 5.1. Rank-Order Comparison of Media and Public Agendas
Source: based on McCombs and Shaw (1972).

is much older. Lippman (1922) argued that the mass media create images of events in people's minds, and warned of the serious responsibility of the press as purveyors and interpreters of events in society. In identifying the functions of the press, Lazarsfeld and Merton (1948) recognized its ability to confer status upon topics it emphasizes. Long (1958) and Lang and Lang (1959) also wrote of the tendency for the media to force attention on certain issues. And in his study of foreign policy, Cohen wrote the press "may not be successful much of the time in telling people what to think, but it is stunningly successful in telling its readers *what to think about.* And it follows from this that the world looks different to different people, depending not only on their personal interests, but also on the map that is drawn for them by the writers, editors and publishers of the papers they read" (1963, p. 13, italics added). From this intellectual heritage, McCombs and Shaw provided the first systematic study of "agenda-setting" and established a straightforward methodology for testing it, the simple comparison of a media content analysis with a survey of the public agenda.

Key Concepts

Put simply, media agenda-setting is the process whereby the news media lead the public in assigning relative importance to various public issues. The media accomplish this agenda-setting function not by directly telling the public that one issue is more important than another, which has proven to be ineffective; instead, the media signal the importance of certain issues by giving these issues preferential treatment, such as more frequent coverage and more prominent positions. In short, the agenda-setting hypothesis involves two concepts (*media agenda* and *public agenda*) and postulates a causal relationship between them (the media agenda influences the public agenda).

Media Agenda. Media agenda refers to a list of issues or events that receive news coverage. An issue refers to a long-term problem or series of events that involves continual coverage, such as the war in Vietnam, Watergate, AIDS, or the recession. In contrast, an event is characterized by a quick-onset happening over a discrete period of time, attracting intense but short-term media attention. The Los Angeles riots of 1992 and the bombing of the World Trade Center in New York are examples of events. A sequence of events may evolve into an issue, although the process of such evolution itself is an interesting but understudied topic in agenda-setting research. For conceptual clarity, Rogers and Dearing (1988) pointed out that it is important to differentiate issues from events when conducting agenda-setting research as they may differ in terms of timing and salience or importance.

The media agenda is often measured by how frequently and how prominently an issue is covered in the news, weighting factors such as column inches for press stories, or amount of air time for television, or position in newspaper or program (Gormley, 1975; Williams & Semlak, 1978). How broadly an issue is defined is important when measuring issue salience (Roberts & Maccoby, 1985). A very broad definition such as "economic conditions" may not provide sufficient variance for an agenda-setting effect to be detected.

Public Agenda. Public agenda refers to the list of issues that are on the minds of the public. Typically, the public agenda is gauged by a survey of peoples' responses to the open-ended question, "What is the most important problem facing our nation today?" McLeod, Becker, and Byrnes (1974) identified three operational versions of public agenda: an intrapersonal agenda (i.e., how important an issue is to the person him/herself); an interpersonal agenda (how important an issue is to others); and a community agenda (how important an issue is to the community/nation). While these different-level agendas interact with each other to some extent, research has shown that the media agenda-setting effect is most noticeable in shaping the community agenda.

Some researchers have gone beyond simple measures of issue salience, exploring instead the extent of people's knowledge about the issues. For example, Benton and Frazier (1976) measured people's awareness of certain issues, and the causes of and possible solutions to these issues. Tichenor and Wackman (1973) used open-ended survey items to measure people's knowledge concerning a local sewage dumping controversy, and showed that what people believed about the issue was a function of which papers they read.

Underlying Assumptions

Despite its apparent simplicity, the agenda-setting hypothesis draws on several assumptions, many of which have not been explicitly stated. For example, in their 1972 article, McCombs and Shaw noted that media agenda-setting is a *content-specific* effect (by matching what the media report on certain issues with what the public think about these issues) and an *aggregate-level* effect (by using an overall statistic to summarize individuals' issue concerns). An implicit assumption here is that a content-specific effect is superior to a content-free effect because the former has more face validity than the latter.

A second assumption, perhaps somewhat controversial, is that the aggregate-level effect by its own is as important, if not more important, than an individual-level effect. As McCombs and Shaw (1972) showed, the media are capable of creating an agenda for the community as a whole, even though each individual member of the community may have his/her own agenda that could be different from the community agenda. This aggregate-level analysis has drawn some criticism (e.g., McLeod et al., 1974). But as Fan (1988) and Noelle-Neumann (1974) have argued, the totality of public opinion, or the perception of an aggregate public opinion, can be a very powerful institution in the political process, capable of turning, for example, a silent majority into a real minority through a spiral of silence process.

Beyond the level of analysis, more central is the assumption concerning the ultimate effects of agenda-setting. As described above, agenda-setting research has established that the media are capable of telling the public "what to think about." What is so remarkable about this seemingly modest and indirect form of media effect? As several lines of research have illustrated, agenda-setting can have far-reaching consequences. For example, public concerns about certain issues, triggered by news coverage, can affect the policy-making process (Page & Shapiro, 1992). Often media agenda setting plays a critical role in the emergence and subsequent political force of a social movement (e.g., antitechnologies, Mazur, 1981; or antiwar movements, Mueller, 1973). And, by drawing attention to some issues over others, the media provide cues for the public to judge, for instance, political candidates on the basis of themes the media emphasize, a mechanism known as *priming* (Iyengar and Kinder, 1987). The priming effect has been shown to transfer into actual voting decisions during election times (Weaver, Graber, Mc-Combs, & Eyal, 1981). As evidence of media effects accumulates, we may once again need to revise our view of the power of the media beyond Cohen's assertion that the press is successful only in telling its readers what to think about.

Organizing Power

The publication of McCombs and Shaw (1972) unleashed an unexpected flood of replications and extensions. As counted by Rogers, Dearing, and Bregman (1993), nearly 200 agenda-setting studies have been published since that date, 56 percent of which explicitly cite McCombs and Shaw (1972). The prominence of agenda-setting can be also seen in a recent survey of core communication scholars (138 most cited authors and 96 International Communication Association, Association for Education in Journalism and Mass Communication, and Speech Communication Association officers, deans/chairs, and major journal editors), who were asked to name the most important concepts/theories in their field (So & Chan, 1991). The result is expectedly diverse since the survey involves every subfield of communication. However, agenda-setting still receives the most votes (by 31 respondents), followed by uncertainty reduction (21) and diffusion of innovation (16).

McCombs and Shaw (1993) once described academic research as a laissez-faire market in which scholars freely pursue research topics at will. The question is, then, what is the "invisible hand" that has held so many scholars fast to the pursuit of agenda-setting research? We believe that the following three properties of agenda-setting, its organizing power, its cognitive orientation, and its new methodological paradigm, are responsible for the creation and sustenance of this ever-growing family.

The scholarly significance of agenda-setting extends beyond the voluminous research it has generated. The key concepts underlying agenda-setting are quite simple, and their generality has enabled this conceptualization to be applied, as a metaphor, to investigations of personal agendas, election candidate agendas, stereotyping, status conferral, and to a variety of contexts such as health care, social marketing, political advertising, and organizational communication. Given that agenda-setting addresses the way in which the mass media may influence people's beliefs concerning what is important in their society, such studies are particularly important given that these beliefs are frequently at odds with what is actually happening in society.

As a theory, agenda-setting favorably meets many of the criteria generally applied when evaluating theory (see Chaffee & Berger, 1987). The simplicity of matching two constructs, media content and public opinion, makes agenda-setting a parsimonious theory. It is internally consistent (involving the comparison of the rank orders of two sets of issues), heuristically provocative (as evidenced by the volume of research it has generated), appears to have fairly strong predictive power, and is falsifiable.

The organizing power of agenda-setting is evidenced by studies within the field of mass communication relating agenda-setting with other communication concepts such as the spiral of silence, the uses and gratifications approach, bandwagon research and media-system dependency. It has also integrated various subfields of research (see McCombs & Shaw, 1993) such as the sociology of news literature (Shoemaker & Reese, 1991), news diffusion (Breed, 1955), and gatekeeping research in journalism (Becker, McCombs, & McLeod, 1975). While it should be noted that conceptualizing agenda-setting as a theory has its critics (for example, see Iyengar & Kinder, 1987) due to its relative naivety and methodological primitiveness, agenda-setting clearly appears to satisfy many of the requirements of a good theory.

Cognitive Orientation

Agenda-setting research was eagerly accepted by the field because it emerged at a time when communication scholars began searching for more powerful mass media effects. After the apparent success of political propaganda during the First World War, and the subsequent rise of charismatic political leaders such as Adolf Hitler and Winston Churchill (who were adept at using mass communications), many people came to view the mass media as capable of wielding enormous influence upon its audience, and were fearful of its potential consequences. This early perspective became known later as the magic bullet theory, a metaphor that captures the swift, sure, and dangerous power that people invested in the media.

Later researchers in the forties and fifties, such as Paul Lazarsfeld, were unable to detect much support for powerful media effects using the more sophisticated survey methods being developed at the time. Neither were those conducting their communication experiments in laboratories, such as Carl Hovland. The absence of powerful-effects findings led contemporary researchers to conclude that the media after all had extremely limited powers of persuasion. This "limited effects" view was best articulated by Joseph Klapper in his book *The Effects of Mass Communication* (1960); he argued that research had demonstrated mass media to be "ordinarily" not a necessary or sufficient cause of audience effects. Instead, it operated as a reinforcer of existing values and attitudes, and media effects were generally seen as mediated by interpersonal relationships and personal experience. While a more careful reading of Klapper's book reveals his belief that there were some conditions under which mass communication could greatly influence society, most contemporary scholars were content to hold a limited-effects perspective, perhaps in response to the more extravagant claims of a powerful and dangerous mass media made earlier.

Since that time there have been developments in other fields which have led to a paradigm shift in communication research and a renewal of the view that the media may have powerful effects (see Roberts & Maccoby, 1985). For instance, the emergence of cognitive psychology during the 1960s (Neisser, 1967) heralded a new school of thought which reconceptualized people as active information seekers. In communication research this led to a search for media effects in the form of cognitive change rather than attitude change in audiences. Meanwhile, in voting studies, researchers were forced to explain voting behavior which was no longer determined by traditional variables such as socioeconomic status, causing them to look again at the media as a source of influence. Finally, the field of communication itself was changing due to a growing number of scholars with actual communication qualifications and experienced media practitioners joining its ranks, all of whom were more inclined to hold powerful effects views (see figure 5.2). It is not surprising then that the first agenda-setting study was received with such interest and enthusiasm.

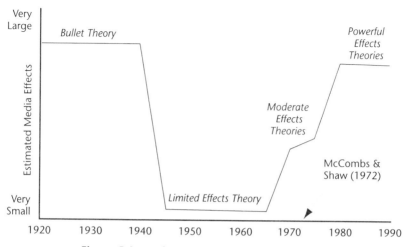

Figure 5.2. Evolution of Media Effects Theory
Source: Modified from W. J. Severin & J. W. Tankard Jr.
(1992, p. 261).

A New Methodological Paradigm

The value of linking media content with public opinion which is the methodology of agenda-setting had been recognized by earlier scholars. Neuman (1989) points out that as early as 1910 Weber called for a joint systematic study of the press and public opinion. Yet communication research has tended to move along two separate lines: media content research which concentrates only on the content of the media and ignores audience effects, and audience effects research which focuses on surveys of audience responses and accepts media content as given. Each strategy on its own has limitations. In survey research, it is often impossible to determine with complete certainty to what media content respondents are actually exposed. Researchers often have to assume exposure to the tested message based on audience self-reports. On the other hand, content analysis of media programming on its own is merely descriptive, and problems of inference (i.e., assuming the message has reached the targeted audience) arise. The gap between the two fields and their limitations has been widely noted and new directions of research called for to address the gap, notably parallel content analysis proposed by Neuman and defined as "the systematic and simultaneous measurement of media content and audience response" (1989, p. 212). By comparing media content analysis with survey research, agenda-setting clearly follows this strategy and overcomes the limitations of media content and audience effects style research.

RELEVANT EXTENSIONS

Over the last two decades, agenda-setting has grown from a simple proposition involving only two variables (i.e., media agenda and public agenda) to a complex theoretical framework encompassing various auxiliary concepts and hypotheses. Numerous new concepts have been added to the original hypothesis as controlling, intervening, or moderating variables. Of the various extensions, research on the causal direction, the contingent conditions, and the substantive context of agenda-setting are among the most important.

Causality of Agenda-Setting

The original study by McCombs and Shaw (1972) reported only a match between media agenda and public agenda, but conveyed an assumption that the media agenda precedes and causes the public agenda. Scholars quickly pointed out three competing hypotheses to explain the correspondence between media agenda and public agenda: the media indeed set the agenda for the public; the media merely reflect the public's sentiment; or the media and the public reinforce each other's issue salience. Much of the agenda-setting research since 1972 has been devoted to resolving this intriguing causal question, with a variety of methodological approaches from the social sciences arsenal.

The first technique employed was the *panel design with cross-lagged correlation*, adopted by McCombs and Shaw in their second study, known as the Charlotte study. This analytic strategy compares the correlation between the media agenda at time one and the public agenda at time two with the correlation between the public agenda at time one and the media agenda at time two in order to determine whether the media influences public opinion at a later date, or vice versa (figure 5.3). The Charlotte study (Shaw & McCombs, 1977) was conducted in Charlotte, North Carolina during the 1972 presidential election, using a panel sample of respondents interviewed at several points throughout the campaign to measure their issue salience, and then matching it with the issue emphasis by the Charlotte newspaper and two broadcast news

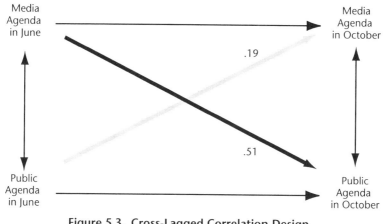

Figure 5.3. Cross-Lagged Correlation Design
Source: Based on Shaw & McCombs (1977).

programs during the same period. Cross-lagged correlation results showed that the correlation between the newspaper agenda at time period 1 and the public agenda at time period 2 was much larger than the correlation the other way around, although this pattern was not detected for the television data. Because this cross-lagged design provides a straightforward means of establishing causality, it has been widely used in many later studies of agenda-setting (e.g.,Tipton, Haney, & Baseheart, 1975; Weaver et al., 1981).

Where the panel design with cross-lagged correlation continued the convention of an aggregate unit of analysis, Iyengar and Kinder (1987) adopted the *laboratory experiment* to study the agenda-setting effect at the individual level. In a series of controlled experiments subjects watched television news dealing with several issues such as inflation, unemployment, and defense. Then investigators compared the viewers' perceived importance of these issues with the responses of nonviewers. The results were unequivocal; even a week after their exposure to the news programs, viewers still attached much higher importance to these issues than did nonviewers.

Given the problem of external validity usually associated with laboratory experimentation, other scholars have chosen the *field experiment* to test the causal process between the media agenda and the public agenda in a more realistic setting. For example, with help from local television stations, Protess and his colleagues at Northwestern University (Protess et al., 1991) conducted a series of field experiments in which they interviewed a random sample of Chicago residents a few weeks before and after the airing of several investigative newscasts. Such a design permits the researchers to trace any change in public opinion between the two surveys to the content of the television newscasts. Given the various types of noise inevitably introduced into field experiments, Protess and his colleagues found agenda-setting effects to be weaker than those in Iyengar and Kinder's laboratory experiment. However, the more realistic setting of their studies may provide a greater degree of confidence in the validity of effects found.

Structural equation modeling (SEM) techniques have also been used to establish the direction of causality in the agenda-setting process (e.g., Hugel, Degenhardt, & Weiss, 1989). SEM is a versatile analytical tool, allowing for measurement error, decomposition of direct and indirect effects, and comparison of alternative causal paths. In this study (Hugel et al., 1989), SEM enabled the researchers to detect an agenda-setting effect after controlling for interpersonal communication, issue obtrusiveness, and other intervening variables. Both Iyengar (1988) and Kosicki (1993) believe that SEM has considerable potential in advancing agenda-setting research.

Finally, a number of scholars (e.g., Behr & Iyengar, 1985; Beniger, 1978; Brosius & Kepplinger, 1990; Funkhouser, 1973; MacKuen, 1981; Neuman, 1990; Rogers, Dearing, & Chang, 1991; Smith, 1980; Zhu, 1992; Zhu et al., 1993) have employed *time series analysis* (TSA) to study agenda-setting. Operating at the aggregate level of analysis by using public opinion data, TSA has several advantages over the methods mentioned above, as noted elsewhere (Zhu, 1992). For example, TSA usually involves many more time points than other methods and is therefore a more appropriate means of studying agenda-setting as a process, and further, is more sensitive to longer-term agenda-setting effects. TSA enables one to examine time lags of various lengths in order to determine the optimum time window for agenda-setting effects to take place, and to detect cycles of media coverage and public attention (Downs, 1972). TSA can also incorporate "real world" indicators into the analysis (e.g., inflation, unemployment, and energy consumption, see Behr & Iyengar, 1985; or casualties in Vietnam, MacKuen, 1981), by which a spurious relationship between the media agenda and the public agenda can be eliminated. As will be discussed in more detail later, TSA also enables investigators to treat agenda-setting as a competitive, nonlinear, or other more complicated or realistic process.

Despite variations in design and analysis from study to study, these multiple methods have demonstrated a clear causal influence of the media agenda upon the public agenda. It is likely that no other theoretical hypothesis in human communication research has received as much empirical attention by so many scholars and with such diverse methods as has agenda-setting. It should be noted that some studies have reported a so-called "reversed agenda-setting effect" in which public issue concerns lead to media coverage, and others a "reciprocal agenda-setting effect" where the media agenda and public agenda mutually reinforce each other. Rogers and Dearing (1988) point out that short-term studies on specific events tend to reveal a one-way direction of influence, but longer-term studies may reveal a two-way relationship between the media agenda and public agenda over time that seems more realistic given the drive by media personnel to present news of interest to their audiences. For breaking news events where there is no previous public concern, one can expect a one-way influence of the media upon the public agenda. But for more persistent issues for which people are likely to have some personal experience and prior public opinion (i.e., an obtrusive issue like inflation), public concern may well lead to agenda-setting effects upon the media. This pattern appears to have held in a German study on the agenda-setting function of television news (Brosius & Kepplinger, 1990), which showed that for some issues characterized by a sudden onset of media interest, the media influenced public opinion. However, in the case of other issues where there was long-term public awareness with little variation, the public agenda appeared to drive the news.

Contingent Conditions

Another enduring question that has attracted the attention of agenda-setting researchers is whether agenda-setting is a universal effect or only happens to certain people under certain conditions. Almost everyone, including McCombs and Shaw, believes the latter because the former sounds uncomfortably reminiscent of the magic bullet theory. In their seminal article, McCombs and Shaw (1972) compared agenda-setting effects across voter groups (Democrats, Republicans, and Independents), across issues (receiving high or low prominence from the media) and across media outlets (newspapers, newsmagazines, and television). They explicitly stated that the purpose of the between-group analyses was to examine the "individual differences" that might be lost in the overall design of "lumping all the voters together in an analysis" (p. 181). Other scholars have since joined in the search for what Erbring, Golden-berg, and Miller (1980) called a " contingent theory" of agenda-setting. In particular, the search has focused on three sets of contin-gent conditions: audience characteristics, issue characteristics, and media characteristics (Winter, 1981).

Audience Characteristics

While most of the conventional demographic and socioeco-nomic variables have demonstrated a very limited role in qualify-ing the agenda-setting effect, scholars have found various dimen-sions of audience involvement to be an important contingent condition. Audience involvement has been measured by such vari-ables as political partisanship (Iyengar & Kinder, 1987; McCombs & Shaw, 1972; McLeod et al., 1974), campaign interest (McLeod et al., 1974; Weaver et al., 1981), and media preference (Benton & Frazier, 1976) or media dependency (Salwen, 1987). These variables are ei-ther used as controlling variables to eliminate a possible spurious effect of the media agenda on public agenda, or as a moderator variable to detect differential effects of the media agenda on vari-ous audience groups. The general findings are that the more in-volved an audience is, the more susceptible the audience is to media agenda-setting, with some exceptions (most notably Iyengar & Kinder, 1987, where the more involved audiences were less sub-ject to the agenda-setting effect, a finding we attribute to their labo-ratory setting).

Why are more involved audiences more likely to be influenced by agenda-setting? There are at least two plausible explanations. The first concerns the notion of "Need for Orientation" (NFO, see Weaver, 1977). An individual is said to have a high NFO when he/she is highly interested in (or strongly believes in the relevance of) a public issue, but is also highly uncertain about the issue. A high level of NFO will lead to active use of the mass media, which opens the door for an agenda-setting influence. Empirical investi-gations (e.g., McCombs & Weaver, 1973; Schoenbach & Weaver, 1985; Weaver, 1977; Weaver et al., 1981) have found support for the role of NFO in the agenda-setting process, although the results are not always consistent across studies in terms of the magnitude of its influence.

MacKuen (1981) proposed another, perhaps more elaborate, theorization of audience involvement. He posited two competing models—audience attentiveness versus cognitive framework. The attentiveness model suggests that the audiences' susceptibility to media agenda-setting is a function of their attentiveness toward incoming information and their cognitive ability to process the information. There appear to be some parallels between the attentiveness model and Weaver's need for orientation construct (NFO). Operationally, MacKuen measured attentiveness by interest in politics, as rated by respondents on a scale ranging from low to high. Cognitive ability was operationalized as years of education. The higher the political interest and/or educational level a person has, the more susceptible the person should be to media agenda-setting, according to the attentiveness model. The cognitive framework model suggests a rival hypothesis where those with more education and higher political interest should have more effective self-defense mechanisms against the influence of media agenda-setting. In a series of empirical tests, MacKuen found evidence supporting the attentiveness model, findings that are also consistent with the research on NFO.

While the consensus has been that there are likely to be variations in individuals' susceptibility to agenda-setting, we probably should not overstate the differences too much. As DeFleur and Ball-Rokeach (1982) have argued in their media dependency theory, there are broad strata of people in our society with sufficient similarities that cause them to share the same problems and concerns, regardless of their differences. A longitudinal study currently being conducted by Zhu and his associates will attempt to show that various sectors of the public may appear to be heterogeneous at any given point in terms of their concerns about social problems; however, the sectors become more homogenous when one traces their issue concerns over a long period of time.

Issue Characteristics

The most important theorization concerning issue characteristics is the notion of issue obtrusiveness (Zucker, 1978). According to Zucker, an issue is obtrusive if the public has direct experience with it, or unobtrusive if the public has no direct contact with it. Domestic economic issues such as inflation and unemployment are often cited as examples of obtrusive issues, whereas foreign affairs is considered an unobtrusive issue. The distinction between obtrusive and unobtrusive issues has been empirically verified. For example, through a factor analysis procedure, Eyal (1979) identified two distinctive groups among eleven issues. The obtrusive issue group included inflation, unemployment, the economy, and so on, while the unobtrusive issue group included welfare, the environment, and foreign affairs. Blood (1981) reported that respondents in a survey rated inflation as the most obtrusive issue, and the Iran hostage issue as the least obtrusive, with recession roughly in the middle.

Media agenda-setting effects are stronger for unobtrusive issues, Zucker argued, because audiences have to rely on the media for information about these issues. On the other hand, audiences are less susceptible to agenda-setting effects on obtrusive issues because they learn about these issues from their own experience, or personal networks, rather than from the media. A number of authors have found evidence supporting these arguments. For example, Eyal (1979), Hugel and colleagues (1989), and Zucker (1978) found a stronger media agenda-setting effect for unobtrusive issues, and Hugel and colleagues (1989), Iyengar (1979), Palmgreen and Clarke (1977), and Winter (1980) found a weaker or even null agenda-setting effect for obtrusive issues. These patterns generally hold up after controlling for real world indictors in the analysis. For instance, MacKuen (1981) found that for obtrusive economic issues the public were more likely to be influenced by the "real world" than by the media. On the other hand, some findings have shown that the extent of media coverage on certain issues is out of proportion with respect to objective indicators and that public perception tends to be more influenced by media portrayals rather than "objective" reality (Funkhouser, 1973; Blood, 1994).

There are also other formulations of issue characteristics. For example, a more recent study by Yagade and Dozier (1990) distinguishes issues into "concreteness" versus "abstractness." The authors reported that media agenda-setting power is enhanced for concrete issues but diminished for abstract issues. As the authors acknowledged, however, the role of issue concreteness may have been confounded with audiences' cognitive ability. Further research is needed to shed light on this and other dimensions of issue characteristics.

Media Characteristics

The debate over which media outlet—newspapers or television—is a better agenda-setter has attracted intense research interest. Of course, this is based on the assumption that newspapers and television have different issue agendas. In McCombs and Shaw's (1972) classic study, four types of media were examined: local newspapers, national newspapers, newsmagazines, and television networks. The results showed that there was a high degree of similarity in issue agenda within each medium and only a modest similarity between media; national newspapers demonstrated the strongest agenda-setting effects, followed by television. Hugel and colleagues (1989) presented a more elaborate study involving individual-level data to test the differential roles of print and broadcasting media in agenda-setting. In their study, investigators matched the content of national television programming and thirteen daily newspapers to measures of national voters' media exposure. A path analysis based on structural equation modeling found that voters were influenced by the newspaper agenda but not by the television agenda on an unobtrusive issue (foreign affairs); however, voters did not respond to either newspaper or television agendas on an obtrusive issue (social security). Several other studies also report that newspapers have a stronger agenda-setting effect than does television (Benton & Frazier, 1976; Eyal, 1979; McCombs, 1977; Patterson & McClure, 1976; Weaver, 1977).

More recent scholars have criticized earlier studies for paying too much attention to newspapers and too little to television (e.g., Brosius & Kepplinger, 1990). The case for studying television is best articulated by Iyengar and Kinder (1987, pp. 1–2) in their opening statement: "Our purpose here is to establish that television news is in fact an educator virtually without peer, that it shapes the American public's conception of political life in pervasive ways; that television news is news that matters." The view on the primacy of television may be well grounded, since the public spends more time watching television than reading newspapers (Robinson & Levy, 1986), and has more confidence in television than newspapers (Roper Organization, 1984). However, the advocates of television research have focused exclusively on television newscasts in their empirical investigations. By using a single-media design, it is impossible to compare the impact of television and newspapers.

It is evident that, in spite of the impressive effort devoted to exploring contingent conditions, our understanding of the qualifying effects of audience, issue, and media characteristics upon agenda-setting is far from conclusive. The cumulative evidence has been mixed, sometimes even discrepant. Some studies find no significant contingent effects on the agenda-setting process where others detect some contingent effects, but with the magnitude and direction of the effect varying from one study to another. Despite the inconsistencies, however, it is this very search for a better understanding of the contingent conditions that has kept agenda-setting research alive and well over the last two decades, and that will continue attracting scholars to this research domain.

Context of Agenda-Setting

As described above, agenda-setting research was originally conducted in the context of national and local political elections. Once researchers had established that news could influence what readers thought to be the most important election campaign issues, it was not long before they extended this notion to other types of issues in other contexts. In the last twenty years, many applications of agenda-setting have been made to topics as diverse as advertising, organizational management, criminal justice, semiotics, peace activism, and sports medicine. A brief review of some of these applications illustrates the significant insights gained from applying this metaphor, originating from the communication sciences, to problems pertaining to other fields.

One context that has gained in importance has been the impact of economic news on *consumer confidence* (Fan, 1993) Given the fact that individual consumer spending accounts for two-thirds of the U.S. national expenditure, it is therefore pertinent to ask, "What causes consumer confidence to rise and fall?" Contrary to conventional "pocket-book determinism" (i.e., consumer confidence is based on the well-being of the economy), agenda-setting scholars have shown that news coverage of the economy may play a greater role than economic reality. For example, Stevenson, Gonzenbach, and David (1991) examined the interrelationship between economic news coverage, consumer confidence, and the actual state of the economy, and found that consumer confidence influenced media coverage over the economy when controlling for reality, but the media in turn picked up on public concern and influenced public perception at a later date. Using a set of new techniques that has been developed to handle nonstationary data, Blood (1994) found strong evidence that newspaper headlines concerning the U.S. recession lowered consumer confidence in the U.S. economy over and above the direct effects of a poor economy upon public sentiment.

Sutherland and Galloway (1981) were the first to use the agenda-setting concept to cast the role of *commercial advertising* in a new light. Now, instead of seeing advertising's purpose as persuading the audience to buy its touted product, the more achievable goal of advertising is to focus the consumer's attention on what values, brands, and attributes to think about when considering purchasing a product. This has been established as an important and necessary first step in the marketing process, ultimately ending in sales. Agenda-setting research techniques have also been applied to assessing the effectiveness of *political advertising*. In a state senate campaign, newspaper advertisements were shown to be fairly effective in communicating information about issues to voters (Kaid, 1976).

Other functions within *business organizations* have benefited from applying an agenda-setting framework, such as public relations, personnel management, organizational management, consulting, and strategic planning. Managerial writers have noted that across businesses and industries, effective managers display similarities in their focus on agenda-setting for their business, and creating networks to accomplish them (e.g., Kotter, 1983). Yet others have argued that businesses are very slow at becoming involved in the agenda-setting arena of politics. Nolan (1985) even suggested that there is a need for "issue analysts" in business, who can identify and promote issues in the company's interests, and foster effective relations with the media.

The emergence of public policy issues such as *consumer protection* in the United States and abroad has been explained within the framework of agenda-setting. Mayer (1991) described the process of how consumer problems are transformed into consumer issues by moving through three stages: consumer problems attract media attention, which in turn arouses public opinion, and finally are addressed by policymakers. Harrison and Hoberg (1991) investigated why the government is attentive to certain *environmental problems* but not others. By comparing the U.S. and Canadian governments' handling of indoor radon and dioxin, they found that media coverage of these problems set the issue priority for their governments.

Other sorts of policy issues have achieved their status from the early use of agenda-setting, such as school finance reform, collective bargaining, comparable worth, and social security. Sustained media coverage on child abuse succeeded in making it a public policy issue (Nelson, 1984). A dramatic example of how the press affects federal policy making through agenda-setting concerned President Carter's decision not to deploy the neutron bomb, a weapon which was described to the public as capable of killing people yet leaving buildings standing. After *Washington Post* reporter Walter Pincus revealed that the neutron bomb was being developed through obscure Pentagon funding, the ensuing public and congressional outcry ultimately forced the decision not to deploy the bomb (Linsky et al., 1986).

The agenda-setting metaphor has been applied to issues concerning *public health*. Researchers have reevaluated media educational programs such as those directed at AIDS, sexually transmitted disease, drug abuse in professional sports, abortion, and the use of seat belts. Using an agenda-setting framework that focuses on issue salience, they have been more likely to find the campaigns to be effective than when looking for direct effects upon behavior. Some unintended agenda-setting effects on health have also been considered. For example, Atkin (1989) looked at the agenda-setting effects of television programs on risky driving behaviors by teenagers.

There have also been a number of investigations into the agenda-setting effects of *crime* stories on topics as diverse as homicides, rape, and police brutality. David Pritchard has conducted a series of studies on how news coverage of crimes has affected the number of police officers subsequently allocated to cities (Pritchard & Berkowitz, 1993), or public prosecutors' decisions on pre-bargains in homicide cases (Pritchard, 1984). The latter study showed that the more publicity a homicide case receives, which presumably creates more public attention to the case, the less likely the prosecutor in charge of the case is willing to make a pre-bargain deal with the defendant.

The successes and failures of *civil rights* movements have been illuminated by using an agenda-setting approach in their analysis. Case studies documenting successful minority rights passage invariably reveal active agenda-setting on the part of groups these legislations are intended to protect. On the other hand, a case study of the failure of the Immigration Reform and Control Act of 1986 revealed that the Hispanic perspective was not represented in the early agenda-setting phases (Arp, 1990). And a close comparison of the issues relating to the claims made by Alaskan natives showed that there were significant differences in understanding of the problem on the part of testifying Alaskan natives and the senators who received their testimony (Korsmo, 1990).

NEW FRONTIERS

Recently, Maxwell McCombs organized a series of activities, including a panel discussion at the joint conference of the World Association for Public Opinion Research and the American Association for Public Opinion Research and a special collection of articles each for the *Journalism Quarterly* and the *Journal of Communication* (see McCombs, 1992; McCombs & Shaw, 1993), to review the last two decades of agenda-setting research and to envision the future. We take the opportunity here to join in this exercise and offer our thoughts and anticipations concerning the future of agenda-setting. While important work continues on the major extensions to agenda-setting, as described above, several new frontiers have emerged in recent years. The following is a brief account of what we believe will be the most exciting prospects for agenda-setting research in the years to come.

Issue Competition

Passing reference has already been made to one of the central but implicit assumptions underlying the original formulation of the agenda-setting hypothesis: the notion of issue competition. Though never explicitly stated, when using rank-order correlation to compare a list of issues on the media agenda with a list of issues on the public agenda, McCombs and Shaw (1972) assumed that each list reflected the relative importance the media and the audience assigned to each issue. Many follow-up studies have used this rank-order design, and the implications of issue competition have not been fully recognized or addressed. Thus, some scholars (e.g., Winter & Eyal, 1981) have criticized the rank-order comparison for ignoring the idiosyncratic characteristics of these issues by aggregating them into a single analysis. These criticisms make methodological sense, but the single-issue analysis does not permit the researcher to test issue competition as the rank-order comparison design can.

Zhu (1992) takes a fresh look at the pros and cons of rank-order comparison. Drawing on research from the fields of human cognitive processing, media organization, policymaking and interest groups, he uses a "zero-sum game" metaphor to explicate the implicit assumption of issue competition underlying the agenda-setting process. The zero-sum perspective argues that agenda-setting is a process whereby various social groups compete to attract the attention of the media, the public, and the policymakers to their issues. Because the media, the public, and the policymaking body all have a limited carrying capacity (e.g., limited space or time on the part of the media, limited attention span by the public, and limited resources of the system), the rise of one issue in the "public arenas" (Hilgartner & Bosk, 1988) is at the expense of another. While the notion of issue competition in agenda-setting research has been assumed since its inception, all the conventional methodologies as reviewed earlier have not been able to provide a ready way to test this dynamic process. Zhu (1992) develops a mathematical model to make this test possible. The model incorporates both multiple issues (as required by the zero-sum principle) and time series technique into one analysis. A test of the model with data on three major issues in 1990–91, the federal budget deficit, the Persian Gulf War, and the recession, lends support to the zero-sum notion.

Recognizing that this "promises to be one of the most exciting venues of research" (McCombs, 1992, p. 823), McCombs and Zhu (1995) moved on to explore if the zero-sum perspective provides a reasonable explanation for the often-observed volatility in the public issue agenda (e.g., the issue of the federal deficit or crime can rise to and fall from the top of public concerns within a matter of weeks). The volatility may result, they hypothesized, from a growing gap between the rising standard of education in the population, which leads to an expansion of issue interest, and the relative constant size of the public agenda which has a limited carrying capacity. They examined the change in the American public's issue agenda from 1954 to 1994, as registered by Gallup Poll's question "What is most important problem facing this country?" The results show that there has been an increase in the number of smaller issues (as measured by the size of their constituencies) crowding on the public agenda, and probably as a consequence, the duration of issues on the public agenda has decreased.

Thus, the public agenda has become more volatile. While these are only preliminary results of work in progress, it is clear that this line of approach to understanding the *dynamic* nature of public agenda, an often-criticized weakness of past agenda-setting research (e.g., Swanson, 1988), shows promise.

Nonlinear Models

Traditionally, agenda-setting has been treated as a linear model in which the public's concern about an issue is a linear function of news coverage on the issue; this amounts to no coverage, no concern; more coverage, higher concerns. One can readily see problems with this linear perspective. For example, under the linear model, issue concerns will increase infinitely as long as they receive news coverage, whereas in reality there is always an upper-ceiling (saturation point) for any issue salience. Also, the linear model treats the agenda-setting effect as a constant over time, whereas, in real life, media impact is often time-varying. Several recent studies

(Brosius & Kepplinger, 1992; Neuman, 1990; Watt, Mazza, & Snyder, 1993; Zhu et al., 1993) have begun to develop nonlinear models of the agenda-setting process. Among these, Neuman (1990) is particularly appealing.

In search of an answer to the question "Would a nonlinear response function make more sense?," Neuman proposed a logistic curve (i.e., S-curve, see figure 5.4) to model how the public responds to the media coverage of an issue. Essentially, the public's attention follows a three-stage path: it remains low when an issue is initially covered by the media; it rises rapidly once the coverage accumulates to a take-off threshold; and eventually it levels off after a saturation point. Neuman's empirical test of the logistic model produced some very interesting findings. For example, he found that the *threshold* of public attention for an issue is within the range of 5–20 percent (i.e., the proportion of the public being concerned about that particular issue). Based on the maximum and the slope of the logistic curve, Neuman developed an issue typology. He termed those issues with a maximum of around 50 percent of public concern and a steep slope (.7 or above) as "crises" (e.g., Vietnam war, racial unrest, and energy crisis). "Symbolic crises" are those issues with a lower maximum of public concern (about 20 percent) and a slower slope (.3–.5), such as Watergate, drug abuse, pollution, and poverty. There are certain issues with a high maximum of public concern (60 percent or higher) but with an almost flat slope, such as inflation and unemployment; he labeled these simple "problems" or "nonproblems."

While nonlinear modeling is a promising approach, as demonstrated by Neuman and others, two notes of caution are in order. First, while more conceptually appealing, nonlinear modeling is inferior to linear models at the present time on a number of technical grounds. When assumptions are met, linear regression models yield unbiased, normally distributed, and minimum variance estimators whereas nonlinear models achieve these properties only asymptotically, that is, as the sample sizes approach infinity (Ratkowsky, 1990). Further, mathematical theory is complete for linear models but mostly incomplete for nonlinear models. For example, linear models, if specified correctly, always have a unique solution, whereas solutions for many nonlinear models have not been developed.

Second, nonlinear modeling should be more theory-driven than data-driven, because there is only one functional form in any linear model whereas there are an infinite number of nonlinear

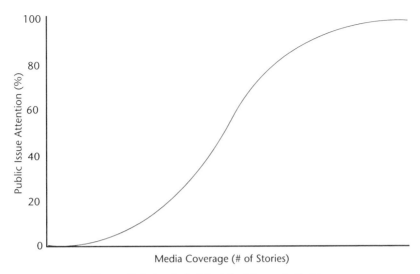

Figure 5.4. Logistic Model of Agenda-Setting
Source: Based on Neuman (1990), as modified in Zhu et al.
(1993, p. 10).

functional forms to consider. The theory-driven approach superimposes a functional form, and if necessary, certain parameter values, to the model (e.g., Neuman, 1990). This approach requires a priori knowledge of the process under study, which, unfortunately, is often not available. A theory-driven model needs to be empirically tested. Here the primary concern is not so much about whether the model is the "best-fit" to a particular dataset, but, rather, whether the model fits the data with reasonably small error, which can be viewed as evidence for the plausibility of the model structure as well as the underlying assumptions.

On the other hand, the empirically-driven strategy searches for a best-fit model among various candidates, and then tries to provide ad hoc explanations for the chosen model (e.g., Brosius & Kepplinger, 1992). While the a priori approach cannot rule out rival models, the empirically driven, best-fit approach can hardly exhaust all possible models either, because there can be an infinite number of models to choose from. A case in point comes from Iglesias and Chirife (1982) who reported 501 alternative empirical models for a simple bivariate relationship: the water activity and the moisture content of a food product. We certainly do not need 501 empirically derived nonlinear models of agenda-setting!

Psychological Mechanism

One of the criticisms that has been leveled against agenda-setting is a lack of theorization (e.g., Iyengar, 1988; Swanson, 1988). What is meant by "theory" here is a psychological account of how the agenda-setting effect takes place within the individual. While agenda-setting was originally conceptualized as a sociological (i.e., aggregate) process, many investigators are also interested in unearthing the psychological mechanisms behind the phenomenon. Here two lines of research focusing on the psychological process of agenda-setting are worth noting.

Iyengar and his colleagues have investigated the role of three psychological concepts, including *counterargument*, *source credibility*, and *emotional arousal*, in mediating the agenda-setting effect upon individuals. They argued that individuals are not passive recipients of incoming media agenda; instead, audiences contrast the issue agenda presented by the media against counterarguments available to them at the time, and will also take into account the source's credibility. While these responses to media messages represent active cognitive processing, there is the alternative possibility that audiences will respond primarily to the affective appeal of the media. In a series of laboratory experiments in which these cognitive and emotional processes were manipulated (Iyengar, Peters & Kinder, 1982; Iyengar & Kinder, 1985), the authors found emotional arousal to be the most significant mediator of the agenda-setting effect, followed by perceived source credibility. There was little support for the impact of counterargument.

Watt et al. (1993) investigated the role of *memory*, another key element of the psychological process underlying the agenda-setting effect. They reconceptualized the media agenda-setting effect on the audiences as a memory forgetting process, which decays exponentially over time. To sustain an issue on the public agenda, the media need to keep feeding stories on the same issue to the public in order to compensate for the *forgetting curve*. The authors developed a nonlinear model to represent this process, and tested it with data involving aggregate issue salience and television coverage on a daily basis. The results, though needing to be verified with individual-level data, appear to be consistent with memory decay theory and the agenda-setting literature.

While there are probably many other psychological concepts that could be applied productively to agenda-setting, these two lines of inquiry certainly shed new light on our understanding of the agenda-setting process and may provide answers to some of its most puzzling aspects. For example, how are the media, especially television, capable of mobilizing, seemingly overnight, intense public concern about certain issues (e.g., nuclear waste) that may not have any real consequences for the individuals they alarm? The media's ability to trigger affective responses, as demonstrated by Iyengar and his colleagues, seems a plausible explanation. Also, why do some issues linger on the public agenda longer than others? In addition to the way issues are handled by the media, factors such as the audience's familiarity with the issues, which counterbalances memory decay, may determine how long issues remain on the public's mind. Continuing work on these and other psychological processes will surely be an important part of agenda-setting research in the future.

Integrating Mass and Interpersonal Communication

The role of interpersonal communication in agenda-setting has long been acknowledged. However, empirical investigations have produced a mixed picture: interpersonal communication appears to enhance media agenda-setting in some cases, inhibit media agenda-setting in other cases, and have no impact at all in still others. More recent studies have made some progress in providing more consistent and better theorized results. For example, Wanta and Wu (1992) made a distinction between two types of issues depending on how much media coverage each receives. For those receiving extensive media attention, interpersonal communication reinforces the media agenda-setting effect, while for those issues ignored by the media, interpersonal communication becomes the main source of influence and thus competes with the media agenda-setting effect.

Drawing on a model initially proposed by Diana Mutz (1991), Weaver, Zhu, and Willnat (1992) proposed that people learn about issues from three sources, including their direct experience, conversations with others, and exposure to the media; and each of these information sources plays a different role in shaping people's issue perception. An audience's direct experience with an issue often leads the individual to perceive it as a personal problem, while media-relayed information makes the individual look upon the issue as a societal problem, and interpersonal communication *bridges* these two levels of issue perception. For example, through conversations, the individual may *generalize* a personal problem to a social problem (as found in both Mutz, 1991 and Weaver et al., 1992), or *localize* a social problem to a personal problem (which is theoretically plausible but has not been empirically confirmed).

In the study by Hugel and colleagues (1989), interpersonal communication was conceptualized as a moderator variable producing differential effects of media agenda-setting. For an unobtrusive issue (e.g., foreign affairs), the authors demonstrated through structural equation modeling that interpersonal communication enhances newspapers' agenda-setting effect (which is consistent with Wanta and Wu, 1992) but suppresses television's effect, which is a new finding. Interpersonal communication, however, does not appear to operate as a moderator variable in agenda-setting for obtrusive issues.

Finally, Zhu and colleagues (1993) developed a mathematical model to incorporate both media and interpersonal communication into an integrated model of agenda-setting. As the two-step flow of information theory suggests, interpersonal communication about a public issue often follows media coverage, but its influence can exceed the media's, depending on the nature of the issue under discussion. The empirical test of their model shows that the media component plays a central role in three unobtrusive issues (e.g., relations with the Soviet Union, the American hostages in Iran, and the Persian Gulf War), whereas the interpersonal communication component is more important in setting the public agenda for three, more obtrusive issues (inflation, recession, and the deficit).

Beyond the Public Agenda

Although many mysteries remain concerning the processes and effects of media agenda-setting, a number of scholars have made the call to look beyond agenda-setting. Two lines of inquiry have dutifully emerged: the antecedents of media agenda-setting (also known as "media agenda-building"), and the consequences of media-setting ("policy agenda-setting"). While both are important extensions of media agenda-setting, we believe the former to be more exciting from a communications research perspective, because it provides a framework for integrating several important domains of research, including media organizational behavior (e.g., Semetko et al., 1991; Reese, 1991), news content (Shoemaker & Reese, 1990) and framing (Kosocki, 1993).

We propose an additional line of inquiry, that of placing

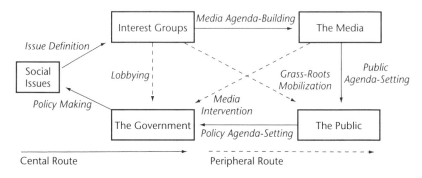

Figure 5.5. Issue Process in Democratic Society

agenda-setting into the broader context of the democratic process. In figure 5.5, four major players (interest groups, the media, the public, and the government) are connected through various routes in terms of their respective roles in the social issue process, and agenda-setting now becomes only one piece of the big picture. We consider three routes as *central*, including media agenda-building, public agenda-setting, and policy agenda-setting, and the remaining routes as *peripheral*, such as direct lobbying, grass roots mobilization, and media direct intervention. While there may be little disagreement about the inclusion of these players in the political process, there certainly are different perspectives about the causal direction and the relative importance of these routes. For example, Graber (1993) offered alternative ways to look at the same process. Despite the different emphases, each route has been studied separately in its own domain of research, spanning mass communication, political science, sociology, and public administration. Agenda-setting appears to be well placed to pull this diverse body of literature together, by using the life and times of a social issue as the connecting thread. This is a truly interdisciplinary endeavor on a fascinating and boundless frontier for scholars to explore.

6

New Rhetoric and New Social Movements

Gerard A. Hauser & Susan Whalen

The study of communication in the Western tradition dates to the early Sophists, who were practicing their craft in Asia Minor during the fourth and fifth centuries B.C. Their speculations on argumentation, stylistics, and the psychology of *logos* were codified under the rubric of rhetoric during the fifth century B.C., and from that time forward became a part of Western culture through its inclusion in the curriculum. As taught in the schools of Greek and Roman rhetoricians, and later in the Church academies and secular universities until this century, rhetoric was the study of how to use language to influence the judgment and actions of others. There were exceptions, of course, such as the speculations of DeQuincy in the last century, but for the most part rhetoric was theorized and learned as a practical art concerned with the production of messages designed to achieve an intended effect. The residue of more than two millennia of association with instrumental considerations remains in common usage and lay perception, where "rhetoric" is almost always synonymous with the study of persuasion.

One would be hard pressed to imagine a serious discussion of rhetorical communication in which instrumental considerations were not tacitly present. And in the case of some schools and traditions, where rhetoric is theorized as a design art, they remain the central concern. However, at the end of the nineteenth century, rhetoric's conceptual topography changed with a formulation that expanded its frontiers to include more profound questions about the nature of language, discourse, and the formation of social reality. That discussion, which still continues, shifted the intellectual agenda of rhetorical studies from instrumental concerns with the production and effects of messages to constitutive concerns with discourse as a social practice. This shift represents a significant development that is producing a *new* rhetoric whose theoretical concern is to articulate the rhetorical character of social action. Its development transcends disciplinary bounds and intellectual traditions with such diverse schools as deconstructionism, new historicism, post structuralism, hermeneutics, neopragmatism, postmodernism, and interpretive studies generally appropriating rhetoric as a category of inquiry and a mode of analysis.

A detailed chart of the scope and complexity of the new rhetoric is a project waiting to be written. Our ambition is more modestly to develop a partial discussion which offers a snapshot of the new rhetoric's philosophical, theoretical, and practical dimensions. We will review its underlying presupposition that rhetoric is constitutive of social formation, then we will discuss the extension of this constitutive view in the rhetorical character of new social movement theory, and finally we will consider how this theory is manifested at the level of praxis by briefly considering one controversy exemplary of a rhetorically formed new social movement.

THE CONSTITUTIVE NATURE
OF THE NEW RHETORIC

From its inception the study of rhetoric had two primary missions: it was an art of production and a method of civic discourse. As an art of production, rhetoric emphasized the important considerations one made in composing a speech or an essay to achieve an intended effect. Aristotle gave an economic appraisal of these considerations by tying them to the end of judgment (*kresis*). The Romans were more expansive, positing doctrines attuned to considerations of language and presentation that suited the ends of *movere, docere,* and *delectare,* or moving, teaching, and pleasing. As a method of civic discourse, rhetoric was theorized as a praxis by which disputes were resolved and official action was taken. For example, Aristotle valorized rhetoric's rational possibilities by insisting that arguments (*pisteis*) were at the heart of responsible public discourse. Cicero, by comparison, presented a more encompassing vision of rhetoric's interactive dynamic when he placed *actio,* or the joint activity of speaker and listener creating a common verdict, at its center. These strands achieved canonical status under the rubrics of *rhetorica docens*, which dealt with the precepts of rhetorical production as taught in the schools, and *rhetorica utens*, which concerned the use of rhetorical discourse as a method for resolving civic issues. Importantly, *rhetorica docens* and *rhetorica utens* aligned both theory and practice with processes of invention (Hauser, 1995). The lay audience's relative authority to influence society's political, social, and even religious practices lent importance to mental interpretations of a contingent world. In this milieu, rhetoric's concern with finding and making suasory arguments placed it at the center of devising and evaluating human decisions (Howell, 1966).

The traditional understanding of rhetoric developed during the Greek and Roman period was dominant until the age of science in the seventeenth and eighteenth centuries. The rise of rationalism and then empiricism displaced rhetoric as the dominant method for discovery. The rational ideals of Frances Bacon and René Descartes uncoupled logic from communication, and its place in the service of mental inquiry, and joined it to science, with a new status in the service of investigating the laws of nature. Human knowledge was modeled on the basis of the natural order, which became paradigmatic for all reality claims, and mathematics replaced argument as their logic of certification. Scientific method dislodged topical reasoning as the means for establishing truth and rhetoric's inventional concerns were supplanted by more modest managerial ones. The Enlightenment, especially the Scottish Enlightenment, brought a new rhetoric into being (Howell, 1967; Hauser, 1970). It secreted the dynamic possibilities of discourse to shape social reality behind instrumental concerns for adapting knowledge to the psychological needs of listeners and readers. Under the influence of Newtonian physics, it was an enterprise guided by a scientific understanding of the mind, as represented by the then prevalent faculty psychology. Thus the Scottish Enlightenment moved rhetoric from behind the podium to language uses at large and reformulated its ends as psychological concerns of enlightening the *understanding*, pleasing the *imagination*, moving the *passions*, and influencing the *will* (Campbell, 1963, p. 1). One achieved these ends through messages that emphasized facticity, presentational accounts that conformed with nature and experience, and evocation of emotion and action through verbal portraiture rather than artistic appeals that were products of human invention (Hauser, 1970; Hipple, 1957).

There were intellectual countermovements, however, to the new rhetoric of the Enlightenment. They resisted the rationalism of

Cartesian method as reductionistic and unable to encompass all of human experience. Among Descartes's critics was Giambatista Vico (1990), who argued for a world apart from nature—a human world—which could be constructed in manifold ways. Not all reality, he thought, lent itself to the logical geometry of Cartesian reason. Humans also created reality through shared understandings that regulated behavior. He argued for such a world as a rhetorical product, a rhetorical invention or discovery made possible through *ingenium* and *fantasia*. Nearly two centuries later Nietzsche continued Vico's attack by arguing that human realities are the products of interpretation. In his seminal essay, "On Truth and Lies in a Nonmoral Sense," he wrote:

> What then is truth? A movable host of metaphors, metonymies, and anthropomorphisms: in short, a sum of human relations which have been poetically and rhetorically intensified, transferred, and embellished, and which after long usage, seem to a people to be fixed, canonical, and binding. Truths are illusions which we have forgotten are illusions; they are metaphors that have become drained of sensuous force, coins which have lost their embossing and are now considered as metal and no longer as coins. (1990, p. 891)

Nietzsche's claim introduced a linguistic turn to our understanding of reality and truth. In contradistinction to the positivity and rationality of assuming an objectively real world that could be known and on which discourse should be based, Nietzsche maintained that we were prisoners of language, that our realities were not based on truth but on our uses of language. This contention introduced a philosophical orientation with profound implications for understanding rhetorical practices and their status as social realities, paving the way for still another *new* rhetoric that is still being theorized.

The linguistic turn itself can be summarized in the claim that the human world is a product of cultural meaning, not fixed variables. This meaning is expressed in discourse, broadly understood, and is manifested in the uses and misuses of symbolic forms, of which language is an instantiation. Discourse itself is polyvocal and polysemic by definition. It does not speak with one voice but echoes the dialogue of cultural voices. Nor does it utter a single message but multiple messages that are brought to the surface through interpretation. Because polysemy cannot be reduced to predefined elements such as a priori speech acts, preestablished dyadic relations, or posited assumptions, interpretation itself is nonreductionistic. Rather, it attempts to elucidate the shared world of meaning on which intentionality and empathy are based and within which the subjects of human discourse constitute themselves.

Although the theme of constitutive rhetoric is a relatively recent development, its foundations were established by the writings of Kenneth Burke. Burke's dramatistic theory (1969) extended the social interactionism of the Chicago school by maintaining that social joining was grounded in the suasory inflections inherent to symbols. Burke established the impossibility of employing symbols without issuing a hortatory appeal, without inducing an attitude. This insight is encapsuled in his theory of identification, which Burke regarded as the central concept of the new rhetoric and as distinguishing it from the old rhetoric based on persuasion.

A central tenet of Burke's dramatism is its distinction between a representational and presentational orientation toward language. The former view maintains that reality exists apart from language and is represented by human symbols. The latter maintains that human reality emerges through discourse; it is bodied forth by choices of image, argument, and strategy. The reality to which humans respond is that which is presented in discourse.

Charles Taylor (1971) has advanced the thesis that these baseline realities are practices that cannot be separated from the language we use to describe them. By that he means that humans are self-interpreting and self-defining animals. Meanings may appear to be fixed but, in fact, they are unstable interpretations. Moreover, the instability of meaning ushers in a corresponding awareness of the instability of human realities which they underwrite. The Enlightenment ideal of a rationally ordered world in which decisions are based on the strength of warranted assent to true arguments cannot be redeemed because it rests on a counterfactual presupposition of stability. There are no true arguments, only interpretations. As Nietzsche would have it, there is no outside world from which we gather brute data of reality; we have only interpretations of interpretations on which to base our understanding. We cannot escape the inherent circularity in all cultural interpretations; interpretation is a perpetual activity. Taylor's thesis leads to the conclusion that the human world is a nonformal and interpretive creation.

This line of analysis, which is developed by a variety of sources and in a variety of intellectual schools, points to human discourse as the basis for understanding cultural and social realities and to the de-centering or displacement of the individual as subject. They suggest that by examining the rhetoric of social actors we can gain insight into how they constitute themselves (or are constituted) as subjects and as a culture or society. Hence, a new understanding of rhetoric has developed—*rhetoric as a social practice*.

On its surface, studying rhetoric as a social practice may seem to offer nothing particularly novel. Has it not always been such? Is this more than a novel way of expressing its ancient instrumentalism? We believe it represents a radical departure.

The *old* rhetoric was based on assumptions of rationality. Aristotle's emphasis on the argument as the heart and soul of rhetoric, Cicero's emphasis on the method of argumentation, the medieval and even renaissance preoccupation with elaborating topical analysis (as in Boethius's *De topicis differentiis* and Agricola's *De inventione dialectica libre tres*), through the work of Perelman and Olbrechts-Tyteca (1969) in the twentieth century equate rhetoric with public moral argument and monumentalize reason as its foundation. They presuppose stability of meaning and the presence of an audience already given and enabled to reach a judgment that will meet at least cultural norms for rationality. The *new* rhetoric finds its heritage in Sophistic speculations about the gulf between language and phenomena, the instability of meaning, the social relativity of truth, and the inherent deceptiveness (*apatē*) of all discourse (Gorgias, 1972). Its trajectory passes through Longinus's speculation on the sublime, through Vico's observations on the human world as a discursive formation and Nietzsche's rather explicit echoes of Sophistic insistence on the instability of meaning and the consequent fissure between language and truth, to the (for lack of a better covering term) postmodern contentions about the instability of meaning, the discontinuity of history, the loss of permanence, the decline of the grand narrative (and perhaps displacement of narrativity itself), the decentering of the subject, and the overall politics inherent in the discursive formation of knowledge/power. It theorizes rhetoric in a milieu specifically lacking a priori criteria for rationality and envisions the rhetoricity of social practices as entailing the discursive deployment of symbolic resources to constitute the very *world* in which social actors find themselves and their identity in it.

The paradoxical nature of the new rhetoric is that it both shares and disavows ancient insights about the possibilities of rhetoric. From antiquity, the new rhetoric borrows an understanding of rhetoric's methodological possibilities for creating publicly shared reality. Historically, the weakest rhetorical models have had their roles inscribed against a backdrop of prevailing assumptions about being, knowing, or acting. These rhetorics have been largely managerial of metaphysical, epistemological, or pragmatic orthodoxies. Conversely, the strongest models of rhetoric have emerged in eras that freed conduct from truth grounded in a dominant set of a priori assumptions.

The conditions of postmodernity have invited fresh thought about a strong rhetorical theory. Conditions of diversity, pluralism, rapid technological innovation, social change, mass diffusion of information, and widespread interdependence have precluded the possibility of consensus based on shared assumptions. Instead, they have encouraged an environment of shifting political alliances. Under conditions that foster instability, rhetoric becomes the dominant democratic alternative to repression. Richard McKeon has argued that rhetoric can serve as a method for coordinating social action under present conditions because it does not privilege one vision of reality over another. Interdependence among parties with diverse ideological and class interests precludes the possibility of solving common problems on the basis of their respective assumptive frameworks. Mutual satisfaction can only be achieved by shifting the focus from shared ideas and values to their shared problems and the consequences for rhetorical partners from this or that solution. A strong understanding of rhetoric locates reality in the agreements established through discourse. It is *constitutive* of a shared world of coordinated social action. Instead of basing the justification for shared action on common presuppositions about being, knowing, or doing, cooperation rests on all parties finding their own justifications for the acceptability of these solutions and the specific configurations they give to a common world. In this sense, McKeon contends, rhetoric is suited to serve as the architectonic productive art for a technological age (1971).

McKeon's argument for the architectonic character of rhetoric reconfigures the nature of interests as the basis for political relations. It abandons any a priori position that makes interests a product of class or ideology. Although such interests exist and remain relevant concerns for those who hold them, they cannot be the starting point for solving a common problem (Hauser & Cushman, 1973). Since contesting parties seldom if ever share class or ideological interests, they lack rhetorical force beyond their own adherents. The only interests relevant are ones that promote cooperation, and these are defined in terms of shared problems and the need to find an efficacious solution to which all involved parties can commit and on which future action can be based. The new rhetoric's commitment to the force of *shared experiences of sharing* common problems presupposes tolerance of interpretive differences in understanding the problems themselves. It envisions a society which McKeon has characterized as composed of social actors who are of one mind in the truth (i.e., that truth is discursively constituted) without being of one opinion (1957, p. 99). For the new rhetoric, *interests are rhetorically constituted.*[1]

McKeon's assumption of a tolerant society whose members "possess reason to judge statements of truth, understanding to appreciate statements of their own values and those of others, desires ordered under freedom, and love of the common good for which men are associated" (p. 99), which incidentally also appears in less rhetorically sympathetic garb in Habermas's procedural model of truth, posits an already existing set of audiences whose assent is contingent upon the rational justification of a solution within their respective frames of reference. The paradox of the new rhetoric arises from its disavowal of ancient theory's depiction of the audience as pregiven. Instead it denies the metaphysics of essence and proceeds on the assumption that audiences are discursive formations.

Twenty-five years ago Edwin Black (1970) published his influential essay, "The Second Persona," in which he examined the uses of the "cancer" metaphor by Robert Welch, guru to the radical right-wing John Birch society. Welch's use of this metaphor to depict the nature of communism in America was typical of the radical right of that period and Black argued that its use was not incidental. Most obviously such a metaphor implied a world of beliefs, values, and actions. More significantly, it also implied an auditor ideally suited to resonate to its call. This paradigm case bespoke a fundamental trait that follows from rhetoric's character as addressed discourse. In attempting to persuade, it envisions an identity for those who would feel the force of its appeals and be moved. It answers the modern "quest for identity" by offering hints "at whom we should become" (p. 113).

Black's argument underscores the textuality of audience and forecasts the fundamental difference between an instrumentalist and constitutive theory of rhetoric. The instrumental view takes the audience to be pregiven. Its identity is known and the effort of rhetoric is to find those means of persuasion that will secure an accommodation between its commitments and the ends of the rhetor. Constitutive theory discards the assumption that our social being is pregiven and unitary. Barbara Biesecker (1989) argues that rhetoric deconstructs the unitary and transcendent subject by calling it to embrace an identity that is not present and known. Rhetorical situations do not exist as objective events structured by a logic of influence but as discursive events structured by a logic of articulation (p. 126). Each rhetorical situation makes personal and collective identity possible because it problematizes the preexisting subject, dividing it from itself through the interplay of alternative possibilities for its own meaning and for intersubjective connection. Maurice Charland (1987) contends that these interconnections occur through the process of inscribing the subject into an ideology that is part of every rhetorical situation. He illustrates this point with the case of the separatist movement in Quebec. Through its famous white paper outlining a different narrative of the French-speaking majority, the Quebec government appropriated a history in which the existing identity as *Canadien français* was replaced by *Québécois*. Following Althusser, who labels this process "interpellation" or hailing someone in a way that demands an answer, Charland observes, "Interpellation occurs at the very moment one enters into a rhetorical situation, that is, as soon as an individual recognizes and acknowledges being addressed. An interpellated subject participates in the discourse that addresses him. Thus, to be interpellated is to become one of Black's personae and be a position in a discourse" (p. 138).

Put differently, the postmodern negation of a fixed subject may be read as a call to de-emphasize the subject as the preconstituted center of society. In line with Nietzsche's denial of the thinking subject who reasons logically and causally, the more extreme views hold the autonomous subject to be a fiction. In the philosophies of Derrida and Foucault, for example, the subject is not the origin of action but is only a position of language, constituted through society's discursive formations.

Historically, rhetoric has held out the possibility of free and independent subjects affirming a common world of beliefs, values, and actions. The new rhetoric has called this assumption into question by denying an autonomous individual and collective identity that exists free and independent of discourse. Although we may join the quest for identity Black mentions, its realization is not a discovery of an inherent self-identity but a process of formation constituted by heeding the inherent call of rhetoric to "be" a subject of a certain type in a world that is discursively constituted and ordered. This position manifests itself in the theory of new social movements, to which we now turn.

THE RHETORICAL THEORY
OF NEW SOCIAL MOVEMENTS

Twenty years ago, social theorists working in a variety of disciplines observed a new type of social movement arrive on the scene of social conflict in countries operating under conditions of advanced industrialism or late capitalism. Prior to the mid-1960s, movement theorists of many stripes focused on those common perceptions of economic grievance, typical understandings of the sources of material injustice, and, perhaps most importantly, broad relationships of class in which social movement activity was seemingly rooted. Communication theorists in turn developed a substantial body of essays that examined the rhetorical strategies through which these common perceptions of grievance and injustice entered and compelled the social imaginary.

Research on new social movements (NSMs) takes as its focus a different sort of structural and psychological collective occurrence of social conflict. These new movements are thought to "stretch the explanatory capacities of older theoretical perspectives" (Johnston, Larana, & Gusfield, 1994, p. 3) and have thus forced social movement researchers into fresh speculation regarding the theoretical and empirical bases of their work (see, e.g., Habermas, 1981; Eder, 1985; Melucci, 1985, 1989, 1994; Offe, 1985; Aronowitz, 1992; Touraine, 1988; Taylor, & Whittier, 1992; Johnston et al., 1994). As conceived in these new forms of movement and the attendant forms of social explanation, the primary distinction between old and new social movements *is captured in a tendency away from struggles of ideology/class, toward issues of identity.*

Examples of NSMs include spiritual/New Age religious movements (e.g., the holistic health movement and Scientology), movements based on gender (e.g., contemporary incarnations of the women's movement), movements based on sexual orientation (e.g., Act Up! and the ecolesbianfeminist movement), ethnic revivalist movements (e.g., the movements aimed toward reappropriations of ethnicity such as the Canadian *Québécois* and Spanish Catalan movements), nationalist movements, and environmental movements (e.g., Earth First!). What distinguishes these new forms of collective political activity from the old is in part the insistence of involved social actors on assertions of self-image; the personal; the intimate; the spiritual; in short, assertions of the quotidian in the *longue durée* of social and political life.

Noticing a newly articulated "sensitivity" on the part of researchers toward the "ethical and cultural themes" of identity, Touraine (1988) remarks:

> How can one fail to establish a relation between such an interest taken by psychologists and sociologists and the appearance, or development, all over the world and in nearly all areas of social life, of claims, social or national movements that appeal for defense of personal or collective identity? (p. 75)

Importantly, Touraine (1988) writes that the appeal to identity "is an appeal to a nonsocial definition of the social actor. . . . A rejection of roles, or, more precisely, a refusal of the social definition of the roles that must be played by the actor" (p. 75), It is "no longer an appeal to a mode of being but the claim to a capacity for action and for change. [Identity] is defined in terms of choice and not in terms of substance, essence, or tradition" (p. 81). As Mellucci succinctly puts it, "The freedom to have which characterized . . . industrial society has been replaced by the freedom to be" (1989, pp. 177–78).

During the last decade, rhetoricians have joined in pointed debate on issues related to theorizing movement rhetoric. Leland Griffin's seminal essay dealing with the rhetoric of historical movements (1952) set the terms for future theorizing by arguing that communication scholars should settle their attention on the rhetorical strategies used by establishment and anti-establishment forces during the course of conflict. Only three studies on movements were published between the appearance of Griffin's essay and Black's (1965) influential description of the generic features of social movement rhetoric. Black's sanctioning of social movement research as a legitimate and promising area of research is widely heralded as having provided the impetus for the substantial increase in scholarly attention paid to social movements in the communication field during the 1970s. These essays uniformly focus upon (1) rhetorical strategies extended by particular movement spokespersons or factions; (2) the rhetorical configurations of single events within a movement; and (3) the rhetoric of competing ideologies from both within and without the movement. In addition, there is the odd essay that focuses upon the generic dimensions of

the rhetoric of a particular movement, or perhaps judges movement rhetoric according to a particular canon (e.g., an aesthetic
criticism of a particular speaker's style).

Yet despite wide agreement among communication scholars regarding the importance of movement studies to the field, there
seems to be an abiding sense that the work has been unable to escape some indefinable point of theoretical and thus critical stall.
Fifteen years ago, Riches and Sillars (1980, p. 287) argued that "critics clearly appear to share no overriding theoretical framework
within which they carry out their analyses . . . [and] seem generally
unresponsive to such theorizing," resulting in rhetorical movement
studies "which appear to be in an undifferentiated and near infant
stage." This concern is echoed in a plethora of essays through that
decade, eventuating in Lucas's claim that "scholarship in the rhetoric of social movements is moribund" (1988, p. 243) and Henry's
final lament that "it is the dearth [of social movement research] . . .
that draws note" (1989, p. 97). Lacking the sort of rich theoretical
underpinning that might direct the critic of movements to more
penetrating understandings of the phenomena and epiphenomena
of the formation of social will, the consequent focus on strategy
seems to have eventuated in catalogues of tactics and attendant mi-
dlevel theories, studies that are discretely useful and absorbing but
leave an often maddeningly ambiguous picture of the distinctive
rhetorical dimensions of social movements or, more precisely, the
rhetorical consciousness of social movement actors.

Michael McGee (1980) warned of the possibility of this occurrence in an early theoretical essay dealing with social movements.
He argued that rhetorical social movement studies had erred "egre-
giously" in unthinkingly borrowing their theoretical and conceptual tools from empirical sociology. The consequence of this appro-
priation was the positivist premise that "movements are
phenomena," lending to movements a certain objective status and
paradigmatic character. The problem with this theoretical move
was that movements now were studied as though they were in
themselves social facts. Movements are better thought of as "meaning" than "phenomena," argued McGee, better theorized herme-
neutically than according to the terms of a behavioral science, as
accounts of human consciousness rather than organizational behavior. "I see no phenomenon at all, but only a series of words with
meanings to be discovered and verified," he wrote (p. 244). McGee's
essay provoked some strong but short-lived controversy (Simons,
1980; Riches & Sillars, 1980; Zarefsky, 1980), but his prescription

has remained unheeded in the theorizing of the rhetoric of social movements.

The dramatic turn to the problematic of "identity" in social theory specific to new social movements seems to us to provide a sudden opening, an occasion for an elaboration of the rhetorical consciousness of social movement actors and activity specific to the characteristics of the new movements that remains undertheorized in work done by communication scholars to this point. We find much to value in McGee's interpretive orientation to the study of social movements and wish to use the hermeneutic turn as the point of departure in developing a set of theoretical statements which may be useful in the study of the rhetoric of contemporary social movements. We thus set forth a series of propositional statements related to the role of rhetoric in new social movements. These are stated as general theory propositions, and specified in terms of the special discursive characteristics of NSMs:

1. The interests upon which social actors act are anchored in material conditions but do not preexist their expression through rhetoric.

Normally, the credentialing of power in a given rhetorical situation is intimately tied to a view of holdings of interests. Giddens has identified the concept of material interest as an essentially contested concept, "as contentious as any in social theory" (1979, p. 188):

> Interests consist of all those things in which one has a stake, whereas one's interest in the singular, one's personal interest or self-interest, consists in the harmonious advancement of all one's interests in the plural. These interests, or perhaps more accurately, the things these interests are *in*, are distinguishable components of a person's well being: he flourishes or languishes as they flourish or languish. (1987, p. 49)

Most social theorists agree that interests are isomorphic with interests as they are disclosed in political behavior or speech in decision making. As Lukes puts it, an interest is realized when an actor "prevails over the contrary preference of others, with respect to key issues" (1974, p. 82).

Rhetoric's relationship to the conception, articulation, and advancement of interest is tremendously complex. Charland's notion of constitutive rhetoric substantially reconfigures the theoretical landscape of this relationship. In arguing that effective rhetoric must do more than mobilize an audience—that, in fact, such rhetoric must actually meet a constitutive criterion—Charland implies a view of interest that bears elaboration.

We began this section of the essay by noting that within the context of an NSM, interests are rooted in the social actor's striving toward a sort of self-actualization mediated through collective activity. Mobilization is no longer wholly rooted in economic interest or grievance; rather, the social actor begins the process of identifying with the collective interests articulated through "membership" in a movement at the moment at which that movement extends a compelling attractive vision of the meaning of everyday life. It is this manner of ideologizing of the personal which attracts actors to the new social movement. The interests articulated through the rhetoric of these movements must offer some whole explanation, some lens through which the private and personal needs of the individual may be essentialized and acted upon. One who identifies as an environmentalist, for example, buys into a worldview which specifies a complete set of practices infiltrating almost all aspects of personal life: which products to buy, what sort of transportation to use, how many children may be borne. The interests articulated through the rhetoric of new movements must comport with a view of the good, a good which may be social in aspect but personal in practice.

2. Social movement actors must negotiate between discursively articulated sets of individual and collective meanings that are essentially unstable.

A minimal criterion for "membership" in a contemporary social movements is that the change agent must see him/herself as acting out beliefs in a manner similar to those of distant members. This is, in fact, a defining condition of movement membership. This criterion was not difficult to meet in the old social movements in which physical proximity was a set circumstance. In a traditional class-based action, for example (and here we are generalizing), a grievance was quite conceivably local in its manifestations; one lived and may have worked with movement companions. But in contemporary society in which citizens are geographically dispersed, transient, and often living lives in which many significant local institutional commitments may be ephemeral, a devotion to movement membership must of necessity be experienced as an individual practice.

Thus, rhetoric attendant to new social movements must maintain some sort of strong equilibrium between personal meaning and collective behavior, between anomie and felt fidelity to whatever vision of the public good is offered by a specific movement. Where engagement in social movement action once offered the very real pleasures of companionship during the course of action, contemporary movement activity may be experienced within the context of dramatic factual dissociation of the individual from the collective. The rhetoric issuing from new movements must thus work inventively and consistently to exercise moral control over individuals who may mightily believe but are not immediately accountable to the collective for their practices.

This sort of rhetorical consciousness is especially consequential for movements which articulate interests which remain at a particularly far distance from the members' everyday lives. Caring about the ozone while one lives and breathes at 1,600 feet, caring about saving the whales while one lives landlocked in Iowa, caring about preserving the rainforests while one calls the arid Arizona desert home seemingly may be the stuff of only the most short-lived movement; and yet as submovements of the general environmental movement, they prevail. This sort of "membership" is only possible if the movement is capable of engaging in articulatory practices that constantly and undeviatingly reassert individual movement members within the context of the movement itself.

In an influential piece of theoretical sociology published a decade ago, Lipset and Schneider (1987) captured the specific senses in which Americans wholly distrust institutions and their companion organizations, choosing instead to invest their trust in individuals. Using public opinion data culled from several decades of polling from a wide variety of sources, *The Confidence Gap* had implications that were far-reaching: Americans could love political life and be fully engaged in issues of the day, yet never register to vote and dismiss all possibilities for real civic involvement; Americans could believe that workers should earn a living wage and believe in the basic decency of the American worker, yet completely distrust unions and develop a particular dislike for union leaders; Americans could hold all manner of strong personal convictions that were deeply felt, yet never fully realized within the context of public activity.

This research finding seems to hold particular resonance for the behavior of social actors within the context of new social movements; for these new movements often specify acts of protest and engagement that are political in most meaningful senses of that term, and perhaps even civic in intent; but importantly, these forms of engagement can be wholly individual, wholly private. Thus, social movement researchers cannot *only* latch on to social movement organizations, or to geographically locatable institutions, in order to get a real sense of public opinion and attendant possibilities for public action. In this regard, Johnston and colleagues (1994) note:

> Though [new social movements] may have no clear class or structural base, the movement becomes the focus for the individual's definition of himself or herself, and action within the movement is a complex mix of the collective and individual confirmations of identity. (p. 8)

A social movement scholar thus errs in primarily searching for explanations rooted in the institutional or organizational components of movement activity, or for rhetoric issuing from those concerns. Indeed, as we have noted, new social movements may lack any real "institutional" component at all, in the traditional senses of that term.

3. Rhetorical situations are the product of choices made by the social actor; rhetorical situations are changing and mercurial responses to actor's conduct.

Touraine writes:

> A social movement is the action, both culturally oriented and socially conflictual, of a social class defined by its position of domination or dependency in the mode of appropriation of historicity, of the cultural models of investment, knowledge, and morality, toward which the social movement itself is oriented. (1988, p. 68)

Touraine thus argues that *social movements are not themselves situations, but are instead actions*. Put another way, social actors are not often willing, not always able—in fact, would not often find it necessary—to articulate the political bases for their actions at the level of the metasocial, in the form of metanarratives. An example at this point will prove instructive. In examining oral histories executed by a sociologist interviewing two industrial laborers in the 1970s, one of the authors encountered a passage telling for the gap that too often exists between the experience of political actors and the scholarly narratives developed to account for them. The interviewer was trying to determine the factional bases for a strike initiated by the two men at a steel mill in eastern Pennsylvania. "John," she said, speaking to one of the men, "contemporary social theory holds that the modern worker is alienated from the means of production, in a condition of permanent political anomie, fixated on minor ineffective modes of control because of the ever-widening gap between production and ownership. How do you respond to that?" "Well, Alice," said John, "I'd have to say that I have some good days, and I have some bad days." The point we wish to make here is a simple one: social facts, including those with a strongly rhetorical dimension, must be explained at their own level. Though this point was first and most compellingly made by Durkheim over one hundred years ago, it is a procedural warning, specifying an orientation to forms of explanation, that bodes well for those interested in rhetorical analysis of discourses stemming from new social movements. A social movement is an action, an action of social actor who is renegotiating the terms of historicity, as Touraine instructs.

This *return of the actor*, though heralded and procedurally inculcated in the theoretical writings of interpretivists in most of the human disciplines, has yet to be internalized or routinized at the level of rhetorical theories aimed at providing modes of explanation and verification of social movement activity. Practically, it might mean: develop forms of explanation that are isomorphic with actors' sense of what they are up to when engaging in movement activity; exhibit a willingness to theorize the private and personal as subtexts of abstract social explanations stemming from new movement rhetorics; account theoretically for what Giddens (1984) has termed "discursive consciousness" (what actors are able to say, or give verbal expression to, about social conditions, including especially the conditions of their own action; awareness that has a discursive form) and practical consciousness (what actors know [believe] about social conditions, including especially the conditions of their own action, but cannot necessarily express discursively) by paying particular attention to the symbols, beliefs, values associated with the NSM as they comport with members' self-image and new senses of the meaning of life, given to them as the token gifts of NSM membership.

CONSTITUTIVE PRAXIS
OF NEW SOCIAL MOVEMENTS

The three theoretical postulates we have been discussing have practical implications for the discursive tendencies of new social movements and for the critical evaluation of their practices. They suggest that at the level of praxis, interests are not manifested in terms of material conditions of class, economics, or labor but in terms of articulatory practices. In other words, *the new rhetoric regards interests as interpretations of material conditions.*

These interpretations take a variety of forms, as were alluded to earlier. Thus, we find that the materiality of gender, sexuality, biology, ethnicity, alien status, environmental conditions, ecological balance, social role, religious faith and practice, and a host of other conditions become the source of such causes as ERA, open housing, Right to Life, bilingual education, Proposition 184, antismoking, Save the Spotted Owl, and the Promise Keepers, among others. Such movements are different from those of the pre–Vietnam War era in that their boundaries are amorphous. There are no clearly defined material resources that demarcate the preserve of those who have banded together to work for change, such as with the labor movement during the twenties and thirties, or the civil rights movement of the fifties and sixties. Those movements grew from specific conditions related to the right to work, to receive fair compensation for one's labor, to vote, to have equal access to public facilities and institutions, to receive compensation on the basis of work performed, or to have an equal educational opportunity. They were based in overt disparities based on class, race, and gender that created asymmetrical relations of power and wealth. Movements were at odds with establishment forces over the distribution of society's resources and their wars were often waged through physical acts intended to reappropriate them in order to resolve political and economic inequalities.

By contrast NSM wars are over language. They center on highly charged labels and constitute members' awareness of material conditions through a personalized and moralized rhetoric. It is not just that antivivisectionists, for instance, are opposed to laboratory experimentation that involves the use of live animals, but they mount their opposition in a way that transforms the laboratory from the antiseptic site for clinical observation to a torture chamber in which helpless creatures are put to death for corporate profit and personal gain. They bring the public to consciousness of the practices of research universities and the pharmaceutical and cosmetic industries in a way that inveighs against the moral compass of their research scientists by labeling them as "cruel," "torturers," and even "murderers," while appropriating to themselves the honorific title of "animal rights activists."[2]

The consequences of unstable meanings, which contribute so heavily to these language wars, have been noted by scholars since at least the 1960s when David Riesman's influential study *The Lonely Crowd* (1961) appeared. Riesman distinguished between inner- and outer-directed societies on the basis of the presence or absence of a shared set of stable social beliefs and values. An inner-directed society, which was present and perhaps prevalent in the United States even as recently as the World War II era, was marked by individuals who had an "internal gyroscope" that provided their orientation to right and wrong and a basis for judging their conduct in terms of community values. The inner-directed person did not have to ask others for certification of his or her moral compass because affiliations of class, religion, and community provided a narrative of traditions and values in which one found a personal sense of meaning and place. The inner-directed person not only belonged to a shared world of ideas and sentiments but *knew* they were shared with others in the community. By contrast, the post–World War II experience has witnessed a deterioration of traditional beliefs and loss of confidence in institutions. Riesman thought this decline of meaningful and satisfying structures for shared experience was accompanied by a loss of shared social orientation. The outer-directed person he found so prevalent in society was a manifestation of an increased need to seek certification of personal meaning and self-worth from others.

Reisman's argument projected a developmental curve in which the social actor of the future would be an autonomous self who oriented toward the world freed from the twin tyrannies of traditional and institutional forces, on the one hand, and conformism to popular opinion, on the other. However, widespread conditions of rapid change have only exacerbated the instability of self-identity he greatly lamented.

This instability is reflected in NSM rhetoric, which centers on the problem of loss of identity and the need for engagement in redemptive discourses of self-discovery. At a time when the relevance of the past is increasingly questioned and people have forgotten how to think historically, NSM rhetoric understandably differs from the group appeals previously so dominant in movement discourse. Yet without a shared sense of the past, ahistorical appeals lack a contextualizing framework—a common tongue—from which to develop shared meanings and common commitments.

The claim that language is both the weapon and spoils in the wars of new social movements is pointedly illustrated in the contemporary debate over political correctness, a primary dialect of the movement known as *multiculturalism*. Debates over multiculturalism are raging on campuses of American universities and colleges, in Congress, in the popular media, and in the corporate boardroom. The themes of multiculturalism fan the incendiary narratives of some of the most prominent modern-day riots of American intellectual life. As Gusfield (1994) argues, social movements occur when they are perceived to be occurring; and though different in form and content from historical social movements, multiculturalism is identified as a political movement of the first order by a wide variety sources. Gerald Graff's *Beyond the Culture Wars*, Roger Kimball's *Tenured Radicals*, Charles Syke's *A Nation of Victims*, Dinesh D'Souza's *Illiberal Education,* and Robert Hughes's *Culture of Complaint* join Eagleton, Gates, Bromwich, Schlesinger, Paglia, Lehman, Bloom, Sykes, Rorty, and Gitlin in powerfully depicting multiculturalism as either the savior or assassin of modern civic experience. The December 1991 issue of *Harper's* published two essays with contrasting views on the debate over multiculturalism that are exemplary of these current writings. These essays—Louis Menand's "What Are Universities For? The Real Crisis on Campus Is One of Identity"; and Rosa Ehrenreich's "What Campus Radicals? The P.C. Undergrad Is a Useful Specter"—along with letters to the editor provoked by them (February 1992, March 1992)—illustrate how meaning wars have superseded contests over interests.

On the question of whether Harvard provides its undergraduates with adequate instruction in the Western core, Harvard grads Rosa Ehrenreich and Caleb Nelson give contrasting readings to the same course offerings. In an essay published in *Atlantic Monthly*, Nelson objects that Harvard's existing core courses were "chosen for the curriculum without regard for substantive content" and are more concerned with developing intellectual skills than with imparting substance. For Nelson, the substantive content should give students an understanding of what important figures actually thought. In her *Harper's* essay, Ehrenreich retorts that emphasis on what great minds thought "is to teach students a set body of facts." For her, imparting the facts of "Western civ" is not and should not be the core's intent. Without a common touchstone to contextualize their respective assertions on educational philosophy, facts assume whatever meaning each wishes since there is no common interpretive framework to ground the claims they derive from them.

In a responsive letter to *Harper's*, Nelson then advances an argument that goes to the heart of multicultural discourses related to the theory and practice of the academic canon. Nelson objects to recent developments in the Harvard curriculum that stipulate course offerings on specialized topics such as fiction produced by African-American women writers. "By designing a curriculum without defining a canon," he writes, "Harvard escapes the controversial task of defining a canon." For Nelson, the concept of canon is compromised at Harvard due to the curricular emphasis on modes of analysis over the transmission of a "specific quantum of information." A canon of this sort would provide undergraduates with a "firm grounding," learning that is "coherent" and "solid"; this characterization is in contrast to the "gaping holes" produced in the curriculum when multicultural interests drive the professorate. Nelson's reminiscence of and longing for a fixed canon, and Ehrenreich's preference for the vagaries of an "uncanoned" specialized core, exemplify the manner in which the praxis of the new rhetoric may be driven by unstable meanings deeply informed by unstable sociopolitical relationships. The new rhetoric in fact would deconstruct "canon" as an archive, or topoi specifying sets of discourses privileged over other sets of competing discourses, whose skies are changeable.

The discovery of identity in NSMs has special meaning for the impulse that instigates rhetorical activity. As we argued above, social action is grounded in relationship and relationship precedes situation as the anchoring concept for NSM rhetoric. However, when the base of relationship is the identity established through membership in a movement rather than shared material interests, the implications of change bear special relevance for the practical realities of message design strategies. The old rhetoric entailed a concept of audience that was to be addressed in terms of shared interests. These provided a common ground from which a rhetor might build persuasive appeals. The theoretical capital of this conception of audience has been expended. Conditions of rapid change, instant dissemination of information, and universal access to messages make it unlikely that those who receive, endorse, and act on public discourse are bonded by shared material interests. Now public messages are attended to by a nameless, faceless, anonymous aggregate of strangers whose influence gains validation insofar as it is recognized as a public that is able to provide some form of legitimation.

Publics differ from the political ideal of *the* public in that they are more than a political reification. They are inferred from patterns of empirical evidence of response offered by a broad cross-section of the population to issues with which they are confronted. In a society which substitutes identity for class as the defining impulse for participation in a social movement, the characteristics of those whose support it solicits are not pregiven nor can its existence be assumed. Publics are rhetorically constituted. They are brought into being by discourses that can communicate a sense of identification with causes that lack clear boundaries and that bestow identity by framing issues in ways that cast individual praxis as an indication of one's being. Ehrenreich, for example, presents her stand on political correctness with claims designed to align her support of curricular reform with traditional American values. She juxtaposes her assertion that the issue is freedom of choice by individuals "who are old enough to *choose* what they want to learn" with her own choices, which happen to have been those advocated by her opposition—traditional contents of Western civilization that emphasized the writings and accomplishments of white European males. Such discourse has a pentimento-like quality in that, like the shadow of the original painting whose textures intrude upon new work superimposed on its surface, the old values of relationships based in class and tradition are insinuated as lurking beneath the surface of relationships of identity. The generic constraints of class relationships and group affiliation that bore upon and informed the old movement rhetoric and that established the borders within which the movement defined its interests may no longer apply, but neither can the more amorphous rhetoric of identity be severed completely from a social and political past. It faces the practical necessity of intimating, at least vaguely, connections between the identity that lies at the heart of the movement's cause with culturally resonant causes of the past.

A significant part of this resonance relies on an agonistic rhetoric in which a movement attempts to mobilize the society to bring about change. Intervention in the trajectory of the existing order is justified through portrayal of its opposition as an entrenched and intractable establishment that must be resisted and even destroyed. Our national history of violence that accompanied such historical movements as the World War I veterans protest in the twenties, the labor strikes of the thirties, and the civil rights and antiwar movements of the fifties, sixties, and seventies is indicative of the extremes to which such opposition might lead.

The displacement of class or group interests by identity causes does not lessen the intensity of conflict that accompanies NSMs, but the combat is less likely to be orchestrated or waged at the institutional level. NSMs do not have an organization or a headquarters like those associated with, say, the labor movement, which presented its members and its public with a discourse of identity. Since identity movements lack institutions that create the rhetoric of identity, they must be found in the more general social practices. The critic's attention focuses on rhetorics that express identificatory interests—"I recycle," "I am *Québécois*," "I teach my children Catalan instead of Spanish." The new rhetoric requires *vernacular* expression to establish social meaning and social action without community. The disparate and diffused membership of NSMs and of the publics that attend to their rhetoric and whose support they elicit depend on developing vernacular codes by which affiliation can be expressed in a way that makes a personal assertion of identity and support.

Vernacular discourses, such as bumper stickers, personal garb, and social practices of, say, recycling, make public assertions of who we are and the values we hold. They provide a sense of social support for causes and an injunction to others about correct behavior. They rub against other social practices in ways that challenge them by asserting an alternative identity. It is not just that, for example, Harvard professor of history Stephan Thernstrom is accused of making racially insensitive remarks in his lectures, but that he is perceived as a "racist." It is not just that students who were disturbed by his comments raised their concerns in the *Harvard Crimson*, but that by raising them there they make him a victim through smears "too vague to be refuted." The dialogic interaction between Thernstrom and Ehrenreich is a war of words to be sure. But they are also interesting in that they reference the vernacular exchanges among students, faculty, and the greater society by which political thoughts and sentiments are inferred from comments that remain unelaborated or even uninterrogated to discern their true meaning. For example, Thernstrom professes that his life was made wretched by a full two months of discourse on the matter in the *Harvard Crimson*. Thernstrom claims to have been made the object of a "witch hunt" reminiscent of "the 1950s menace to academic freedom" that propelled him to consider "Nixon-like" surveillance techniques when speaking to undergraduates in office hours. Thernstrom found the entire debacle to be so "Kafkaesque"—obscure meanings sequestered in the form of charges of political crimes issued by faceless authorities—that he decided he should no longer offer the course in question. Ehrenreich in contrast infers that the issues blew over in a few days because most students lost interest and paid no attention to stories in the *Crimson*. Their respective inferences grow from the meanings they attach to such considerations as the length of time spent on a question, the places in which discourse does or does not occur (here, a file of clippings from the *Crimson* competes with the common sense of the student body), the vernacular codes for interpreting charges of "racial insensitivity" versus "racist," matters of precisely how identity is then extrapolated from these dialogic exchanges, and finally how such exchanges eventuate in moral claims about the individual's worth.

It is in this specific sense that multiculturalism takes its form as a political movement agitating for rights connected to identity. This identity is in turn interpolated, given its first breath, by the subnarratives of the discourse of multiculturalism. In this universe of discourse, to deny a student a class sprung from a "specialized" archive is to make a political choice that denies that student the narratives which are now seen to constitute identity—narratives of race or gender, for example—*thus denying that student the identity per se.* It is fair to assume that had multiculturalism never come to assume its salience in academic discourse, women would continue to be women; ethnic Americans would not demographically disappear. But for movement adherents, multicultural rhetorics provide the defining characteristics, the essential meanings, of those identities, by attaching specific literatures and new historical narratives to them. Responses to the Menand and Ehrenreich essays additionally point to a perception of multicultural rhetorics as flaccid forms of political protest. "Mere semantic utopianism" couched in the vernacular of "moral arrogance," wrote one professor of English who found student protests in the sixties more "meaningful." Proponents of multiculturalism in turn wrote letters that told of fear of persecution if views were made public among peers; one woman compared the political movement to a Holocaust experience.

A most sparkling lesson of American intellectual history is that debates that seem primarily conceptual—speculative debates whose referents exist in the abstract—are never what they seem to be. We conclude by noting that the multicultural debate is not in this regard markedly different from other theoretical conflicts in American history; as Rieff (1993) argues, multiculturalism is "not simply an idea, sprung from the minds of intellectuals, but rather [is] a product or corollary of a specific material integument"— which is to say, the newly globalized consumer economy. What is so rhetorically fascinating about multiculturalism as a rather perfect example of new social movements is its internal insistence that to win at language is to win the prize with the highest possible commodity value; that how we speak about a social relationship constitutes the whole of how we experience it; that this prize of language exists apart from the economic structures that necessarily shape it and from which it necessarily springs; that this language flourishes as a political movement even as welfare mothers are demonized, union workers are deunionized, the poor in America grow poorer. At this point, the rhetoric of multiculturalism has not demonstrated a strong inclination to join with sociopolitical rhetorics framed in nonacademic terms—or as Ehrenreich puts it, "real discussion" of "more pressing issues *outside* the academy." In short, the debate over multiculturalisms poses the perfect postmodern contradiction for the contemporary scholar of movement rhetoric: wildly successful language that remains hermetic, negotiating carefully between individual narrative and collective need, discerning no requirement to comport with the material realities of the culture which at every level situates it and in which it is situated.

NOTES

1. We do not mean to suggest that the issue of the relationship between discourse and material interests is in any manner settled in contemporary theory, with the materialist argument buckling under the pressures of the linguistic turn. In fact, quite the opposite is true. Some materialists working in a variety of disciplines—most especially interpretive sociology and history—have taken strong exception to studies which consider discourse to be a force in production. For a summary of arguments, see Palmer, 1990.

2. One of the authors recalls attending a meeting with the American College of Laboratory Animal Medicine (ACLAM) to discuss the political problem they faced in presenting their work to the public. This group of veterinarians, whose job is to enforce National Science Foundation and National Institutes of Health guidelines that regulate the care and treatment of laboratory animals used in medical research, see their mission as protecting the humane rights of these animals. At this meeting they were addressed by a legislator from the Maryland Assembly, who explained why the state had passed a law prohibiting researchers from acquiring animals

from local pounds for experimental purposes. In sum, the legislator claimed that "the animal rights activists" had done a better job of lobbying to protect animal interests. When one of the veterinarians objected that his group considered themselves to be the true proponents of animal rights and the protectors of their humane treatment, and that they resented the claim of activists to speak for "animal rights," the legislator responded that it was too late; the activists had laid stake to the title and the researchers would have to find another one for themselves. For a discussion of the rhetorics of animal rights played out in the public sphere, see Olson and Goodnight, 1994.

7

Managing Government Competitiveness
The Changing Role of Communications

Ron B. Cullen

> *Our governments are in deep trouble today. In government after government and public system after public system, reinvention is the only option left. But the lack of a vision— a new paradigm—holds us back.*
> —Osborne and Gaebler, *Reinventing Government*

The recent recession served to crystallize changes in the role of government in many countries. Gobalization of the world economy has reduced the sovereignty of individual nations. Some nations have responded more effectively than others. Where effective responses have occured, nations appear to have created a source of national competitive advantage; where countries have failed to meet standards of performance set by the global community, nations have been cut. The implications for national autonomy and development seem clear.

Most recessions since the 1930s can be seen as part of the ongoing business cycle. The challenge for governments was not to solve the problem or to change the role of government; the challenge was to ameliorate the pain of recession, to await and then take credit for the inevitable recovery. Unlike these previous recessions, the recent recession was associated with important and essentially noncyclical shifts in direction in many countries.

These noncyclical changes demand new approaches to the management of nations and new roles for national and regional governments. In recent years, the reform of government and government administration has tended to lag behind reform in the business sector. There can be little doubt that improving the competitiveness of nations now requires new approaches to government and government administration. While some of these approaches can be adapted from business experience, others cannot. New approaches to government administration must improve the fit between problems and solutions, and must reduce the risks of failure to more acceptable levels.

The challenge of implementing change for most governments is the challenge of delivering tangible results while also maintaining a broad support for change. The implementation of change has been constrained by the reality that many nations seem to have become less governable. In addition, systems of government decision making and administration that worked well enough in the past have increasingly become obstacles to national performance. There is a growing realization that countries, to be world-competitive, require a competitive government as well as a competitive business sector.

This chapter proposes a new model of government administration and uses it to examine the changing role of government and the effectiveness of some of the prescriptions for government reform that are now emerging. The analysis suggests that the current crisis in government has been caused by attempts to respond to new global pressures with old values and systems or, alternatively, with tools borrowed piecemeal from the private sector. Interestingly, the solution to the crisis for many governments is to adopt new approaches to government management that have been sadly missing from the score sheet of many, though not all, governments in recent years.

GLOBAL TRENDS ARE RESHAPING
NATIONAL COMPETITIVENESS

An isle is emerging that is no bigger than a continent—the Interlinked Economy (ILE) of the Triad (the United States, Europe, and Japan), joined by aggressive economies such as Taiwan, Hong Kong, and Singapore.

It is becoming so powerful that it has swallowed most consumers and corporations, made traditional national borders almost disappear, and pushed bureaucrats, politicans, and the military toward the status of declining industries.
—Kenichi Ohmae, *The Borderless World*

Fundamental trends are altering the way in which business must operate to succeed and the way in which wealth is created and distributed between and within nations. These same trends are altering the role of government and the way in which government and the private sector must operate to compete. While Kenichi Ohmae is probably mistaken in forecasting the decline of government and while he almost certainly overstates the role of markets in the present and future world, he presents a compelling picture of the changes that are underway and of the need for major changes in the role of government.

Five external trends are driving changes in the way in which governments are managed and in the relationship between the private and public sectors: globalization; competition for scarce resources; technology development and transfer that are altering fundamentally the value chain of many industries and revolutionizing approaches to integration and control in both the private and public sectors; major increases in the level of diversity between nations, regions, and interest groups; and the need to manage these issues under the glare of mass information that highlights differences and inequities in the process of government.

Globalization

The traditional model for external relationships was to manage them to contribute to the domestic economy of a nation by buffering the domestic economy from undesirable external pressures.

The capacity of nations to buffer their values and development from external influences has all but passed. This has created new external threats and opportunities. Governments can no longer respond effectively to recession or deliver economic growth and employment in isolation. Nations need to access global resources and technologies and markets. The price for this access is the need to meet external needs and expectations.

Competition

Nations must compete externally for a share of global resources and for access to markets and technologies. The traditional model for competition conveniently separated the role of government and business: government was required to regulate markets; business and industry groups were required to operate independently to create added value. This approach has proved unable to cope with external changes; in the new global economy, government and industry need to work together to optimize the share of global resources accessed by a nation or region.

Global resources are increasingly allocated by business networks such as multinationals, by international trade and investment, and by agencies such as the World Bank that seek to facilitate development. Nations that fail to respond effectively are accessing a decreasing share of these global resources.

The role of the public sector can no longer be studied separately from the rest of the economy. The way in which the two sectors interact is no longer fixed; it has become a key variable in new approaches to government. The boundaries between the two sectors are changing as integration between the public and private sectors become more critical. Government must work with the private sector to gain a share of global resources and to develop the internal resources required to exploit global markets and technologies.

Technology

To compete, nations must access and apply developing technologies cost-effectively. The development of technology has made technology access and technology transfer, the application of new technology, and advanced technological information and processes, key issues for the economic competitiveness of nations.

Old technology tends to be reflected in established production values and practices; new technology requires adaptation of those values and practices to facilitate technology transfer.

The traditional model for technology transfer was to develop a technology base hierarchically, starting with low technologies and leading to higher technologies and then upgrading and developing the base incrementally. These strategies are no longer effective. Pursued in the current global environment, they are a prescription for disaster and economic exploitation.

To develop as part of the global economy, countries need: to recognize that many technology changes are necessarily discontinuous; to access technologies strategically at all levels; to apply and exploit technologies to produce competitive advantage; and, finally, to position themselves to exploit emerging technologies.

These strategies in turn require nations: to develop international alliances; to reform labor markets; to review approaches to education and training; to accept and manage technological redundancy as a cost of remaining competitive; and to develop public and private sector partnerships to access key technologies. Generic skills are no longer enough; governments must ensure that there is a strategic fit between the demand and supply sides of the education and training system.

Diversity

In addition to globalization and competition for resources and markets, governments must manage major increases in the level of diversity between nations, regions, and interest groups. This requires new approaches by governments, which have favored and often sought to engineer common values and who have come to believe that the majority is the whole.

The traditional model for managing diversity was to focus on common values and consensus and to isolate and reduce anomalies. Integration of economic and political factors at the regional and industry levels can no longer be presumed. High response demands devolution. The need for change and for priorities means that difficult political consensus issues must also be devolved.

Increasingly, the old search for consensus is being seen as counterproductive. Nations are learning to manage their affairs within a comfort zone within which key groups are not motivated to oppose change. This requires political systems able to recognize and negotiate needs with interest groups and an administrative system able to deliver results while managing negative impacts.

The administrative challenge for governments today can be reduced to the twin challenges of meeting public expectations for real impacts rather than rhetoric while simultaneously managing within the comfort zone to accomodate diversity and maintain the scope for change. The myriad of new administrative tools developed in recent times can be seen as responses to these two challenges. The techniques reduce to two new approaches to government administration; performance management and confort-zone management.

Information

The traditional approach to communication was to control and shape reporting to reinforce established values and approaches. In the 1970s, when the political and entertainment businesses found much common ground, the objective was still to manipulate mass communications to support established priorities and values and to conceal differences and failures. Simple communicable ideas rather that prescriptions for action were the hallmarks of successful governments.

Governments can no longer convince the public that their interests are synonymous with the national or even the public interest. It is difficult to convince people that they are moving ahead or even leading the world when the nightly telecasts reflect a more compelling reality.

The speed and saturation of today's mass communications have outflanked these old strategies in many countries. Information about the performance of governments is more readily available, as is information about the performance of other nations.

Performance or the lack of it can no longer be hidden, and public expectations are now more demanding. The grand plans and platitudes that characterized much national planning are no longer persuasive, either to key interest groups within a country or to external groups that increasingly require evidence of performance as a prerequisite for investment and trade.

THE NEW CHALLENGE FOR GOVERNMENT

Who's to say whether Osborne and Gaebler have it right (I think they mostly do). The point is that government—in America, Japan, or France—hasn't been reinvented, and the world of commerce mostly has (though the task is far from finished). —Tom Peters, *Liberation Management*

Governments have three core roles: they must work with business to optimize the resources available to a country, by accessing a share of world resources and building a world-competitive industrial base; they must optimize both the short- and long-term well-being of their citizens by regulating the framework within which these resources are distributed within the country and by addressing the needs of disadvantaged groups; and they must maintain the scope to govern. While these core roles have not changed, the way in which they must be approached is light years removed from approaches that seemed to work well enough even a decade ago.

In defining the role of government, there is a tendency to confuse means with ends. For example, governments address these core roles by leveraging private and public sector resources, by regulating markets, by providing infrastructure and services, by addressing access to international markets and research and technology, and by ensuring that the education and training system delivers world-competitive work skills. Governments also need to balance available resources against the growing list of competing needs, and they must avoid waste and deal equitably with citizens and business. In evaluating government competitiveness, it is important to benchmark performance against the three core roles of government before considering the success or failure of particular solutions.

Comparisons of the effectiveness of government between nations tend to be cluttered by various factors. They include differences between political systems, between per capita levels of wealth, and between stages of economic and social development. Comparisons that have been made seem to suggest that effective government management is an important determinant of national performance. The old idea that government can control, regulate, or even service some static notion of national interest seems dead. Government today must be competitive. Competitive government differs from trends to introduce competition into the delivery of government services. The benchmarks are the performance of government in other countries.

Interestingly, the concepts of speed and strategic response that have proved so powerful in the business sector also seem to be fundamental to improving the performance of the government sector. Except perhaps in times of major crisis, government management has not been noted for its speed of response or for its capacity to monitor external developments. Even where responses involve little more than removing the maze of regulations that prevent the private sector responding, the evidence suggests that the public sector has difficulty seeing the woods for the trees.

As governments moved to change old approaches and facilitate the move to high-response management, the fragile consensus that supports governance has been severely challenged in many countries. The management and communications changes required to move to a high-speed response model of government are essential parts of the reinvention of government this time around. In the process, concepts of leadership in government management will need to be rewritten.

Benchmarking National Competitiveness

In responding to the external pressures discussed above, nations need to maximize added value. Three assumptions are suggested to benchmark added value.

1. That added value is best measured in terms of increased national competitveness.

2. That the most effective measures are therefore relative measures which compare one country with another.

3. That the comparisons also need to extend to the key factors (access to markets and technology, workforce and management

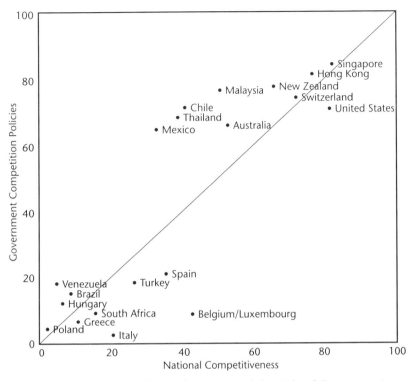

Figure 7.1. National Competitiveness and the Role of Government in Selected Countries

Source: Indices derived from World Economic Forum, *The World Competitiveness Report 1994* (14th ed.), Geneva, Switzerland.

skills, the provision of infrastructure, etc.) that underpin overall national competitiveness.

Nations differ markedly in their effectiveness, and differences are readily benchmarked and communicated. Such information is making it more difficult for nations that seek to buffer and develop differently.

Figure 7.1 compares evaluations for selected countries on the basis of national competitiveness and the contribution of governments to national competitiveness. The differences between countries are clear from these data, and these differences can be explored in terms of the way in which countries have sought to manage development and change. Three more specific points can be made about these data.

1. Countries that rank low on the contribution of government policies to competition also rank low on overall national competitiveness. They include Hungary, Poland, Italy, and Greece.

2. Some countries that rank high on national competitiveness also rank high on the contribution of government policies. They include Singapore, Hong Kong, the United States, New Zealand, and Switzerland.

3. Some countries rank in the upper quartile for competition policies but have not yet delivered national competitiveness. They include Malaysia, Chile, Thailand, Australia, and Mexico.

Performance Management:
Governments can learn from and adapt business solutions

Initial responses to the new global challenges discussed above tended to use old government management solutions; however, they were too insular to address global trends and too process-oriented to be strategic. When the need for new approaches to government became apparent, many nations looked to the experience of the business sector (Cullen, 1995).

The search to apply business solutions is not surprising; three out of the four core problems facing public administration today have parallels in the business sector. The three problems that have parallels in the challenges addressed by business in the 1980s are: the need to adjust value chains to respond more rapidly; the need to produce real outcomes rather than to consume resources or deliver processes; and the need to rationalize functions and focus on core values. However, attempts to transplant business solutions have created almost as many problems as they have solved.

Current reforms in government administration seek to draw on tools developed to meet the needs of business enterprises. There are three problems with this approach. First, transplanting solutions from one situation to another is always a risky business, especially when the theory surrounding many of the solutions remains underdeveloped. Second, the solutions had frequently failed in particular business situations. Third, the business analogy does not encompass the fourth core problem facing government management today: namely, the need to manage and develop the fragile consensus necessary for governments to govern and to implement change.

While governments can learn from business they cannot be managed as a business. Table 7.1 contrasts management priorities required to manage the interrelated missions in the public sector with the strategic management model that has helped the private sector to cope with change. The traditional model of government has been anti-evaluative, and many approaches to government management embrace this rather restrictive value system. While minimizing evaluation may have maintained an uneasy political consenus, the public has become increasingly critical of the failure of governments to deliver on even the simplest reforms. This lowering of expectations has created major opportunties to develop new approaches to public sector management that shorten cycle time and manage impacts and evaluate performance more directly.

Business solutions require evaluation and a related focus for action that has traditionally been avoided by government administration. This focus can be developed using performance management techniques and can provide a basis for strategic control and evaluation. However, the impacts associated with action planning need to be managed differently. Continuous evaluation needs to be used as a guide to action rather than as evidence of failure. The traditional generalities that surround government programs need to be complemented by a new commitment to action.

There are traps for those who see the business-government analogy in simple terms. For example, attempts to use the traditional plans and budgets developed by government as a basis for the sort of accountability and evaluation required by new business management solutions seem bound to fail. Plans and budgets developed by government are quite different from the plans and budgets developed by business. Because government plans and budgets must summarize the complex negotations with interest groups required to maintain the scope to govern, they seldom provide the simple guides to action required to drive conventional business solutions. Attempts to convert government plans and budgets to provide a strategic focus tend to destroy the political consensus required to support change in a complex system.

The idea of empowerment that has driven many successful business reforms must be approached differently in the public sector; devolution of power to act must also be contained by the need to manage comfort zones and diversity. Conventional attempts to centralize the management of comfort zones and decentralize the management of service delivery presume that the fit between these systems can be maintained. Often it cannot.

TABLE 7.1. Management in Government and Business

Management Variables	Private Sector	Public Sector
Goals	Externally linked, focused, hierarchical. Renegotiation rare and linked to major external changes.	Political consensus goals tend to be diverse, nonhierarchical, and targeted to comfort-zone maintenance and the solution of common problems. Service delivery and infrastructure goals tend to be general and nonevaluative in order to minimize the impact on comfort zones.
Culture	Uniform and focused to support missions and goals. Developed through communications and by staff selection.	Diverse and focused on simple ideas, a respect for differences, and on the solution of common problems.
Planning	A general mandate for both action and evaluation.	A vehicle for the negotiation of comfort zones and for demonstrating respect for diverse needs.
Communication	Development of common values. Understanding change. Evaluation of results.	Development of common solutions. Respect for differences. Maintenance of comfort zones.
Budgets	A vehicle for implementation and control.	Ratification of comfort zones. Resources allocated to meet key interests, and to provide service delivery and infrastructure objectives.
Core Management Values	Strategic. Performance and results oriented. Devolution of powers to individual managers within agreed plans and a common value system.	Management of the fit between political consensus, service delivery, and resource efficiency and availability. Management of comfort zones. Delivery of services within the constraints generated by the need to manage the impact on comfort zones. Repositioning of the role and functions of the public sector to respond to external change.

Comfort-Zone Management:
Governments can be competitive while managing diversity and retaining the scope to govern

The changes that are underway are testing the internal consensus for change in many countries and in many political systems. A key element of this model of government is the need to develop and maintain a consensus for change, not in terms of high levels of acceptance for each proposal, but in terms of the maintenance of a comfort zone that recognizes and protects key interests to the point where opposition to key changes is contained. The issue is not simply to develop a political consensus, which is proving difficult enough in many countries, but also to manage a consensus for change among the key interest groups with the capacity to stop each change.

The concept of comfort-zone management explains many of the differences between private sector and public sector management models. It explains some of the interesting differences between ideas of leadership in the public and private sectors. The difficulty the public experiences with performance evaluation and the fascination with processes and inputs are not simply vestiges of old bureaucratic values; they reflect the need to manage the impact of government on a complex system of interest groups.

The techniques for managing comfort zones, including respect for differences and a focus on solutions offering specific value rather than common values, are central to successful public sector management. While there are some interesting parallels with the values required to manage multinational enterprises, many business solutions do not address these techniques. Many attempts to apply business solutions to government management problems fail to translate the solutions to address even the rudimentary requirements of modern comfort-zone management.

Governments have sought to address the growing problem of managing comfort zones in various ways: some have sought to use participative planning to alter community attitudes and protect key interests; some have used crisis management and temporary coercion; other have used nonpublic processes to support key priorities; and others have sought to remove them from the public sector by privatizing them.

TOWARD COMPETITIVE GOVERNMENT

Underpinning the ideas discussed above is an emerging paradigm for the management of nations that focuses on speed, consensus, and performance.

Most theories of government management are confined to the public sector, most see internal factors as dominamt, most are driven by notions of efficiency or equity or autonomy rather than by the need to respond rapidly to external changes, and most presume an autonomy for nations that today is already an illusion.

There are at least four different approaches to the theory of government: some theories concentrate on policies; some theories focus on political sector decision making and power; other theories concentrate on public sector delivery and management; and finally, some newer solutions address grassroots strategies for altering delivery and removing the blockages that have devastated public sector performance in recent years. All of these theories underrate the impact of the external trends discussed above.

Each approach has validity and each in some respects complements the other. Unfortunately, each approach tends to adopt its perspective as dominant and sees the alternatives as raising subordinate issues. No assumption could be more limiting to the development of effective theory. No assumption could be further from the realities faced by governments today.

A New Model of Government

Any new model of government must be able to explore the reasons why some countries are performing more effectively than others, it must shed light on the reasons why business solutions are both effective and ineffective, and it must provide a focus for the development of future ideas and a basis for action.

Three related propositions provide the basis for such a model.

1. That nations are managing strategic transitions to accommodate new external realities. These solutions are best seen in terms of transitions within a continuum of management responses bounded by three basic modes of management: high production, high autonomy, and high response. Effective responses need to involve trade-offs that shift national management toward the high-response model.

2. That the successful implementation of change requires new approaches to the management of grassroots impacts on both national competitiveness and the comfort zones that provide government with the scope to implement change. Government administrative systems must manage both types of impacts at the same time. The tools for ensuring that projects lead to operational outputs and real added value constitute performance management. The tools for ensuring that comfort zones are maintained and resistance to changes minimized constitute comfort-zone

management. The keys to these new approaches to management are more flexible approaches to planning, more effective management of impacts, and the management of cycle time to increase the speed of many government responses.

3. That competitive government must find ways to manage the timing of projects more strategically. The first imperative is to alter lead times to enable government to work with business to exploit windows of opportunity as they arise. The second imperative is to reduce cycle time in order to deliver results before opposition to change erodes support for implementation. Many current reforms in government administration avoid this issue. Some reforms actually increase response time; for example, legislative budgeting and planning processes continue to be developed to increase accountabilty at almost any cost. Ironically, these developments often commence projects at the wrong time and increase cycle time, and place at risk the very performance they seek to stimulate.

MANAGING TRANSITIONS

Solutions are best seen in terms of transitions within a continuum of management: high production, high autonomy, and high response.

Frameworks developed to analyze organizations can be applied to the management of regions, nations, and groups of nations. Such an analysis provides new insights into the changing role of government, the ways in which the private and public sector need to interact to respond to changes in markets and technology and communications, and the role of the political process in developing the consensus required to support change.

A study of national differences evaluated against various external and internal variables identifies three limiting models of government. Each of the three models of management has different strengths and weaknesses. Each solution requires a different contribution from the public and private sectors. Each faces different transitions to cope with the external changes that all nations must now address. This framework explains differences between nations in terms of transitions rather than static positions. Figure 7.2 compares a number of different transitions. The transitions are themselves a function of where a nation is placed in the model and where it seeks to move to. Within this overall framework, nations

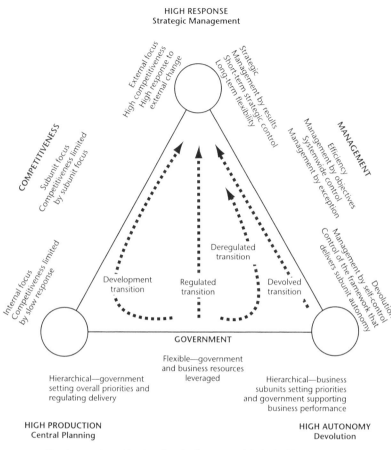

HIGH RESPONSE
Strategic Management

External focus
High competitiveness
High response to
external change

Strategic
Management by results
Short-term strategic control
Long-term flexibility

MANAGEMENT

Efficiency
Management by objectives
Systemwide control
Management by exception

COMPETITIVENESS

Subunit focus
Competitiveness limited
by subunit focus

Management by self-control
Control of the framework that
delivers subunit autonomy

Devolution

Internal focus
Competitiveness limited
by slow response

Deregulated
transition

Development
transition

Regulated
transition

Devolved
transition

GOVERNMENT

Flexible—government
and business resources
leveraged

Hierarchical—government
setting overall priorities and
regulating delivery

Hierarchical—business
subunits setting priorities
and government supporting
business performance

HIGH PRODUCTION
Central Planning

HIGH AUTONOMY
Devolution

Developmental transition: based on development models that build production
capacity as a base for achieving high response
Deregulated transition: based on the deregulation of various planned economies
Regulated transition: based on regulated expansion and internal development
Devolved transition: based on devolution and the empowerment of subunits

Figure 7.2. A Tri-Modal Model of National Management

can begin the process of managing transitions and of optimizing their performance.

The three limiting modes of management are titled "high response," "high production," and "high autonomy." High-response government monitors and responds to external changes. The objective is to position a nation to exploit external change and optimize national benefits. The challenge is to develop and maintain a consensus for change. High-production government seeks to optimize internal efficiencies through national priorities and planning. The challenge is to buffer the system from external pressures and to develop a culture that supports production priorities. The high-autonomy model optimizes the autonomy of subunits and relies on such units to adapt and respond and deliver wealth. The high-autonomy model works spectacularly well when there is an effective fit between the priorities of subunits and of the nation. However, attempts to alter the priorities of subunits tend to be seen as eroding autonomy and are often resisted. The challenge is to gain the benefits of high autonomy within a framework of priorities that can coordinate effective responses.

The modes do not define three separate types of management but comprise a continuum, within which management changes can be described and within which the mix of management variables must be optimized. Table 7.2 explores differences between selected variables. However, in many respects, the three limiting modes are mutually exclusive. The high-production mode necessarily trades off both response and autonomy to achieve its production priority. The high-autonomy mode necessarily trades off production efficiency and response in order to maximize subunit autonomy. The high-response mode necessarily trades off both production efficiency and autonomy in order to respond effectively to external factors. Each of the limiting modes is clearly different. The variables appear to be continuous and each can be used to rank the three modes.

The tri-modal model can be used to explore the emerging crisis in government management and to provide some insights into solutions:

- The model illustrates the dangers of glossing over differences and of assuming that there are either optimal positions for a given nation or optimal solutions for managing all transitions. The transitions required depend upon where, on the model grid, a nation starts, and where it wishes to go. In addition, there are choices about the nature of the transition and the trade-offs required to optimize the management mix.

- The general direction that transitions need to address is clear, although not all nations achieve such shifts in practice. The external trends discussed earlier are forcing governments to be more responsive and to dismantle cross-boader and internal barriers to performance. This in turn requires a management shift toward the high-response mode.

TABLE 7.2. The Boundaries of Effective Management

	High Production	High Response	High Autonomy
Focus	Focuses on optimizing production. This mode works best when the economy is buffered from external forces. Structures focus on specialization and coordination.	The high-response mode increases the power of the environment over both individuals and enterprises within a nation. The changes required almost always contain an element of discontinuous change.	The high-autonomy mode maximizes the autonomy of individuals and enterprises. Major activities are presumed to occur at other levels. The management role is to provide an environment that supports the activities of subunits.
Management	Management priorities are to eliminate waste and malfunctions by refining processes and structures.	Management aims to implement effective change by focusing on impacts and performance. A major challenge is to use external crises to build and manage political consensus.	Management aims to develop and maintain a consensus about the limits to subunit autonomy and to provide a framework within which subunits can pursue effective change without impacting adversely on other subunits.
Technology	Technology has contributed to coordination and has made work roles less restrictive.	Technology has made the coordination required simpler.	Technology has made comparisons between the treatment of subunits easier and has opened up options to increase control and reduce autonomy.

TABLE 7.2. The Boundaries of Effective Management (cont'd)

	High Production	High Response	High Autonomy
Objectives	Priorities tend to be imposed through central planning or by major interventions to regulate economic activity.	Dynamic strategic planning that addresses results, key delivery processes, and inputs. Detailed planning must be devolved and high-autonomy structures must adjust to new priorities that impact differently on people within a nation.	The focus is away from planning to deliver results and toward the use of planning to develop consensus, explore impacts, and define boundaries and key interests.
Evaluation and control	Exception against plan.	Tight control of short-term impacts, flexible evaluation against long-term threats and opportunities.	Control to protect subunit autonomy and deliver equal treatment.
Government/ business leverage	This solution requires a strong public sector and a subordinate private sector.	This solution requires strategic coordination of the public and private sectors to produce integrated outcomes. The relationships need to be flexible, related to current priorities, and they need to be managed within short performance-oriented cycles.	This mode requires only limited coordination between the sectors. The role of government is to buffer the national economy from external forces, negotiate key alliances, provide infrastructure, and ensure that autonomy is protected and people are treated equitably. The private sector operates independently within this overall framework.

- The nature and extent of these shifts depend on whether a nation needs to develop underlying production strengths and whether it is moving from a position of high productivity or high autonomy. At least four different transition strategies can be identified.

- Each of these transitions can be interpreted as an attempt to respond to external changes by moving toward the high-response mode. Each requires different tools and must address different threats.

Transitions Based on Development Models
That Create Competitive Production Capacity
as a Base for Achieving High Response

Japan used a development model to achieve many of the characteristics of the high-production mode and then to develop high response through networks of multinational companies. A number of the high-growth Asian economies have chosen this development path. The intial development of high production was based on a development model that buffered external forces and focused internal development, built large, efficient companies with clear competitive advantages, and then used those companies to access world markets.

The Singapore transition presents a simpler and interesting variation on this model. As a modern city-state, Singapore has been able to adopt strategies not available to larger, more diverse nations.

The various development models have been remarkably successful. Development goals tend to be accepted initially as a means of catching up with other nations, and acceptance is reinforced when programs deliver added value. The transition is to the left and upward on the model (figure 7.2). The key to success is acceptance of overall strategic priorities, the development of production strengths, and the use of early gains to support further change.

The transition requires the development of industry strengths, and the initial development of high-response needs to address external opportunities. Empowerment and devolution occurred within this framework.

Three threats need to be neutralized in managing this type of transition. First, nations may not be able to buffer development from global pressures while at the same time accessing critical resources. Second, nations may scan the environment poorly and respond to trends that are not sustained or cannot be exploited.

Finally, the strategy depends on maintaining a consensus for focusing resources on national priorities and development. The factors that underpin that consensus are changing. Pressures to open markets and increase autonomy can destory that consensus.

Transitions Based on the Deregulation of Various Planned Economies

The centrally planned economics of Eastern Europe were buffered from external forces. Central planning was not associated with environmental scanning or benchmarking. The focus tended to be internal.

Recent transitions have opened these economies to internal and external market forces. The results have been sadly predictable. The strategies of benchmarking industry development, which the Asian model used, do not seem to have been employed; instead, privatization programs and open markets were presumed to be the way to increase efficiency. Often, the focus on evaluation and infrastructure support that worked so well in Asia was not present. The key multinationals required to generate wealth in a high-autonomy model did not exist, and strategies to harness existing multinationals to national priorities appear to have met with only limited success.

The transitions appear to have focused on increasing autonomy without increasing production. They have dismantled many of the barriers to change that bedeviled the central planning model, but they do not appear to have improved the capacity of these nations to respond to external changes. So far, the transition seems to have moved horizontally. Whether the current crisis experienced by these transitions will provide the basis to develop production and response strengths in these economies remains an open question. Some countries appear to be improving competitiveness; others look to be regressing to the old central planning models that will reduce competitiveness over time. The role of government and the approach taken to public sector management is likely to prove critical for many of these transitions.

Transitions Based on Regulated Expansion and Internal Development

The Western European experience is diverse. However, it is characterized by a tradition of central government and planning, and by attempts to maintain a more traditional role for government.

While the role of national governments is changing, many of the traditional government roles are simply shifting to the European Community (EC) level. The development strategy has been to buffer national economies from external, particularly non-EC, forces and to develop consensus through central planning while reducing national barriers. Like the development transition discussed earlier, the transition sought is to the left and upward on the model (fig. 7.2), at least at the overall EC level.

There are parallels and differences with the development-based transitions discussed earlier. The aim of development is similar; however, the focus for subunit development is different. In the European model, the focus is at least in part national rather than industry-based. The issues of consensus management and comfort-zone management, which must be addressed to manage such a transition, are clearly more difficult than for the Asian development models.

The model can also be applied to particular nations within the EC. Expansion of markets and competition generated by opening up internal borders offer major opportunities. Consensus at the national level tends to involve government, unions, and business. The United Kingdom under Thatcher arguably severed many of these constraints and moved to a high-autonomy model. Germany and France retained a centralized model. While the German model appears to focus on a negotiated public sector/private sector interface, the French model retains more of the characteristics of the traditional government planning and regulatory model.

There are interesting issues raised by the United Kingdom transition. The United Kingdom has a more international focus, and has sought to become competitive at the cost of employment and various social services. It has reduced the tripartite consensus model and has sought to enable companies to access Europe and the global markets.

The breakdown of barriers to the Eastern European countries represents both a major opportunity and a major threat to the transitional consensus process.

Transitions Based on Devolution and the Empowerment of Subunits

The United States is a high-autonomy mode of government with established industrial strengths. The transition sought is upward and to the left on the model (figure 7.2). This requires some realignment of industry policies and performance, and requires government to address critical infrastructure and support priorities. The United States fell behind in the competitiveness stakes in the 1970s and the 1980s. The response has been to examine and benchmark the competition, and to develop a group of highly effective and large multinational corporations. Instead of buffering its economy, the United States opened it and exposed industry to major pressures.

The U.S. government focus has been to manage diversity and achieve political consensus at the national and regional levels. The process is managed almost independently of the industry policy process discussed above. The focus for response is the multinational corporation. Government has supported the interests of these multinationals, and has sought to assist them to access markets. Government has also supported the process by infrastructure and education and training investment, and by assisting corporations to gain competitive advantages from various government projects.

The transition based on devolution and the empowerment of subunits produced many challenges. The threats are similar to those faced by all high-autonomy organizations, that gridlock will develop and governments will not be able to deliver needed infrastructure and services, or that the latter will not be coordinated with industry policies and the need to access the global economy.

However, recent improvements in competitiveness suggest that the transition is occcuring. The United States government has experienced major comfort-zone restraints. It is not surprising that the reform of government has become a major priority to support the current transition.

MANAGING IMPLEMENTATION

An effective reform strategy needs to be supported with effective implementation strategies and tools. Many governments with a sound agenda for reform have found themselves unable to manage implementation.

Effective national responses to external pressures involve shortening response times and strategically managing ongoing improvements in national competitiveness. Strategic management in open-ended situations must balance the tensions between the need for short-term controls and the need for long-term flexibilty. Understanding such processes and benchmarking the performance of nations requires a study of transitions. Managing transitions requires strategies and tools that manage grassroots benefits, manage other, often unintended, impacts, and build an ongoing momentum for future change.

The implementation of change requires new approaches to the management of grassroot impacts, on both national competitiveness and the comfort zones that provide government with the scope to implement change.

Figure 7.3 summarizes an implementation model that can be used to explain the high failure rate associated with recent government reform. This model suggests that government administrators must manage both project performance and comfort zones at the same time.

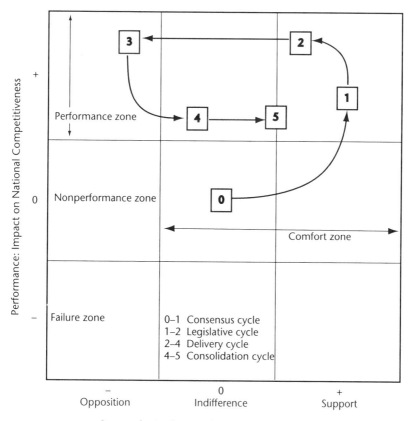

Figure 7.3. Implementation-Impact Model

The objective is to manage impacts to maintain each project in both the positive performance zone and in the comfort zone. Governments that trade off popularity for value-added results tend to find that popularity without performance is an increasingly short-lived phenomenon.

Governments that seek change at any cost create conflict and, over time, erode their capacity to govern. Governments pursuing the traditional strategy of compromise to stay out of trouble increasingly find they achieve neither added value nor popularity.

The implementation impact model provides a useful tool for mapping government implementation performance. However, it is most powerful when used to manage cycle dynamics.

The Management of Cycle Dynamics

The management of cycle dynamics has three components:

1. The management of overall cycle time by engineering government value chains to reduce cycle time and enable projects to exploit external events and deliver benefits before initial support erodes;

2. The management of cycle impacts by scheduling impacts on interest groups to maintain perceptions of net added value, even when negative impacts must occur;

3. The support of the process with pro-active cycle-focused communications strategies that balance expectations against delivery, manage the dynamics of negative impacts, and consolidate project benefits when they are available.

Competitive government must find ways to manage the timing of projects more strategically, to exploit windows of opportunity as they arise, and to reduce cycle time in order to deliver results before opposition to change erodes support for implementation.

As nations pursue transitions to high-performance government, cycle time management becomes a key variable for managing the fit between the different missions of government. The high-response model requires corporate priorities to be superordinate, restricting and perhaps threatening to individual priorities. The management challenge is to plan the process to deliver corporate priorities that optimize individual autonomy. This requires shorter cycle times within which specific impacts, positive and negative, real and perceived, can be actively managed. This in turn requires new concepts of leadership and communication for the public sector.

Figure 7.3 uses the implementation impact model to examine movement over time. The numbers divide implementation into four cycles: a consensus cycle (0–1); a legislative cycle (1–2); a delivery cycle (2–4); and a consolidation cycle (4–5).

In managing the consensus cycle (0–1), the challenge is to build support for the changes needed to commit the reforms. Government can usually control information to focus on benefits and avoid discussion of specific negative impacts. On the other hand, history is littered with governments that have oversold solutions only to find that the public rate success a failure. It is important to balance expectations against the prospects of delivery. Timing is often critical to launching projects and building consensus.

In managing the legislative cycle (1–2), the challenge is to access the legislative approvals and resources required to implement change. Where key interest groups seem likely to stop specific projects, trade-offs and negotiations are required. The objective is to gain authorization with minimum trade-offs and constraints. Gaining legislative approval is seldom the end of negotiations with groups opposed to change.

In managing the delivery cycle (2–4), the challenge is to schedule and evaluate both positive and negative impacts to maintain sufficient support to complete reform projects. Managers need to manage the dynamics of project impacts by either bringing forward positive impacts or shortening cycle time in order to sell end benefits as imminent. Another challenge is to manage negative impacts. Not everyone benefits from every project, and some individuals and interest groups may be disadvantaged. Planning must address these realities, and organize timing and communication strategies to neutralize resistance. The added value of a project can diminish considerably during the delivery stage, as constituencies lobby to offset perceived disadvantages. Leadership requires the negotiation of such impacts. The challenge is to position implementation within a comfort zone that enables implementation to proceed without sacrificing results to the point where reform fails to add value.

In managing the consolidation cycle (4–5), the challenge is to communicate benefits, to manage the gap between public expectations and actual delivery, and to consolidate the benefits by ensuring that opponents cannot erode them too readily. Clearly this phase can move projects in various directions on the model grid. However, for the purposes of this discussion, a horizontal movement to the right is assumed (fig. 7.3). This reflects a maintenance of added value and a growing support for reform as benefits are appreciated and understood.

An examination of actual implementation reveals many different cycle patterns. However, three general points can be derived from this application of the model to the implementation problems faced by government:

1. Governments are rarely able to deliver the added value they first envisage.

2. The extent of the reductions they must accept is determined by: the effectiveness of particular reform programs; their capacity to reduce cycle time and achieve short-run control over change; and the threshold levels that define the comfort zone.

3. The chances of a government consolidating to the right (fig. 7.3) on the model depend on whether competitiveness increases, and on the size of the gap between public perceptions of government objectives and the reality of delivery at the grassroots level.

COMMUNICATIONS AND COMPETITIVE GOVERNMENT

Change in the role of government has created the need for new approaches to communications. Three shifts illustrate the new functions that must be delivered to support the transition to competitive government: communications must now address the need to add value as well as to sell ideas; communications must become involved in the scheduling of impacts as well as seeking to cosmeticize them; and communications need to focus on the consolidation of public evaluation of government performance, rather than on the short-term packaging and sale of achievements in isolation combined with strategic damage control. New approaches to communications in government need to be supported by a new theory, which uses communications to add value to the performance of government by assisting government to evaluate performance and manage cycle dynamics effectively.

Traditional objectives for communications in government have focused on: the development of a positive image using grand plans; an emphasis on consensus; and the avoidance of both the idea of and responsibility for failure. The use of polling as a diagnostic tool and as a means of supporting traditional communications strategies has become more newsworthy than the policies or the politicians they seek to evaluate. Often the polls address short-term consensus issues that do not relate directly to the sort of comfort-zone impacts suggested above. Often they do not address directly the issue of competitiveness and added value.

The traditional approach to government segments the task of adding value from the task of selling that value to various publics. The presumption underpinning this approach is that, since most programs add value, negative public responses must be a problem of communication. Where programs are clearly seen to have failed, the communications challenge is not to address failure, but to contain the short-run impact on public perceptions of government performance.

A new role for communications in government is emerging that cannot be evaluated in isolation from either the need to add value to national competitiveness or the need to maintain the scope to govern. Three features differentiate this new role from the traditional approach discussed above:

1. Communications need to manage the focus on external benchmarks and realities, and to build internal consensus about added value and national competitiveness. With the notable exception of governments undertaking development transitions, such external issues are not a major focus for traditional government communications.

2. Communications need to contribute pro-actively to decisions about the timing of projects. In the traditional model, timing is set by other government processes: by election; by rigid legislative and budget cycles; by the need to ration resources over many projects; by the need to maximize internal efficiency rather than external effectiveness; and by the need to comply with the plethora of government regulatory regimes that are assumed to lead to effective government. At best, communications strategies are able to select from a smorgasbord of possibilities and to block unpopular initiatives. Communications specialists tend to become involved when there are routine communications to conduct, when there are achievements to be packaged and sold, or when there is a problem. As cycle time reduces, the scope for communications strategies to address the timing of projects differently increases; when this occurs, new opportunities can be created and many problems can be avoided.

3. Communications strategies need to become involved in the implementation and consolidation stages of the government project
cycle. In particular, they must be pro-actively involved in cycle
management to ensure that the consolidation phase is to the right
on the Implementation-Impact Model (fig. 7.3). This requires a
new attention to cycle dynamics that encompasses speed, consensus, and performance. New approaches to the management of
cycle dynamics enable government to balance perceptions of positive and negative impacts throughout the cycle. Successful consolidation depends on whether a project meets public expectations of net value. Traditional approaches to communications
tend to oversell value and underrate negative impacts. Project implementation tends to occur independently of communications
until a problem emerges; at that stage, comfort zones have usualy
been breached, and damage control is often the only option left.
Although there have been some brilliant short-term damage control operations, they usually involve deception, the excessive use
of public resources to buy support, or the erosion of the added
value the project or program sought to deliver. All these strategies
can lead to the sort of long-term disillusionment with government that is difficult to reverse.

The idea that government must shorten cycle time and manage
cycle dynamics challenges many traditional values and priorities.
The responses of government, to both the need to rationalize and
the limited resources available to buy popularity, have been to seek
efficiency, to audit inputs, and generally to extend cycle time rather
than reduce it. This decreases the chances of projects and government testing the limits of the comfort zone, and places pressures on
the communications function to deliver remedial solutions.

The idea that government must manage diversity challenges
the twin desires of politicians to find consensus and of bureaucrats
to create an orderly and uniform world. Neither of these preferences reflects reality. Both establish the preconditions for major
and unnecessary failure. Many solutions developed by government
focus on maintaining majority public support; yet it is minority interests that often determine the limit of the comfort zone for government.

It should surprise no one that current changes in government
and national management also require a shift in the role of communications in government. The need to address competitiveness
in the new globalized economy has led business to reduce cycle
time and to develop new approaches to communications. Similar
external pressures are also responsible for changes in government.

However, the ways in which successful governments are moving to increase national competitiveness, to manage cycle dynamics, and to use communications as a key management variable, differ in important respects from the changes that have occurred in business.

8

A Pluralistic View of the Emerging Theories of Human Communication

Branislav Kovačić & Donald P. Cushman

At a time of increased politicization and radicalization of the intellectual processes involved in theoretic inquiry, there is a need to stand back from these processes and locate a pluralistic standpoint that can help us deal with progress or lack of progress toward understanding the human communication processes. Such a pluralistic standpoint entails, of course, human preferences and therefore is subject to discussion and debate. However, it is in the discussion and debate about where we have been, what we now know, and where we need to go next that constructive inquiry furthers our knowledge of human communication processes.

Thus, in order to think, talk, and write about emerging communication theories productively, one is advised to pose and then attempt to answer three questions: (1) What is theory?, (2) How do we judge theory?, and (3) Why do we theorize? It is the purpose of this chapter to venture to ask the three questions and supply our answers. First, we provide a pluralistic framework of social scientific tradition within which to embed our discussion of emerging communication theories. Second, we apply our pluralistic framework to each chapter in the book to (1) throw into a sharp relief unique new contributions of every chapter, (2) delineate the areas of overlap among them, (3) stake out regions of contrast and difference, (4) point out the major weaknesses and, (5) adumbrate some promising paths of further development and mutual enrichment of emerging theories of communication. Finally, we provide a summary of our argument developed in the chapter.

THEORY, ITS EVALUATION, AND
REASONS FOR THEORIZING

Theory may be defined as a form of social knowledge, a subset of components of a particular social scientific tradition. Such components spread from the nonempirical/nonfactual pole to the empirical/factual position (Alexander, 1987) to the practical pole (Cushman & Kovačić, 1995).

A Conception of Theory

Cushman and Kovačić's (1995) philosophic level of a social scientific tradition consists of general presuppositions and ideological orientations (Alexander, 1987). General presuppositions are assumptions about the nature of communication, the nature of action, and the problem of social order. Ideological orientations are conservative, liberal, and radical political beliefs of the social scientists. The theoretic level of social scientific traditions includes models—simplified and abstract representations of the world—concepts, and complex and simple propositions (Alexander, 1987) that may specify a precisely verifiable set of relationships between a web of concepts (Cusman & Kovačić, 1995). The empirical/factual level comprises correlations, observations, and methodological assumptions such as preferences for quantitative or qualitative techniques, comparative or case-study analyses, and microscopic (individuals, interpersonal relationships, and groups) versus macroscopic (institutions or societies as a whole) empirical foci (Alexander, 1987). Finally, what Cushman and Kovačić (1995) name the practical level of social scientific traditions is intended to link theory with human action in vital contexts. The message strategies or tools of persuasion, tactical steps/sequences, and communication operations or activities to be performed in order to achieve desired outcomes are the elements of the practical level. We turn now to a more detailed discussion of a social scientific tradition. At the philosophical level, general presuppositions, as we mentioned, are assumptions about the nature of communication, the nature of action, and the problem of social order. Theorists usually assume that action is either rational or nonrational. Alexander elaborates:

> In social theory . . . this dichotomy refers to whether people are selfish (rational) or idealistic (nonrational), whether they are normative and moral (nonrational) in their approach to the world or

purely instrumental (rational), whether they act in terms of maxi-
mizing efficiency (rationally) or whether they are governed by
emotions and unconscious desires (nonrationally). All these dichotomies relate to the vital question of the internal versus external reference of action. Rationalistic approaches to action portray
the actor as taking his bearings from forces outside of himself,
whereas nonrational approaches imply that action is motivated
from within. . . . Action may be pottrayed, though it usually is
not, as having both rational and nonrational elements. (Alexander, 1987, p. 10)

The problem of social order concerns social patterns, ways in
which such patterns are produced, and whether they precede any
specific individual act or are the result of individual negotiation.
Alexander clarifies differences between individualistic and collectivist approaches to order:

If thinkers presuppose a collectivist position, they see social patterns as existing prior to any specific individual act, as, in a sense,
the product of history. . . . [C]ollectivists may well acknowledge
that social order exists as much inside the individual as without;
. . . whether it is conceptualized as inside or outside an actor, social order from the collectivist perspective is not seen as the product of purely this-instant, this-moment considerations. . . . [Indi-
vidualistic theorists] insist, all the same, that these patterns are
the result of individual negotiation, that they are the upshot of
individual choice. They believe not simply that structures are
"carried" by individuals but that they are actually produced by
actors in the concrete, ongoing processes of individual interaction. For them, it is not only that individuals have an element of
freedom but that they can alter the fundaments of social order at
every successive point in historical time. Individuals, in this view,
do not carry order inside of them. Rather, they follow or rebel
against social order—even their own values—according to their
individual desires. . . . [However,] assumptions about order do
not entail any particular assumptions about action. (Alexander,
1987, pp. 11, 13)

Assumptions about the nature of communication may be expressed as "the logical permutations" among presuppositions of action and social order—rational-individualistic (the asocial self exercises instrumental self-control), rational-collectivist (the notion of
the self is eliminated by the external material and ideal structures),
normative-individualistic (the asocial individual exercises moral

self-control), and normative-collectivist (the self is socialized by cultural systems)—or as a more complex, multidimensional union of these four dichotomies (see Alexander, 1987). Regardless of the specific position taken, communication is generally viewed as some combination of (1) perceptions/thoughts/interpretations/information processing, (2) talk/interactions, and (3) speechless behavior that occurs before, during, and after talk/interaction (Cushman & Kovačić, 1994). Some theorists, however, reduce communication to interaction/talk and argue that the conceptions of interaction differ as to whether and to what extent it is assumed that interaction is emergent or intelligible only in terms of its own ordering principles (for a discussion, see Sigman, 1995). In this context we may ask a decisive question: What are the sources or generative mechanisms of observed communication patterns/regularities? Communication and other social scientists have proposed essentially three such cross-disciplinary wellsprings of communication patterns: (1) psychological mechanisms such as self-concept and cognitive complexity, (2) principles of the coherent sequence of messages in interaction/talk, and (3) ideal and material structures such as cultural codes and political/economic systems, respectively. At the theoretical level, we find models, concepts, and complex and simple propositions. Functional and institutional models of society as a the place of communicative action are pertinent to our discussion. Alexander adds more detail:

> There are models, for example, which describe society as a functioning system, like the physiological system of the body or the mechanical system of an internal combustion engine. Other models view society as composed of separate inslitutions without any integral, systemic relationship to one another. . . . [Some theorists insist] that if assumptions are made that society is consensual, then models will be chosen that are functional. (Alexander, 1987, p. 8)

Complex and simple propositions may specify a precisely verifiable set of relationships—their type, strength and direction—between a web of concepts. According to Stichcombe (1968), the following types of relationships may be defined: (1) one- or two-way, (2) sequential or coextensive, (3) necessary or substitutable, and (4) deterministic or probable.

The practical level of social scientific traditions—especially in the field of communication—consists of an array of unique but requisite communication skills in the form of actors' overall goals, strategies or general plans for conduct, tactical steps/sequences, and activities to be performed. This level is concerned with how sophisticated actors have to be to achieve desired goals, how actors learn and improve upon their communication skills, how widespread the skills are in a given population, and how generalizable a given level of skill is.

A social scientific tradition is thus an intricate conceptual edifice composed of the four overlapping levels that are both mutually limiting and enriching. Different scientific traditions conceive of these levels and their elements in the unique and suggestive ways and, moreover, rank the importance of the levels and their elements differently. What is important is that growth, development, and stagnation of social scientific traditions can be understood by the interplay of their levels and components.

Judging Theory

The empirical/factual level of social scientific traditions—correlations, observations, and methodological assumptions—is the least controversial. Methodological procedures are relatively unambiguous rules for (1) appropriate research design, (2) research question and hypothesis formulation, (3) proper sampling, (4) analysis, and (5) interpretation of the significance of findings. Methodological procedures thus allow for a reasoned discussion about correction of mistakes/errors, ranking of the significance of findings, and selection of the relevant future research topics. However, we do not have similar rules for judging other components of social scientific traditions—their philosophical, theoretical, and practical levels. Consequently, we propose the concept of a social scientific tradition itself as a pluralistic standard for evaluating its constituent parts, especially its core ingredient—theories. The template of social scientific traditions is general, flexible, and heuristic, and thus an appropriate standard for (1) locating elements of a particular theory, (2) suggesting future areas of its productive development, and (3) comparing and evaluating theories. In our view, communication theories are to be compared and evaluated in terms of their (1) completeness, (2) epistemic power, and (3) moral/practical consequences. Let us clarify the last three points.

A Completeness Principle. We propose that a complete theory consists of explicitly developed theoretical components that are embedded within philosophical constituent parts on the one hand, and empirical and practical arguments on the other.

An Epistemic Power Principle. We operationalize this principle in terms of the three elements: (1) explicitly specified cross-disciplinary generative mechanisms or constraints that produce observable communicative patterns/regularities in a certain number of domains (possible worlds), (2) models that consist of simple or complex propositions specifying these communicative patterns/regularities as a precisely verifiable set of relationships among a web of concepts in a certain number of domains (possible worlds), and (3) important empirical findings yielding over extended periods of time a high ratio of the variance explained to the number of propositions in a theoretical model.[1]

A Principle of Moral/Practical Consequences. We argue for subjecting communication skills derived from a specific theory—strategies, tactics, and activities—to standards of efficiency and effectiveness found in the actors' actual world (see Seidman, 1994). In addition, we suggest that moral/practical consequences of theory-specific communication skills be evaluated by (1) a degree to which theory's ideals intersect with the actors' actual worlds, (2) the goals of theory, and (3) the roles theorists prefer to play when applying their theories to the actual worlds. We now turn to this point.

Reasons for Theorizing

Probably the knottiest question is the one probing into reasons for theorizing. We shall approach this question from three directions. First, the philosophic level of a social scientific tradition may include explicit ideological orientations of the social scientists (Alexander, 1987). Conservative political beliefs may lead scholars to formulate theories to defend the status quo; liberal political beliefs may compel theorists to theoretically articulate reforms of oppressive, inefficient, or ineffective institutions, groups, interpersonal relationships, and individuals; and radical political beliefs may drive scholars to enunciate a theory of radical institutional change. However, theorists more often than not omit or disguise their political beliefs and, moreover, political beliefs often have an indeterminate effect on the theory formation process. Second, theorists may also make a more or less conscious and consistent decision as to what to do with their theories—for what purposes and how to use them. Theories as a form of a social knowledge may be used for goals ranging from bureaucratic social control to tolerance of social differences and conflict (Lyotard, 1984; Seidman, 1994).

Scholars may use their theories by playing at least five roles in any combination. They can play the roles of (1) researcher, (2) consultant/expert, (3) teacher, (4) moral advocate/analyst, and (5) activist (Brown, 1992, Deetz, 1992; Seidman, 1994). Third, regardless of their political and role orientations, communication theorists may want to understand and then influence actors' (1) decision and action preferences/choices, (2) use of and response to imperatives and commands (power and authority), and (3) moral judgments of actions and states of affairs.[2]

We argue that one of the reasons for theorizing is a desire to influence the realm of everyday action. This is why, at the philosophical level, social scientific traditions offer the preferred slices or domains (actual and possible worlds) of communicative reality deemed to be socioculturaly important, stable, and urgent. In general, the narrower is the chosen slice of communicative reality, the more limited is the scope and function of possible theoretical insights and practical implications at a given level of precision. However, regardless of the chosen slice of communicative reality, the theoretical level must isolate significant and stable generative mechanisms of communication patterns in order to construct powerful communicative strategies. It is not that only the philosophic and theoretic level of social scientific traditions have serious formal consequences for the practical level of appropriate communicative strategies and skills. There are also empirical requirements such as a high ratio of the variance explained to the number of propositions in a theoretical model, and necessary (holding in all possible worlds) rather than substitutable relationships between a web of concepts. Equally important is that any significant theory of communication must provide communication strategies and skills with traction on relevant empirical actors. Communication strategies and skills must be based on ideals and emotions (nonrational action) that are not simply residing in ideal, nonactual possible worlds but, rather, are intersecting with the actual (our) world. Otherwise, actors may not need such communication strategies and skills, and may not be able or want to learn, use, and improve them.

EMERGING THEORIES OF HUMAN COMMUNICATION

We may be facing a paradox (Kovačić, 1994). In the current condition of major social—economic, political, and cultural—transformations, communicative practices appear to be the single most important source of temporary social order/patterned stability. Proven mechanisms of social collectivist order such as material and ideal structures, and established mechanisms of individualistic social order such as durable personal values/intentions/preferences seem to be increasingly unstable and fragmented. Thus antecedents of action—preexisting material and ideal patterns and individual preferences—may be relevant only insofar as they serve as temporary starting points. If historical/past communicative patterns (collectivist social order) lose traction on relevant empirical actors, then future goals may compel the actors to modify constellations of these sequences and bring about individualistic social order (Mead, 1932). Generative mechanisms in the form of standardized tasks with their standardized vocabularies then give way to new generative mechanisms in the form of future visions and new tasks, and new/creative vocabularies. Some combination of creative normative and rational social action—following of rules in a novel way (a temporary recombination of rules), and/or acting independently of the old rules—may then lead to individualistic social order.

Guided by future visions and new tasks and vocabularies, communication becomes a means to form temporary alliances as institutional frameworks within which social actors negotiate specific sequences of communicative practices and appropriate topics in order to forge temporarily the consensus for the accomplishment of specific tasks, and to mint temporary personal and group identities. Theorists may become "conceptual strategists" who frequently reinvent generative mechanisms in the form of these future visions/tasks/vocabularies. They resort to either incremental, short-term fine-tuning, or longer-term, transformational redefinitions of future visions/tasks/vocabularies. Consequently, significant communication patterns are to be observed in the interaction/talk itself and its consequences, but not in its antecedents. Stated more formally: future visions/tasks/vocabularies, as a type of "If it were the case that p—which it is not—then q" counterfactual condition, account for observed communicative patterns. As a part of ideal, non-actual possible worlds, they will shape observed patterns only when intersecting with the actual world of empirical actors.

We shall now apply our pluralistic framework of social scientific tradition to each essay on the emerging theories of human communication. We suggested three criteria for judging theory. First, we proposed a completeness criterion that demands that theories—

explicitly developed models, concepts, and complex and simple propositions—be embedded within a larger framework of philosophical, empirical, and practical elements. Second, we proposed an epistemic power critenon that requires that theorists formulate cross-disciplinary generative mechanisms that account for observed communicative patterns/regularities. Our third criterion evaluates moral/practical consequences of theory-specific communication skills.

Most authors state their methodological assumptions rather explicitly. What they do not discuss explicitly, however, is their preferred empirical focus. Our view is that a micro-empirical focus is chosen by Carbaugh and colleagues, who elucidate communication practices within multiple cultural communities (chapter 1); Wiemann and colleagues, who explain communication competence across a range of interpersonal relationships (chapter 2); Cahn, who examines conflict communication in interpersonal relationships (chapter 3); and Donohue, who outlines an interactionist framework for peace (chapter 4). A macro-empirical focus, on the other hand, is preferred by Zhu and Blood, who dissect agenda setting in a democratic political process (chapter 5); Hauser and Whalen, who scrutinize new social movements and their rhetoric (chapter 6); and Cullen, who sketches transitions to competitive government (chapter 7). We will use this tacitly preferred empirical focus of the authors to organize our discussion of the emerging theories of human communication.

Micro-Empirical Focus:
Individuals, Interpersonal Relationships, and Groups

Carbaugh and colleagues (chapter 1) imply that knowledge of culture-specific communicative scenes, communication practice, and discourse is necessary for the most appropriate and effective use of social interaction for cultural performances in multiple communities. Communication scenes and cultural discourses of identification comprise preexisting patterns (collectivist social order) and particular communication practices and their outcomes constitute individualistic social order in this theory of communication and culture. Actors' interactive use of identities implies that both instrumental (rational) and normative/moral (nonrational) forces are operative. Carbaugh and colleagues' communication model of sociocultural life suggests that specific communication scenes entail particular communication practices and cultural discourses of identification. The authors use ethnography of communication that combines a "turtle's eye view" (a rich description of this-instant, this-moment communication activities) and a "bird's eye view" (a placement of this-instant activities into more comprehensive frameworks). They imply that effective and appropriate communication practices require a vision that goes beyond a single community (actual world) to embrace multiple communities (multiple actual worlds). We reckon that such a vision and a task of accomplishing it form a generative mechanism that accounts for observed patterns of communication. Carbaugh and colleagues' arguments lead us to believe that moral/practical consequences of their theoretical endeavor are preservation and enhancement of tolerance of social differences and nondestructive conflict. Their theory is consistent with the roles of (1) researcher, (2) consultant/expert, (3) teacher, (4) moral advocate/analyst, and (5) multicultural activist.

Communication practices and their outcomes are redefined by Wiemann and colleagues (chapter 2) as relational communication competence and relational satisfaction, respectively. Prior patterns of experience of interpersonal relationships amount to collectivist social order in Wiemann and colleagues' theory of relational communication competence. Actors' joint, skillful, and effective co-participation in interactions and the ensuing relational satisfaction outcome constitute individualistic social order. Actors' interactional goals and future expectations are both instrumental (rational) and normative/moral (nonrational). Wiemann and colleagues construct a rather complex relational model of communication competence that includes such concepts as context, individual communicators, interactional goals, relational history, future expectations, process reflexivity (reflection on and accommodation to the relationship), process complexity (cross-situational generalizability of experience), and relational satisfaction. Although the relationships between a web of concepts are not explicitly specified, the model indicates how individuals jointly and competently create and maintain mutually satisfying relationships. The authors state that they are yet to devise some method of empirical assessment of relational communication competence. They suggest that a vision of relational satisfaction and an accompanying task of bringing it about collaboratively by relational partners in a whole range of interpersonal relationships (multiple actual worlds) may constitute a generative mechanism that accounts for observed patterns of relational communication competence. Although the authors stress the application of their model to teaching communication competence skills, the roles of (1) researcher and (2) consultant/expert also seem consistent with this emerging theory of human communication.

Relational communication competence and relational satisfaction form an implicit point of departure for Cahn's (chapter 3) paradigm of conflict communication. Preexisting patterns of interpersonal conflict—collectivist social order—consist of a series of escalating interpersonal events, actors' cognitions such as negative attributions and expectations, and the contested rules for interaction. However, actors can renegotiate such patterns, change the actual world of their relationships, and thus bring about individualistic social order. In doing so, actors are motivated by both ideals and emotions (nonrational, action) and instrumental calculations (rational action). Cahn formulates a model of conflict communication that captures ways of resolving interpersonal conflict in a mutually beneficial way. Some of the major concepts are interpersonal relationships; escalating and de-escalating behaviors, negative, neutral, and positive attributions and expectations; agreed upon rules for conflict management; and forms of conflict. However, relationships between this web of concepts are not explicitly specified. The author states his methodogical preferences as three related observational techinques: (1) observations of dyads, (2) self-reports of interdependent cognitions, and (3) observations of triads and rules that regulate interaction. Cahn suggests that a vision of mutually beneficial interpersonal relationships—the ones with which partners are satisfied and to which they are committed—and an accompanying task of conflict resolution may form a generative mechanism that accounts for observed sequences/patterns in conflict communication. The theory states that interpersonal conflict can be resolved in a mutually beneficial way by (1) introducing de-escalating behaviors, (2) checking for accuracy of negative attributions and expectations, and (3) relying on conflict mediators who design and implement agreed upon rules that help to convert the participants' competitive orientations and actions into cooperative ones. The roles of (1) researcher, (2) teacher, and (3) consultant/expert are consistent with this emerging theory of conflict communication.

Transformation of competitive orientations and actions into cooperative ones is one of the core components of Donohue's interactionist framework for peace (chapter 4). Preexisting patterns of peaceful and nonpeaceful behaviors make up collectivist social order in this emerging theory. Stabilization of interaction patterns into constructive or destructive contexts and the transitions between the various types of peace and aggression constitute individualistic social order. The link between interaction and actors' identity in Donohue's framework for peace suggests that actions are guided by both instrumental (rational) and normative/moral (nonrational) impulses. Donohue mints a model of a range of peaceful and nonpeaceful behaviors. The model includes concepts such as peace, identity, interpersonal aggression and violence, and interpersonal negotiation and mediation. The model also suggests—but does not explicity specify—communicative transitions between clusters of peaceful and nonpeaceful behaviors (transitions between the actual worlds). He describes a phase-mapping analytical technique for ascertaining whether and how messsages respond to one another in a sequential manner. Donohue suggests that a vision of peaceful relationships and an attendant task of transforming competitive/aggressive behaviors into cooperative/friendly ones is an appropriate generative mechanism that elucidates communication patterns of interpersonal aggression and violence as well as negotiation and mediation. Donohue also hints at useful strategies for the enhancement of the actors' joint development of peace patterns over time. Like Carbaugh and colleagues' theory of communication and culture (chapter 1), Donohue's interactionist framework for peace seeks to preserve and enhance tolerance of social differences and nondestructive conflict. Similarly, his theory is consistent with the roles of (1) researcher, (2) consultant/expert, (3) teacher, (4) moral advocate/analyst, and (5) multicultural activist.

Macro-Empirical Focus: Institutions

We should note that Donohue's interactionist framework for peace (chapter 4) marks a transition to macro-empirical focus on communication in and between institutions. Peaceful or aggressive relationships are formed by individuals, groups, and institutions. Zhu and Blood (chapter 5) examine social interaction in terms of mutual, sequential, links between public's and media's role in the agenda-setting process. Patterns that precede an unfolding interaction are collectivist order, and the sequences of interaction and their outcomes are individualistic social order. Actors vying to promote their version of agenda are governed by both instrumental (rational) and normative/moral (nonrational) considerations. Zhu and Blood offer insights into a democratic process of which media agenda setting is but a component. Zhu and Blood construct a communication model of a democratic political process—a major revision of the agenda setting research tradition—with multiple actors who deploy a combination of mass and interpersonal communication strategies. Some of the major concepts of this conflictive, institutional model are the media's and the public's agendas (lists of significant issues or events), issues (long-term problems or a series of events), and events (quick happenings over a discrete period of time). The model proposes multiple types of one- and two-way linear and nonlinear relationships between the public's and the media's agendas. The authors state that their theory should be investigated empirically by a combination of qualitative and quantitative techniques. Zhu and Blood indicate that a vision of a more open and transparent democratic process and a concomitant task of formulating and implementing a preferred agenda by multiple actors embedded in their actual worlds may be a significant generative mechanism for producing effective patterns of mediated and interpersonal, face-to-face, processes of social influence. They also suggest some relevant political and media strategies to be used by multiple actors in a democratic political process. Their approach is consistent with the roles of (1) researcher, (2) consultant/expert, (3) teacher, (4) moral advocate/analyst, and (5) activist.

Hauser and Whalen (chapter 6) focus on actors who attempt to shape and even subvert this democratic political process—new social movements. Prior patterns of engagements and experiences by new social movements constitute collectivist social order in Hauser and Whalen's theory of new rhetoric and new social movements. On the other hand, deployment of new rhetoric by new social movements and outcomes that come afterward—identify formation as a matter of choice, and victories and defeats scored in meaning wars—are examples of individualistic social order. Identity formation and meaning wars strongly suggest that actors take their bearings from both ideals and emotions (nonrational action) and instrumental considerations (rational action). Hauser and Whalen outline an (extra)institutional communication model that includes concepts such as new social movements, new rhetoric as a social practice, identity, "internal" and "external" audience, and meaning wars. The model suggests how new rhetoric as social practice shapes identity as choice. We surmise that case studies based on rhetorical investigation and then their comparative analysis are tacit methodological preferences in accordance with this theory. The authors imply that a task of a successful participation of new social movements and their members in meaning wars demands the temporary and tentative communicative distinction between "us" and "them." Such a task may be a generative mechanism that accounts for observed communication patterns of new rhetoric as a constitutive praxis. Hauser and Whalen argue that new social movements cannot address their members ("internal" audience) or "external" audiences in terms of preexisting shared interests (preexisting consensus). Thus new social movements must devise strategies for waging meaning wars, a topic that Hauser and Whalen do not discuss explicitly. Nevertheless, their approach is consistent with the roles of (1) researcher, (2) consultant/expert, (3) teacher, (4) moral advocate/analyst, and (5) activist.

There seems to be some consensus that effective communication cannot be based on preexisting shared interests (preexisting consensus) between "internal" and "external" audiences. Cullen (chapter 7) offers the comfort zone, a pragmatic consensus defined as a containment of opposition of key groups to key changes, as a staple of institutional communication in the public sector. In Cullen's theory of the management of government competitiveness, two initial modes of the public sector management—high-production and high-autonomy mode—involve preexisting patterns of social order. Four strategies for a transition from these two initial modes of the public sector management to the desired destination—the high-response mode—and the destination itself make individualistic social order. Actors are motivated by both instrumental calculations (rational action) and ideals and emotions (nonrational action). Cullen's communication model of transitions to competitive government consists of constructs such as modes of the public sector management, measurable performance, comfort zones (pragmatic consensus), speed and timing of change in the public sector management, and the public sector leadership and communication. The model traces how a combination of initial modes of the public sector management (high-production and high-autonomy modes) and the selected strategy of change shape a particular implementation cycle and its timing framework that, in turn, lead to the responsive, competitive mode of public sector management. The model calls for a new type of the public sector leadership and communication. We imagine that the author would endorse an empirical approach based on a comparative analysis of case studies of the public sector transformations. Cullen argues that a vision of a competitive government—the high-response mode of the public sector management—and a concomitant task of achieving it form a generative mechanism that accounts for communicative patterns in the management of change in the public sector. The author states that the implementation of change in the public sector requires (1) performance management (projects that lead to observable outputs and real added value), (2) comfort-zone (pragmatic consensus) management involving multiple actors and their actual worlds, and (3) the skillfill timing of change projects and reduction of their cycle time to preempt opposition to change. This theory advances a new mechanism of bureaucratic control in the service of the public sector change and thus seems to have an affinity with the roles of (1) researcher, and (2) consultant/expert.

SUMMARY

We argued that this is a time of increased politicization and radicalization of the intellectual processes involved in theoretic inquiry. In such circumstances there is a need to stand back from these processes and locate a pluralistic standpoint that can help us deal with progress and/or lack of progress toward understanding the human communication processes. The emerging theories of human communication presented in this book attempted to avoid a focus upon extreme claims and procedures that seek to undermine what is common and central to theoretic inquiry. In each of the seven essays we find at the philosophical level only a cursory discussion of general presuppositions, and implicit liberal/reformist ideological orientations. Our reconstruction of the implicit presuppositional arguments finds that each essay offers a multidimensional view of action, social order, and communication. The contributors to the book all start from the premise that the primary purpose of human communication is to share symbolic information to establish, maintain, and change actors' self-concepts as well as to establish, maintain, and terminate relationships among individuals, groups, and human institutions. However, they all attempt to ask new questions or raise new issues regarding these foundational communication processes. What they fail to do is take an explicit philosophic position on the relationship between preexisting and emerging communication patterns. It is our hope that the authors will provide an explicit philosophical justification of the importance of theorizing about communication change. After all, this is what the emerging theories of human communication strive to accomplish.

   At the theoretical level, the essays on emerging theories of human communication did not go beyond the initial arguments about generative mechanisms of observed communication patterns nor beyond the initial attempts to adumbrate theoretical models and specify relationships among a web of concepts. Although these first steps are the main contribution of the emerging theories of human communication, a further elaboration of theoretical models is the crucial future task in accordance with the epistemic power principle.

We cannot but emphasize that the philosophical and theoretical limitations have serious consequences for the practical accomplishments of the emerging theories of human communication. To the extent that they leave philosophical, theoretical, and empirical tasks unfinished, the emerging theories of human communication have a limited capacity to enrich our repertoire of requisite communication skills in the form of our overall goals, strategies or general plans for conduct, tactical steps/sequences, and activities to be performed. We hope that they will soon offer us an explicit body of knowledge needed to avoid the treacherous illusion that we may subjugate, dominate, or avoid the actual worlds of actors whom we do not understand, agree with, or like but whom we cannot ignore. If the emerging theories of human communication fail to identify the requisite communication skills demanded by the multicultural world, if they fail to show us how to learn and improve upon these communication skills, and how widespread the skills are in multiple populations, then this book will have not achieved its purpose. We hope that events will not take this turn.

NOTES

1. In order to enhance epistemic power of theory, scholars often embrace atomism that promises to explain complex phenomena in terms of aggregates of fixed unitary factors. Because symbolic processes involving the use of language in interaction are extremely flexible and fluid, scholars very often feel compelled to find a solution for the problems of mutability and plurality in symbolic processes in terms of aggregates of fixed, irreducible units or elements. We urge that such solutions be resisted by turning initially to modal logic, a type of formal logic consisting of the possible worlds analysis (Nolt, 1984).

Our view is that there *is* a plurality of worlds. We do not have to assume that possible worlds causally influence each other. We shall presuppose, however, that the actual world is the one that *we* are in (our world), and that it is primarily our linguistic acts that separate the actual from the merely possible worlds. We can also accept that there are nonactual possible worlds in the form of sets of propositions and other types of "abstract" objects that are but a useful tool for logic.

Modal logic offers us three fundamental insights. First, it proffers ways of thinking of possibility as propositions true in some possible worlds, and necessity as propositions true in all possible worlds. This amounts to the following standard for evaluating theories: the number and relative significance of possible worlds or domains in which theoretical propositions hold. Second, modal logic advances the view that, because possible worlds or domains are spatially and temporally ordered, actors situated in their actual "world" may establish links with a certain number of spatially accessible possible worlds, and forge temporal links between whatever has happened or will happen within their actual world. Spatial accessibility allows us to theorize about cross-community communication, and temporal dimension permits us to mint communication theories of tradition and change. Third, modal logic enunciates formal links between our actual world and possible worlds. For instance, Kripke (1959) discusses the relation of "relative possibility" or "accessibility" among "possible worlds." A world x is accessible from a world y if and only if the former is possible in (or from the point of view of) the latter. Similarly, Lewis (1983, 1985, 1986) stipulates a "similarity" or "closeness" relationship among "possible world" counterparts expressed by a counterfactual conditional "If p had been true, q would have been."

What we learn from Kripke is that a proposition is true in all worlds x directly accessible from a world y. It is also true in all worlds z to which worlds x are directly accessible and through which all worlds x are accessible to the world y (indirectly). What we learn from Lewis is that a counterfactual conditional can be regarded as true if it is true in all of the most similar worlds to ours in which p is true. A similarity relationship exists when among those possible worlds in which p is true, some world in which q is true is more similar to the actual world (our world) than any world in which q is false. Thus, a counterfactual conditional is true if and only if some world where p and q are the case is more similar to our world than any world where p and *not-q* are the case.

Similarly, in the context of applied logic hypothetical reasoning and counterfactual conditions deal with "known-to-be false antecedents." For example, the counterfactual conditional "If it were the case that p—which it is not—then q" requires an inference to be drawn from the contrary-to-fact thesis represented by its antecedent. Such counterfactual conditions are particularly appropriate to stating regularities pertaining to future-oriented actions.

2. We can draw on three types of practical logic that examine concepts of practice and the logical relations among statements about actions such as choosing, planning, commanding, and permitting. First, the logic of preference (choice) attempts to provide an ordering of the possible worlds

in terms of probability and desirability (utility) of actors' choices (von Wright, 1963, 1971). Second, the logic of commands (instructions, orders, requests) applies the concept of validity to practical reasoning from the value of commands and sets of commands (Rescher, 1966). Third, deontic logic provides normative classifications of actions and states of affairs, such as the permitted, the obligatory, the forbidden, or the meritorious (von Wright, 1951; Fitch, 1966).

References

INTRODUCTION

Aldrich, H. E. (1988). "Paradigm warriors: Donaldson versus the critics of organization theory." *Organization Studies, 9*, 18–25.

Alexander, J. C. (1987). *Twenty lectures: Sociological theory since World War II.* New York: Columbia University Press.

Cushman, D. P., & Kovacic, B. (Eds.). (1995). *Watershed research traditions in human communication theory.* Albany: State University of New York Press.

Wagner, D. (1984). *The growth of sociological theories.* Beverly Hills, Calif.: Sage.

1. A VIEW OF COMMUNICATION AND CULTURE

Baxter, L. (1993). "Talking things through" and "putting it in writing": Two codes of communication in an academic institution. *Journal of Applied Communication Research, 21*, 313–26.

Baxter, L., & Goldsmith, D. (1990). Cultural terms for communication events among some American high school adolescents. *Western Journal of Speech Communication, 54*, 377–94.

Carbaugh, D. (1988). *Talking American: Cultural discourses on* Donohue. Norwood, N.J.: Ablex.

Carbaugh, D. (1988/1989). Deep agony: "Self" vs. "society" in *Donahue* discourse. *Research on Language and Social Interaction, 22*, 179–212.

Carbaugh, D. (1989). Fifty terms for talk: A cross-cultural study. *International and Intercultural Communication Annual, 13*, 93–120.

Carbaugh, D. (Ed.). (1990). *Cultural communication and intercultural contact.* Hillsdale, N.J.: Lawrence Erlbaum.

Carbaugh, D. (1991). Communication and cultural interpretation. *Quarterly Journal of Speech, 77,* 336–42.

Carbaugh, D. (1993). "Soul" and "self": Soviet and American cultures in conversation. *Quarterly Journal of Speech, 79,* 182–200.

Carbaugh, D. (1995). Ethnographic communication theory of Philipsen and associates. In D. Cushman & B. Kovacic, (Eds.). *Watershed research traditions in human communication* (pp. 269–97). Albany: State University of New York Press.

Carbaugh, D. (1996). *Situating selves: The communication of social identities in American scenes.* Albany: State University of New York Press.

Fitch, K. (1994). Culture, ideology, and interpersonal communication research. In S. Deetz (Ed.), *Communication yearbook/17* (pp. 104–35). Thousand Oaks, Calif.: Sage.

Geertz, C. (1973). *The interpretation of cultures.* New York: Bantam.

Geertz, C. (1976). From the native's point-of-view: On the nature of anthropological understanding. In K. Basso & H. Selby (Eds.), *Meaning in anthropology.* Albuquerque: University of New Mexico Press.

Gibson, T. (1995). *The liminal institution: An ethnography of communication at Hampshire College.* Unpublished master's thesis. University of Massachusetts, Amherst.

Hall, B. "J." (1995). "Brown-nosing" as a cultural category in American organizational life. *Research on Language and Social Interaction, 28,* 391–419.

Hymes, D. (1972). Models of the interaction of language and social life. In J. Gumperz & D. Hymes (Eds.), *Directions in sociolinguistics: The ethnography of communication* (pp. 35–71). New York: Holt, Rinehart, and Winston.

Katriel, T. (1991). *Communal webs: Communication and culture in contemporary Israel.* Albany: State University of New York Press.

Malinowski, B. (1935/1965). *The language of magic and gardening: Coral gardens and their magic.* Bloomington: Indiana University Press.

Morris, M. (1981). *Saying and meaning in Puerto Rico: Some problems in the ethnography of discourse.* Oxford: Pergamon.

Philipsen, G. (1987). The prospect for cultural communication. In L. Kincaid (Ed.), *Communication theory: Eastern and Western perspectives* (pp. 245–54). New York: Academic Press.

Philipsen, G. (1989). Speech and the communal function in four cultures. *International and Intercultural Communication Annual, 13*, 79–92.

Philipsen, G. (1992). *Speaking culturally*. Albany: State University of New York Press.

Sousa, A. (1994). *An "observation" of "participation": Interaction between Cheyenne Americans and Anglo-Americans*. Paper prepared for Communication 514: Social uses of language, University of Massachusetts, Amherst.

Turner, V. (1974). *Dramas, fields, and metaphors*. Ithaca, N.Y.: Cornell University Press.

2. A RELATIONAL MODEL OF COMMUNICATION COMPETENCE

Altman, I., & Taylor, D. (1973). *Social penetration: The development of interpersonal relationships*. New York: Holt, Rinehart & Winston.

Bateson, G. (1958). *Naven* (2nd ed). Palo Alto, Calif.: Stanford University Press.

Berger, C. R., & Calabrese, R. J. (1975). Some explorations in initial interaction and beyond: Toward a developmental theory of interpersonal communication. *Human Communication Research, 1*, 99–112.

Bernstein, B. (1964). Elaborated and restricted codes: Their social origins and some consequences. *American Anthropologist, 66*, 55–69.

Bochner, A. P. (1981). On the efficacy of openness in close relationships. In M. Burgoon (Ed.), *Communication yearbook, 5* (pp. 109–24). Newbury Park, Calif.: Sage.

Bochner, A. P., & Kelly, C. (1974). Interpersonal competence: Rationale, philosophy and implementation of a conceptual framework. *Speech Teacher, 23*, 270–301.

Brown, P., & Levinson, S. C. (1987). *Politeness: Some universals in language use*. New York: Cambridge University Press.

Canary, D. J., & Spitzberg, B. H. (1989). A model of competence perceptions of conflict strategies. *Human Communication Research, 15*, 241–68.

Canary, D. J., & Stafford, L. (1994). Maintaining relationships through strategic and routine interaction. In D. J. Canary & L. Stafford (Eds.), *Communication and relational maintenance* (pp. 3–22). San Diego: Academic Press.

Cegala, D. J. (1981). Interaction involvement: A cognitive dimension of communicative competence. *Communication Education, 30,* 109–21.

Cegala, D. J., Savage, G. T., Brunner, C. C., & Conrad, A. (1982). An elaboration of the meaning of interaction involvement: Toward the development of a theoretical concept. *Communication Monographs, 49,* 229–48.

Chomsky, N. (1965). *Aspects of theory of syntax.* Cambridge, Mass.: MIT Press.

Cupach, W. R., & Imahori, T. T. (1993). Identity management theory: Communication competence in intercultural episodes and relationships. In R. L. Wiseman & J. Koester (Eds.), *Intercultural communication competence* (pp. 112–31). Newbury Park, Calif.: Sage.

Cupach, W. R., & Spitzberg, B. H. (1983). Trait versus state: a comparison of dispositional and situational measures of interpersonal communication competence. *Western Journal of Speech Communication, 47,* 364–79.

Duran, R. L. (1992). Communicative adaptability: A review of conceptualization and measurement. *Communication Quarterly, 40,* 253–68.

Gilbert, S. J. (1976). Empirical and theoretical extensions of self-disclosure. In G. R. Miller (Ed.), *Explorations in interpersonal communication* (pp. 197–216). Beverly Hills, Calif.: Sage.

Giles, H., Mulac, A., Bradac, J. J., & Johnson, P. (1987). Speech accommodation theory: The first decade and beyond. In M. L. McLaughlin (Ed.), *Communication yearbook, 10* (pp. 13–48). Newbury Park, Calif.: Sage.

Goffman, E. (1959). *The presentation of self in everyday life.* Garden City, N.Y.: Anchor.

Goffman, E. (1967). *Interaction ritual: Essays on face-to-face interaction.* Garden City, N.Y.: Doubleday.

Gudykunst, W. B. (1993). Toward a theory of effective interpersonal and intergroup communication: An anxiety/uncertainty management (AUM) perspective. In R. L. Wiseman & J. Koester (Eds.), *Intercultural communication competence* (pp. 16–32). Newbury Park, Calif.: Sage.

Gudykunst, W. B., Gao, G., Schmidt, K., Nishida, T., Bond, M., Leung, K., Wang, G., & Barraclough, R. (1992). A cross-cultural study of self-monitoring. *Communication Research Reports, 6,* 7–12.

Gudykunst, W. B., & Hall, B. J. (1994). Strategies for effective communication and adaptation in intergroup contexts. In J. M. Wiemann, & J. A. Daly (Eds.), *Strategic interpersonal communication* (pp. 225–72). Hillsdale, N.J.: Lawrence Erlbaum.

Hall, A. D., & Fagen, R. E. (1956). Definition of system. *General Systems Yearbook, 1,* 18–28.

Hall, E. T. (1976). *Beyond culture.* New York: Doubleday.

Hammer, M. R. (1984). Communication workshop on participants' intercultural communication competence: An exploratory study. *Communication Quarterly, 32,* 252–62.

Hammer, M. R. (1989). Intercultural communication competence. In M. K. Asante & W. B. Gudykunst (Eds.), *Handbook of international and intercultural communication* (pp. 247–60). Newbury Park, Calif.: Sage.

Hammer, M. R., Gudykunst, W. B., & Wiseman, R. L. (1978). Dimensions of intercultural effectiveness: An exploratory study. *International Journal of Intercultural Relations, 2,* 382–92.

Hofstede, G. (1980). *Culture's consequences.* Beverly Hills, Calif.: Sage.

House, J. S., Landis, K. R., & Umberson, D. (1988). Social relationships and health. *Science, 241,* 540–45.

Hymes, D. (1972). On communicative competence. In J. B. Pride & J. Holmes (Eds.), *Sociolinguistics: Selected readings.* Baltimore: Penguin.

Imahori, T. T., & Lanigan, M. (1989). Relational model of intercultural communication competence. *International Journal of Intercultural Relations, 13,* 269–86.

Jourard, S. M. (1968). *Disclosing man to himself.* New York: Van Nostrand.

Kellermann, K. (1992). Communication: Inherently strategic and primarily automatic. *Communication Monographs, 59,* 288–300.

Kim, M. S. (1993). Culture-based interactive constraints in explaining intercultural strategic competence. In R. L. Wiseman, & J. Koester (Eds.), *Intercultural communication competence* (pp. 132–52). Newbury Park, Calif.: Sage.

Kim, Y. Y. (1992). Intercultural communication competence. A systems-theoretic view. In S. Ting-Toomey & F. Korzenny (Eds.), *Cross-cultural interpersonal communication* (pp. 259–75). Newbury Park, Calif.: Sage.

Koester, J., Wiseman, R.L., & Sanders, J. A. (1993). Multiple perspectives of intercultural communication competence. In R. L. Wiseman, & J. Koester (Eds.), *Intercultural communication competence* (pp. 3–15). Newbury Park, Calif.: Sage.

Langer, E. J. (1979). *Mindfulness.* Reading, Mass.: Addison-Wesley.

Markus, H. R., & Kitayama, S. (1991). Culture and the self: Implications for cognition, emotion, and motivation. *Psychological Review, 2,* 224–53.

Martin, J. N. (1993). Intercultural communication competence: A review. In R. L. Wiseman & J. Koester (Eds.), *Intercultural communication competence* (pp. 16–32). Newbury Park, Calif.: Sage.

Mead, G. (1934). *Mind, self, and society*. Chicago: University of Chicago Press.

Millar, F. E., & Rogers, L. E. (1976). A relational approach to interpersonal communication. In G. R. Miller (Ed.), *Explorations in interpersonal communication* (pp. 87–103). Beverly Hills, Calif.: Sage.

Miyahara, A. (1994, July). *Toward a concept of Japanese communication competence: Epistemological and ontological issues in theory building*. Paper presented at the International Communication Association conference, Sydney, Australia.

Nishida, H. (1985). Japanese intercultural communication competence and cross-cultural adjustment. *International Journal of Intercultural Relations, 9*, 247–69.

O'Hair, D., Friedrich, G. W., Wiemann, J. M., & Wiemann, M. O. (1994). *Competent communication*. New York: St. Martin's Press.

Pavitt, C., & Haight, L. (1985). The "competent communicator" as a cognitive prototype. *Human Communication Research, 12*, 225–42.

Rubin, R. B., Graham, E. E., & Mignerey, J. T. (1990). A longitudinal study of college student's communication competence. *Communication Education, 39*, 1–14.

Spitzberg, B. H. (1994). The dark side of (in)competence. In W. R. Cupach & B. H. Spitzberg (Eds.), *The dark side of interpersonal communication* (pp. 25–49). Hillsdale, N.J.: Lawrence Erlbaum.

Spitzberg, B. H., & Canary, D. J. (1985). Loneliness and relationally competent communication. *Journal of Social and Personal Relationships, 2*, 387–402.

Spitzberg, B. H., & Cupach, W. R. (1984). *Interpersonal communication competence*. Beverly Hills, Calif.: Sage.

Spitzberg, B. H., & Cupach, W. R. (1989). *Handbook of interpersonal competence research*. New York: Springer-Verlag.

Spitzberg, B. H., & Hecht, M. (1984). A component model of relational competence. *Human Communication Research, 10*, 575–99.

Takai, J., & Ota, H. (1994). Assessing Japanese interpersonal communication competence. *Japanese Journal of Experimental Social Psychology, 33*, 224–36.

Thibaut, J. W., & Kelley, H. H. (1959). *The psychology of groups*. London: John Wiley.

Ting-Toomey, S. (1989). Identity and interpersonal binding. In M. K. Asante & G. W. Gudykunst (Eds.), *Handbook of international and intercultural communication* (pp. 351–73). Newbury Park, Calif.: Sage.

Ting-Toomey, S. (1993). Communicative resourcefulness: An identity negotiation perspective. In R. L. Wiseman & J. Koester (Eds.), *Intercultural communication competence* (pp. 72–111). Newbury Park, Calif.: Sage.

Triandis, H. C. (1990). Cross-cultural studies of individualism and collectivism. In J. Berman (Ed.), *Nebraska symposium on motivation* (pp. 41–133). Lincoln: University of Nebraska Press.

Walster, E., Walster, G. W., & Berscheid, E. (1978). *Equity: Theory and research*. Boston: Allyn & Bacon.

Watzlavick, P., Beavin, J. H., & Jackson, D. D. (1967). *Pragmatics of human communication: A study of interactional patterns, pathologies, and paradoxes*. New York: Norton.

Wiemann, J. M. (1977), Explication and test of a model of communicative competence. *Human Communication Research*, *3*, 195–213.

Wiemann, J. M., & Backlund, P. (1980). Current theory and research in communicative competence. *Review of Educational Research*, *50*, 185–89.

Wiemann, J. M., & Bradac, J. (1989). Metatheoretical issues in the study of communicative competence. In B. Dervin (Ed.), *Progress in communication science* (vol. 9, pp. 261–84). Norwood, N.J.: Ablex.

Wiemann, J. M., & Kelly, C. W. (1981). Pragmatics of interpersonal competence. In C. Wilder-Mott & J. H. Weakland (Eds.), *Rigor and imagination: Essays from the legacy of Gregory Bateson* (pp. 283–97). New York: Praeger.

Wiseman, J. L., & Koester, J. (Eds.). (1993). *Intercultural communication competence*. Newbury Park, Calif.: Sage.

Zigler, E., & Phillips, L. (1960). Social effectiveness and symptomatic behaviors. *Journal of Abnormal and Social Psychology, 61*, 231–38.

3. CONFLICT COMMUNICATION

Albert, J. K. (1990). The use of humor in managing couples' conflict interactions. In D. D. Cahn (Ed.), *Intimates in conflict: A communication perspective* (pp. 105–20). Hillsdale, N.J.: Lawrence Erlbaum.

Bell, E. C., & Blakeney, R. N. (1977). Personality correlates of conflict resolution modes. *Human Relations, 30*, 849–57.

Billings, A. (1979). Conflict resolution in distressed and nondistressed married couples. *Journal of Consulting and Clinical Psychology, 47*, 368–76.

Braiker, H. B., & Kelley, H. H. (1979). Conflict in the development of close relationships. In R. L. Burgess & T. L. Huston (Eds.), *Social exchange in developing relationships* (pp. 135–68). New York: Academic.

Burrell, N. A., & Cahn, D. D. (1994). Mediating peer conflicts in educational contexts: The maintenance of school relationships. In D. D. Cahn (Ed.), *Conflict in personal relationships* (pp. 79–94), Hillsdale, N.J.: Lawrence Erlbaum.

Cahn, D. D. (1987). *Letting go: A pratical theory of relationship disengagement and reengagement.* Albany: State University of New York Press.

Cahn, D. D. (1992). *Conflict in intimate relationships.* New York: Guilford.

Cahn, D. D. (1994). Conflict communication. In V. S. Ramachandran (Ed.), *Encyclopedia of human behavior* (pp. 675–86). San Diego: Academic.

Cahn, D. D. (1996). Family violence from a communication perspective. In D. D. Cahn & S. Lloyd (Eds.), *Family Violence from a communication perspective.* Newbury Park, Calif.: Sage.

Cahn, D. D. & Hanford, J. T. (1984) Perspectives on human communication research: Behaviorism, phenomenology and an intergrated view. *Western Journal of Speech Communication, 48*, 277–92.

Cupach, W. R., & Spitzberg, B. H. (Ed.). (1994). *The dark side of interpersonal communication.* Hillsdale, N.J.: Lawrence Erlbaum.

Cushman, D. P., & Whiting, G. (1972). An approach to communication theory: Toward consensus on rules. *Journal of Communication, 22*, 217–38.

Danielson, C. (1994). A holistic approach to dispute resolution at a community mediation center. In D. D. Cahn (Ed.), *Conflict in personal relationships* (pp. 203–22), Hillsdale, N.J.: Lawrence Erlbaum.

Donohue, W. A., Allen M., & Burrell, N. (1988). Mediator communicative competence. *Communication Monographs, 55*, 104–19.

Donohue, W. A., & Weider-Hatfield, D. (1988). Communication strategies. In J. Folberg & A. Milne (Eds.), *Divorce mediation: Theory and practice* (pp. 297–315). New York: Guilford.

Fincham, F. D., Bradbury, T. N., & Grych, J. H. (1990). Conflict in close relationships: The role of intrapersonal phenomena. In S. Graham &

V. Folkes (Eds.), *Attribution theory: Applications to achievement, mental health, and interpersonal conflict* (pp. 161–84). Hillsdale, N.J.: Lawrence Erlbaum.

Fitzpatrick, M. A. (1988). *Between husbands & wives: Communication in marriage.* Beverly Hills, Calif.: Sage.

Fitzpatrick, M. A., & Winke, J. (1979). You always hurt the one you love: Strategies and tactics in interpersonal conflict. *Communication Quarterly, 27,* 3–11.

Foa, U. G., & Foa, E. B. (1974). *Societal structures of the mind.* Springfield, Ill.: Thomas.

Fontaine, G. (1990). Cultural diversity in intimate intercultural relationships. In D. D. Cahn (Ed.), *Intimates in conflict: A communication perspective* (pp. 209–24). Hillsdale, N.J.: Lawrence Erlbaum.

Gaelick, L., Bodenhausen, G. V., & Wyer, R. S. (1985). Emotional communication in close relationships. *Journal of Personality and Social Psychology, 49,* 1246–65.

Gottman, J. M. (1970). *Marital interaction: Experimental investigations.* New York: Academic.

Gottman, J. M. (1982a). Emotional responsiveness in marital conversations. *Journal of Communication, 16,* 108–19.

Gottman, J. M. (1982b). Temporal form: Toward a new language for describing relationships. *Journal of Marriage and the Family, 44,* 943–62.

Gottman, J. M., Markman, H., & Notarius, C. (1977). The topography of marital conflict: A sequential analysis of verbal and nonverbal behavior. *Journal of Marriage and the Family, 39,* 461–77.

Halpern, J. (1994). The sandwich generation: Conflicts between adult children and their aging parents. In D. D. Cahn (Ed.), *Conflict in personal relationships* (pp. 143–60), Hillsdale, N.J.: Lawrence Erlbaum.

Hatfield, E., Utne, M. K., & Traupmann, J. (1979). Equity theory and intimate relationships. In R. L. Burgers & T. L. Huston (Eds.), *Social exchange in developing relationships* (pp. 99–133). New York: Academic.

Hawes, L. C., & Smith, D. H. (1973). A critique of assumptions underlying the study of communication in conflict. *Quarterly Journal of Speech, 62,* 423–35.

Hawkins, J. L., Weisberg, C., & Ray, D. (1980). Spouse differences in communication style: Preference, perception, behavior. *Journal of Marriage and the Family, 42,* 585–93.

Healy, J. G., & Bell, R. A. (1990). Assessing alternate responses to conflicts in friendship. In D. D. Cahn (Ed.), *Intimates in conflict: A communication perspective* (pp. 25–48). Hillsdale, N.J.: Lawrence Erlbaum.

Hocker, J. L., & Wilmot, W. W. (1985). *Interpersonal conflict* (2nd ed.). Dubuque, Iowa: William C. Brown.

Lloyd, S. A. (1987). Conflict in premarital relationships: Differential perceptions of males and females. *Family Relations, 36,* 290–94.

Llyod, S. A., & Emery, B. C. (1994). Physically aggressive conflict in romantic relationships. In D. D. Cahn (Ed.), *Conflict in personal relationships* (pp. 27–46). Hillsdale, N.J.: Lawrence Erlbaum.

Margolin, G., & Wampold, B. (1981). Sequential analysis of conflict and accord in distressed and nondistressed marital patterns. *Journal of Consulting and Clinical Psychology, 49,* 554–67.

Menaghan, E. (1982). Measuring coping effectiveness. A panel analysis of marital problems and coping efforts. *Journal of Health and Social Behavior, 23,* 220–34.

Osborne, L. N., & Fincham, F. D. (1994). Conflict between parents and their children. In D. D. Cahn (Ed.), *Conflict in personal relationships* (pp. 117–41). Hillsdale, N.J.: Lawrence Erlbaum.

Patterson, D. G., & Schwartz, P. (1994). The social construction of conflict in intimate same-sex couples. In D. D. Cahn (Ed.), *Conflict in personal relationships* (pp. 3–26), Hillsdale, N.J.: Lawrence Erlbaum.

Pike, G. R., & Sillars, A. L. (1985). Reciprocity of marital communication. *Journal of Social and Personal Relationships, 2,* 303–24.

Rands, M., Levinger, G., & Mellinger, G. D. (1981). Patterns of conflict resolution and marital satisfaction. *Journal of Family Issues, 2,* 297–321.

Raush, H., Barry, W., Hertel, R., & Swain, M. (1974). *Communication, conflict and marriage.* San Francisco: Jossey-Bass.

Rettig, K. D., & Bubolz, M. M. (1983). Interpersonal resource exchanges as indicators of quality of marriage. *Journal of Marriage and the Family, 45,* 497–509.

Roloff, M. E., & Cloven, D. H. (1990). The chilling effect in interpersonal relationships: The reluctance to speak one's mind. In D. D. Cahn (Ed.), *Intimates in conflict: A communication perspective* (pp. 49–76). Hillsdale, N.J.: Lawrence Erlbaum.

Rusbult, C. E., & Zembrodt, I. M. (1983). Responses to dissatisfaction in romantic involvements: A multidimensional scaling analysis. *Journal of Experimental Social Psychology, 19,* 274–93.

Sabatelli, R. M., & Cecil-Pigo, E. F. (1985). Relational interdependence and commitment in marriage. *Journal of Marriage and the Family, 47,* 931–37.

Sillars, A. L. (1980). The sequential and distributional structure of conflict interactions as a function of attributions concerning the locus of responsibilty and stability of conflicts. In D. Nimmo (Ed.), *Commuication yearbook 4* (pp. 217–35). New Brunswick, N.J.: Transaction.

Slaikeu, K. A., Culler, R., Pearson, J., & Thoennes, N. (1985). Process and outcome in divorce mediation. *Mediation Quarterly, 10,* 55–74.

Ting-Tommey, S. (1983). An analysis of verbal communication patterns in high and low marital adjustment groups. *Human Communication Research, 9,* 306–19.

Ting-Toomey, S. (1984). Perceived decision-making power and marital adjustment. *Communication Research Reports, 1,* 15–20.

Ting-Tommey, S. (1994). Managing conflict in intimate intercultural relationships. In D. D. Cahn (Ed.), *Conflict in personal relationships* (pp. 47–78). Hillsdale, N.J.: Lawrence Erlbaum.

Walster, E., Walster, G. W., & Bercheid, E. (1978). *Equity: Theory and research.* Boston: Allyn & Bacon.

Weiss, R. L., & Dehle, C. (1994). Cognitive behavioral perspectives on marital conflict. In D. D. Cahn (Ed.), *Conflict in personal relationships* (pp. 95–116). Hillsdale, N.J.: Lawrence Erlbaum.

Wills, T. A., Weiss, R. L., & Patterson, G. R. (1974). A behavioral analysis of the determinants of marital satisfaction. *Journal of Consulting and Clinical Psychology, 42,* 802–11.

4. AN INTERACTIONIST FRAMEWORK
FOR PEACE

Berkowitz, L. (1989). The frustration-aggression hypothesis: An examination and reformulation. *Psychological Bulletin, 106,* 59–73.

Blake, R. R., & Mouton, J. S. (1964). *The managerial grid.* Houston: Gulf.

Blumer, H. (1969). *Symbolic interaction: Perspective and method.* Englewood Cliffs, N.J.: Prentice Hall.

Boulding, K. E. (1990). *Three faces of power.* Newbury Park, Calif.: Sage.

Carmet, D. (1993). The international dimensions of ethnic conflict: Concepts, indicators, and theory. *Journal of Peace Research, 30,* 137–50.

Deutsch, M. (1973). *The resolution of conflict.* New Haven, Conn.: Yale University Press.

Deutsch, M. (1994). Constructive conflict management for the world today. The *International Journal of Conflict Management, 5,* 111–29.

Donohue, W. A. (1990). Interaction goals in negotiation: A critique. In J. Anderson (Ed.), *Communication yearbook 13* (pp. 417–27). Newbury Park, Calif.: Sage.

Donohue, W. A. (1991). *Communication, marital dispute, and divorce mediation.* Hillsdale, N.J.: Lawrence Erlbaum.

Donohue, W. A., & Ramesh, C. (1993). Relationship development in negotiation. In M. Roloff & L. Putnam (Eds.), *Communication and negotiation* (pp. 99–122). Newbury Park, Calif.: Sage.

Donohue, W. A., & Roberto, A. J. (1993). Relational development as negotiated order in hostage negotiation. *Human Communication Research, 20,* 175–98.

Evans, E. (1993). Peacekeeping: Two views. The U.S. military and peacekeeping operations. *World Affairs, 155,* 143–47.

Felson, R. B., & Tedeschi, J. T. (1993). *Aggression and violence: Social interactionist perspectives.* Washington, D.C.: American Psychological Association.

Galtung, J. (1971). A structural theory of imperialism. *Journal of Peace Research, 8,* 92.

Galtung, J. (1985). Twenty-five years of peace research: Ten challenges and some responses. *Journal of Peace Research, 22,* 141–59.

Gittler, J. B. (1989). *The annual review of conflict knowledge and conflict resolution* (vol. 1). New York: Garland.

Gottman, J. (1994). *Why marriages succeed or fail.* New York: Simon & Schuster.

Greffenius, S., & Gill, J. (1992). Pure coercion vs. carrot-and-stick offers in crisis bargaining. *Journal of Peace Research, 29,* 39–52.

Herek, G. M., Janis, I. L., & Huth, P. (1987). Decision making during international crises: Is quality of process related to outcome? *Journal of Conflict Resolution, 31,* 204–26.

Holmes, M. E., & Poole, M. S. (1991). Longitudinal analysis. In B. Montgomery & S. Duck (Eds.), *Studying interpersonal interaction* (pp. 286–302). New York: Guilford.

Houweling, H., & Siccama, J. G. (1988). Power transitions as a cause of war. *Journal of Conflict Resolution, 32*, 87–102.

Houweling, H., & Siccama, J. G. (1991). Power transitions and critical points as predictors of great power war. *Journal of Conflict Resolution, 35*, 642–58.

Janis, I. L. (1972). *Victims of groupthink*. Boston: Houghton Mifflin.

Kelley, C. E. (1991). Beyond peace as "not war": The search for a transcendent metaphor. In R. Troester & C. Kelley (Eds.), *Peacemaking through communication* (pp. 29–36), Annandale, Va.: Speech Communication Association.

Kelman, H. C. (1981). Reflections on the history and status of peace research. *Conflict Management and Peace Science, 5*, 95–110.

Kelman, H. C. (1991). On the history and development of peace research: Personal reflections. In J. Nobel (Ed.), *The coming of age of peace research* (pp. 25–38). Groningen, The Netherlands: Styx.

Kim, Y. Y. (1989). Explaining inter-ethnic conflict. In J. Gittler (Ed.), *The annual review of conflict knowledge and conflict resolution* (vol 1). New York: Garland.

Morrow, J. D. (1989). A reexamination of the effects of arms races on the occurrence of war. *Journal of Conflict Resolution, 33*, 500–29.

Notarious, C., & Markman, H. (1993). *We can work it out: Making sense of marital conflict*. New York: Putnam.

Putnam, L. L. (1990). Reframing integrative and distributive bargaining: A process perspective. In B. H. Sheppard, M. H. Bazerman, & R. j. Lewicki (Eds.), *Research on negotiation in organizations* (vol. 2, pp. 3–30). Greenwich, Conn.: JAI Press.

Rahim, M. A. (1983). *Rahim organizational conflict inventories*. Palo Alto, Calif.: Consulting Psychologists Press.

Rapoport, A. (1972). Various conceptions of peace research. *Peace Research Society (International) Papers, 19*, 91–106.

Sillars, A. L., Weisberg, J., Burggraf, C. S., & Wilson, E. A. (1987). Content themes in marital conversations. *Human Communication Research, 13*, 495–528.

Singer, J. D. (1990). *The invisible hand, extra-rational considerations, and decisional failure*. Paper presented to the American Political Science Association, San Francisco.

Sorensen, G. (1992). Utopianism in peace research: The Gandhian heritage. *Journal of Peace Research, 29*, 135–44.

Strauss, A. (1978). *Negotiations: Varieties, contexts, processes, and social order.* San Francisco: Jossey Bass.

Suedfeld, P., & Bluck, S. (1988). Changes in integrative complexity prior to surprise attacks. *Journal of Conflict Resolution, 32,* 626–35.

Watzlawick, P., Beavin, J. H., & Jackson, D. D. (1967). *Pragmatics of human communication.* New York: Norton.

Winter, D. G. (1993). Power, affiliation, and war: Three tests of a motivational model. *Journal of Personality and Social Psychology, 65,* 532–45.

5. MEDIA AGENDA-SETTING THEORY

Arp, W. (1990). The exclusion of the illegal Hispanics in agenda setting: The Immigration and Reform and Control Act of 1986. *Policy Studies Review, 9,* 327–38.

Atkin, C. K. (1989). Television socialization and risky driving by teenagers. International Symposium: The social psychology of risky driving. *Alcohol, Drugs and Driving, 5,* 1–11.

Becker, L., McCombs, M. E., & McLeod, J. (1975). The development of political cognitions. In S. Chaffee (Ed.), *Political communication* (pp. 21–63). Beverly Hills, Calif.: Sage.

Behr, J. L., & Iyengar, S. (1985). Television news, real world cues and changes in the public agenda. *Public Opinion Quarterly, 49,* 38–57.

Beniger, J. R. (1978). Media content as social indicators: The Greenfield index of agenda-setting. *Communication Research, 5,* 437–53.

Benton, M., & Frazier, P. J. (1976). The agenda setting function of the mass media at three levels of "information holding." *Communication Research, 3,* 261–74.

Blood, D. (1994, May). *Economic news, consumer sentiment, the state of the economy and presidential popularity: A time series analysis.* Paper presented at the annual meeting of the American Association for Public Opinion Research, Boston.

Blood, R. W. (1981). *Unobtrusive issues in the agenda-setting role of the press.* Unpublished doctoral dissertation. Syracuse University: Syracuse, N.Y.

Breed, W. (1955). Social control in the newsroom. *Social Forces, 33,* 326–33.

Brosius, H. B., & Kepplinger, H. M. (1990). The agenda setting function of television news. *Communication Research, 17,* 183–211.

Brosius, H. B., & Kepplinger, H. M. (1992). Linear and nonlinear models of agenda-setting in television. *Journal of Broadcasting and Electronic Media, 36,* 5–23.

Chaffee, S., & Berger, C. (1987). What Communication Scientists Do? In C. Berger & S. Chaffee (Eds.), *The handbook of communication science,* Newbury Park, Calif.: Sage.

Cohen, B. (1963). *The press and foreign policy.* Princeton, N.J.: Princeton University Press.

DeFleur, M., & Ball-Rokeach, S. (1982). *Theories of mass communication* (4th ed.). White Plains, N.Y.: Longman.

Downs, A. (1972). Up and down with ecology: The "issue-attention cycle." *The Public Interest, 28,* 38–50.

Erbring, L., Goldenberg, E., & Miller, A. (1980). Front-page news and real-world cues: A new look at agenda-setting by the media. *American Journal of Political Science, 24,* 16–49.

Eyal, C. H. (1979, May). *The roles of newspapers and television in agenda-setting.* Paper presented at the annual meetings of the American Associations of Public Opinion Research. Buck Hill Falls, Pa.

Fan, D. P. (1988). *Predictions of public opinion from the mass media: Computer content analysis and mathematical modeling.* Westport, Conn.: Greenwood Press.

Fan, D. P. (1993, May). *Predictions of consumer confidence/sentiment from the press.* Paper presented at the annual meeting of American Association of Public Opinion Research, Chicago.

Funkhouser, G. (1973). Trends in media coverage of the issues of the '60s. *Journalism Quarterly, 50,* 533–38.

Gormley, W. T., Jr. (1975). Newspaper agendas and political elites. *Journalism Quarterly, 52,* 30–38.

Graber, D. A. (1993). *Mass media and American politics* (4th ed.). Washington, D.C.: Congressional Quarterly Press.

Harrison, K., & Hoberg, G. (1991). Setting the environmental agenda in Canada and the United States: The case of dioxin and radon. *Canadian Journal of Political Science, 24,* 3–27.

Hilgartner, S., & Bosk, C. (1988). The rise and fall of social problems: A public arenas model. *American Journal of Sociology, 94,* 53–78.

Hugel, R., Degenhardt, W., & Weiss, H. J. (1989). Structural equation models for the analysis of the agenda-setting process. *European Journal of Communication, 4,* 191–210.

Iglesias, H. A., & Chirife, J. (1982). *Handbook of food isotherms.* New York: Academic Press.

Iyengar, S. (1979). Television news and issue salience: A reexamination of the agenda-setting hypothesis. *American Politics Quarterly, 7,* 395–416.

Iyengar, S. (1988). New directions of agenda-setting research. In J. A. Anderson (Ed.), *Communication yearbook 11* (pp. 595–602). Newbury Park, Calif.: Sage.

Iyengar, S., & Kinder, D. R. (1985). Psychological accounts of media agenda-setting. In S. Kraus & R. Perloff (Eds.), *Mass media and political thought* (pp. 117–40). Newbury Park, Calif.: Sage.

Iyengar, S., & Kinder, D. R. (1987). *News that matters: Agenda setting and priming in a television age.* Chicago: University of Chicago Press.

Iyengar, S., Peters, M. D., & Kinder, D. R. (1982). Experimental demonstrations of the "not-so-minimal" consequences of television news programs. *American Political Science Review, 76,* 848–58.

Kaid, L. L. (1976). Measures of political advertising. *Journal of Advertising Research, 16,* 49–53.

Klapper, J. T. (1960). *The effects of mass communications.* Glencoe, Ill.: Free Press.

Korsmo, F. L. (1990). Problem definition and the Alaska natives: Ethnic identity and policy formation. *Policy Studies Review, 9,* 294–306.

Kosicki, G. M. (1993). Problems and opportunities in agenda-setting research. *Journal of Communication, 43,* 100–27.

Kotter, J. P. (1983). Agenda setting and networking tools of the management trade. *Modern Office Technology, 28,* 10–14.

Lang, G. E., & Lang, K. (1959). The mass media and voting. In E. Burdick & A. J. Brodbeck (Eds.), *American voting behavior* (pp. 217–35). Glencoe, Ill.: Free Press.

Lazarsfeld, P., & Merton, R. K. (1948). Mass communication, popular taste and organized social action. In L. Bryson (Ed.), *The communication of ideas* (pp. 95–118). New York: Institute for Religious and Social Studies.

Linsky, M., Moore, J., O'Donnell, W. & Whitman, D. (1986). *How the press affects federal policymaking: Six case studies.* New York: Norton.

Lippman, W. (1922). *Public opinion.* New York: Harcourt Brace.

Long, N. E. (1958). The local community as an ecology of games. *American Journal of Sociology, 64,* 251–61.

MacKuen, M. (1981). Social communication and the mass policy agenda. In M. B. MacKuen & S. L. Combs (Eds.), *More than news: Media power in public affairs* (pp. 19–144). Beverly Hills, Calif.: Sage.

Mayer, R. N. (1991). Gone yesterday, here today: Consumer issues in the agenda setting process. *Journal of Social Issues, 47*, 21–39.

Mazur, A. (1981). Media coverage and public opinion on scientific controversies. *Journal of Communication, 31*, 106–15.

McCombs, M. E. (1977). Newspaper versus television: Mass communication effects across time. In D. L. Shaw & M. E. McCombs (Eds.), *The emergence of American political issues: The agenda-setting function of the press* (pp. 89–105). St. Paul, Minn.: West.

McCombs, M. E. (1992). Explorers and surveyors: Expanding strategies for agenda-setting research. *Journalism Quarterly, 69*, 813–24.

McCombs, M. E., & Shaw, D. L. (1972). The agenda setting function of mass media. *Public Opinion Quarterly, 36*, 176–85.

McCombs, M. E., & Shaw, D. L. (1993). The evolution of agenda-setting research: Twenty-five years in the marketplace of ideas. *Journal of Communication, 43*, 58–67.

McCombs, M. E., & Weaver, D. H. (1973, April). *Voters' need for orientation and use of mass communication.* Paper presented at the annual meeting of the International Communication Association, Montreal, Canada.

McCombs, M. E., & Zhu, J. H. (1995). Capacity, diversity and volatility of the public agenda: Trends from 1954 to 1994. *Public Opinion Quarterly, 59*, 495–525.

McLeod, J., Becker, L., & Byrnes, J. (1974). Another look at the agenda setting function of the press. *Communication Research, 1*, 131–66.

Miller, A., Goldenberg, E., & Erbring, L. (1979). Type-set politics: Impact of newspapers on public confidence. *American Political Science Review, 73*, 67–84.

Mueller, J. E. (1973). *War, presidents, and public opinion.* New York: John Wiley.

Mutz, D. C. (1989, May). *Yours, mine and ours: Information sources, perceptions of unemployment and their political consequences.* Paper presented at the annual meeting of the International Communication Association, San Francisco.

Neisser, U. (1967). *Cognitive psychology.* Englewood Cliffs, N.J.: Prentice Hall.

Nelson, B. (1984). *Making an issue of child abuse*. Chicago: University of Chicago Press.

Neuman, W. R. (1989). Parallel content analysis. In G. Comstock (Ed.), *Public communication and behavior, vol. 2* (pp. 205–89). Orlando, Fla.: Academic Press.

Neuman, W. R. (1990). The threshold of public attention. *Public Opinion Quarterly, 54*, 159–76.

Noelle-Newmann, E. (1974). The spiral of silence: A theory of public opinion. *Journal of Communication, 24*, 43–51.

Nolan, J. T. (1985). Political surfing when issues break. *Harvard Business Review, 63*, 72–81.

Page, B., & Shapiro, R. (1992). *The rational public: Fifty years of trends in Americans' policy preferences*. Chicago: University of Chicago Press.

Palmgreen, P., & Clark, P. (1977). Agenda setting with local and national issues. *Communication Research, 4*, 435–52.

Patterson, T., & McClure, R. (1976). *The unseeing eye: The myth of television power in national elections*. New York: Putnam.

Pritchard, D. (1984). Homicide and bargained justice: The agenda-setting effect of crime news on prosecutors. *Public Opinion Quarterly, 50*, 143–59.

Pritchard, D., & Berkowitz, D. (1993). The limits of agenda-setting: The press and political responses to crime in the United States, 1950–1980. *International Journal of Public Opinion Research, 5*, 86–91.

Protess, D. L., Cook, F. L., Doppelt, J. C., Ettema, J. S., Gordon, M. T., Leff, D. R., & Miller, P. (1991). *The journalism of outrage*. New York: Guilford.

Ratkowsky, D. A. (1990). *Handbook of nonlinear regression models*. New York: Marcel Dekker.

Reese, S. (1991). Setting the media's agenda: A power balance perspective. In J. A. Anderson (Ed.), *Communication yearbook 14* (pp. 309–40). Newbury Park, Calif.: Sage.

Roberts, D. F., & Maccoby, N. (1985). Effects of mass communication. In G. Lindzey, & E. Aronson (Eds.), *Handbook of social psychology* (pp. 539–98). New York: Random House.

Robinson, J. P., & Levy, M. R. (1986). *The main source: Learning from TV news*. Newbury Park, Calif.: Sage.

Rogers, E. M., & Dearing, J. W. (1988). Agenda-setting research: Where has it been? Where is it going? In J. A. Anderson (Ed.), *Communication yearbook 11* (pp. 555–94). Newbury Park, Calif.: Sage.

Rogers, E. M., Dearing, J. W., & Chang, S. (1991). AIDS in the 1980s: The agenda-setting process for a public issue. *Journalism Monographs, 126.*

Rogers, E. M., Dearing, J. W., & Bregman, D. (1993). The anatomy of agenda-setting research. *Journal of Communication, 43,* 68–84.

Roper Organization. (1984). *Public perception of television and other mass media.* New York: Television Information Office.

Salwen, M. B. (1987). Mass media dependency and agenda setting. *Communication Research Report, 4,* 26–31.

Schoenbach, K., & Weaver, D. H. (1985). Finding the unexpected: cognitive bonding in a political campaign. In S. Kraus & R. M. Perloff (Eds.), *Mass media and public thought* (pp. 157–76). Newbury Park, Calif.: Sage.

Semetko, H., Blumler, J. G., Gurevitch, M., & Weaver, D. H. (1991). *The formation of campaign agendas: A comparative analysis of party and media roles in recent American and British elections.* Hillsdale, N.J.: Lawrence Erlbaum.

Severin, W. J., & Tankard, J. W., Jr. (1992). *Communication theories: Origins, methods and uses in the mass media* (3rd ed.). New York: Longman.

Shaw, D. L., & McCombs, M. E. (1977). *The emergence of American political issues: The agenda setting function of the press.* St. Paul, Minn.: West.

Shoemaker, P., & Reese, S. (1991). *Mediating the message: Theories of influence on mass media content.* New York: Longman.

Sutherland, M., & Galloway, J. (1981). Role of advertising: Persuasion or agenda setting? *Journal of Advertising Research, 21,* 25–29.

Smith, T. (1980). America's most important problem: A trend analysis, 1946–1976. *Public Opinion Quarterly, 44,* 164–80.

So, C. Y. K., & Chan, J. M. (1991, August). *Evaluating and conceptualizing the field of communication: A survey of the core scholars.* Paper presented at the annual meeting of the Association for Education in Journalism and Mass Communication, Boston.

Stevenson, R., Gonzenbach, W., & David, P. (1991, August). *Economic recession and the news.* Paper presented at the annual meeting of the Association for Education in Journalism and Mass Communication, Boston.

Swanson, D. L. (1988). Feeling the elephant: Some observations on agenda-setting research. In J. A. Anderson (Ed.), *Communication yearbook 11* (pp. 603–19). Newbury Park, Calif.: Sage.

Tichenor, P. J., & Wackman, D. B. (1973). Mass media and community public opinion. *American Behavioral Scientist, 16*, 593–606.

Tipton, L., Haney, R. D., & Baseheart, J. R. (1975). Media agenda-setting in city and state election campaigns. *Journalism Quarterly, 52*, 15–22.

Wanta, W., & Wu, Y. C. (1992). Interpersonal communication and the agenda-setting process. *Journalism Quarterly, 69*, 847–55.

Watt, J. H., Mazza, M., & Snyder, L. B. (1993). Agenda-setting effects of television news coverage and the effects decay curve. *Communication Research, 20*, 408–35.

Weaver, D. H. (1977). Political issues and voter need for orientation. In D. L. Shaw & M. E. McCombs (Eds.), *The emergence of American public issues: The agenda setting function of the press* (107–19). St. Paul, Minn.: West.

Weaver, D. H., Graber, D. A., McCombs, M. E., & Eyal, C. H. (1981). *Media agenda setting in a presidential election: Issues, images and interest.* New York: Praeger.

Weaver, D. H., Zhu, J. H., & Willnat, L. (1992). The bridging function of interpersonal communication in media agenda-setting. *Journalism Quarterly, 69*, 856–67.

Williams, W. Jr., & Semlak, W. D. (1978). Structural effects of TV coverage on political agendas. *Journal of Communication, 28*, 114–19.

Winter, J. P. (1980). *Differential media-public agenda-setting effects for selected issues, 1948–1976.* Unpublished doctoral dissertation, Syracuse University: Syracuse, N.Y.

Winter, J. P. (1981). Contingent conditions in the agenda-setting process. In G. C. Wilhoit & H. deBock (Eds.), *Mass communication review yearbook 2.* Beverly Hills, Calif.: Sage.

Winter, J. P., & Eyal, C. H. (1981). Agenda-setting for the civil rights issue. *Public Opinion Quarterly, 45*, 376–83.

Yagade, A., & Dozier, D. M. (1990). The media agenda-setting effect of concrete versus abstract issues. *Journalism Quarterly, 67*, 3–10.

Zhu, J. H. (1992). Issue competition and attention distraction: A zero-sum theory of agenda-setting. *Journalism Quarterly, 69*, 825–36.

Zhu, J. H., Watt, J. H., Snyder, L. B., Yan, J., & Jiang, Y. (1993). Public issue priority formation: Media agenda-setting and social interaction. *Journal of Communication, 43*, 8–29.

Zucker, H. G. (1978). The variable nature of news media influence. In

B. D. Rubin (Ed.), *Communication yearbook 2* (225–45). New Brunswick, N.J.: Transaction.

6. NEW RHETORIC AND NEW SOCIAL MOVEMENTS

Aronowitz, S. (1992). *The politics of identity: Class, culture, social movements.* New York: Routledge.

Biesecker, B. (1989). "Rethinking the rhetorical situation from within the thematic of *différance.*" *Philosophy and Rhetoric, 22,* 110–30.

Black, E. (1970). "The second persona." *Quarterly Journal of Speech, 56,* 109–19.

Burke, K. (1969). *A rhetoric of motives.* Berkeley: University of California Press.

Campbell, G. (1963). *The Philosophy of Rhetoric.* (L. F. Bitzer, Ed.). Carbondale: Southern Illinois University Press.

Charland, M. (1987). Constitutive rhetoric: The case of the *Peuple Québécois. Quarterly Journal of Speech, 73,* 133–50.

Charland, M. (1991). Finding a horizon and telos: The challenge to critical rhetoric. *Quarterly Journal of Speech, 77,* 71–74.

Eder, K. (1985). The "new social movements": Moral crusades, political protest groups, or social movements? *Social Research, 52,* 663–716.

Ehrenreich, R. (1991, December). What are universities for? *Harper's, 283,* 57–61.

Gorgias. (1972). Encomium of Helen. (G. Kennedy, Trans.). In R. Sprague (Ed.), *The older sophists* (pp. 50–54). Columbia: South Carolina University Press.

Griffin, L. M. (1952). The rhetoric of historical movements. *Quarterly Journal of Speech, 38,* 184–88.

Griffin, L. M. (1980). On studying movements. *Central States Speech Journal, 31,* 225–32.

Gusfield, J. R. (1994). The reflexivity of social movements: Collective behavior and mass society theory revisited. In E. Larana, H. Johnston, & J. R. Gusfield (Eds.), *New Social Movements* (pp. 58–78). Philadelphia: Temple University Press.

Habermas, J. (1981). New social movements. *Telos, 49,* 33–37.

Hauser, G. A. (1972). Empiricism, description, and the new rhetoric. *Philosophy and Rhetoric, 5,* 24–44.

Hauser, G. A. (1995). Between philosophy and rhetoric: Interpositions within traditions. P*hilosophy and Rhetoric, 28,* iii–xvii.

Hauser, G. A., and Cushman, D. P. (1973). McKeon's philosophy of communication: The architectonic and interdisciplinary arts. *Philosophy and Rhetoric, 6,* 211–34.

Henry, D. (1989). Recalling the 1960s: The New Left and social movement critism. *Quarterly Journal of Speech, 75,* 97–112.

Henry, D., and Jensen, R. J. (1991). Social movement criticism and the renaissance of public address. *Communication Studies, 42,* 83–93.

Hipple, W. J. (1957). *The beautiful, the sublime, and the picturesque.* Carbondale: Southern Illinois University Press.

Howell, W. S. (1966). Renaissance rhetoric and modern rhetoric: A study in change. In D. C. Bryant (Ed.), *The rhetorical idiom* (pp. 53–70). New York: Russell & Russell.

Howell, W. S. (1967). John Locke and the new rhetoric. *Quarterly Journal of Speech, 53,* 319–33.

Hunt, S. A., Benford, R. D., and Snow, D. A. (1994). Identity fields: Framing processes and the social construction of movement identities. In E. Larana, H. Johnson, & J. R. Gusfield (Eds.), *New social movements* (pp. 185–208). Philadelphia: Temple University Press.

Johnston, H., Larana, E., and Gusfield, J. R. (1994). Identities, grievances, and new social movements. In E. Larana, H. Johnson, & J. R. Gusfield (Eds.), *New social movements* (pp. 3–35). Philadelphia: Temple University Press.

Letters. (1992, February). *Harper's, 284,* 4–5, 70–74, 78.

Letters. (1992, March) *Harper's, 284,* 4–5.

Lipset, S. M., & Schneider, W. (1987). *The confidence gap* (rev. ed.). Baltimore: Johns Hopkins University Press.

Lucas, S. (1980). Coming to terms with movement studies. *Central States Speech Journal, 31,* 255–66.

Lucas, S. (1988). The renaissance of American public address: Text and context in rhetorical criticism. *Quarterly Journal of Speech, 74,* 241–60.

Lukes, S. (1974). *Power: A radical view.* London: Macmillan.

McGee, M. (1980). "Social movement": Phenomenon or meaning? *Central States Speech Journal, 31*, 233–44.

McKeon, R. (1957). Communication, truth, and society. *Ethics, 67*, 89–99.

McKeon, R. (1971). The uses of rhetoric in a technological age: Architectonic productive arts. In L. F. Bitzer & E. Black (Eds.), *The prospect of rhetoric*. Englewood Cliffs, N.J.: Prentice Hall.

Melucci, A. (1985). The symbolic challenge of contemporary movements. *Social Research, 52*, 789–816.

Melucci, A. (1989). *Nomads of the present: Social movements and individual needs in contemporary society*. Philadelphia: Temple University Press.

Melucci, A. (1994). A strange kind of newness: What's "new" in new social movements? In E. Larana, H. Johnston, & J. R. Gusfield (Eds.), *New social movements* (pp. 101–30). Philadelphia: Temple University Press.

Menand, L. (1991, December). What are universities for? *Harper's, 283*, 62–72.

Nietzsche, F. (1990). On truth and lies in a nonmoral sense. In P. Bizzell & B. Herzberg (Eds.), *The rhetorical tradition* (pp. 888–96). Boston: Bedford Books of St. Martin's Press.

Offe, C. (1985). New social movements: Challenging boundaries of institutional politics. *Social Research, 52*, 817–68.

Olson, K. M., & Goodnight, G. T. (1994). Entanglements of consumption, cruelty, privacy, and fashion: The social controversy over fur. *Quarterly Journal of Speech, 80*, 249–76.

Palmer, B. D. (1990). *Descent into discourse: The reification of language and the writing of social history*. Philadephia: Temple University Press.

Perelman, C., & Olbrechts-Tyteca, L. (1969). *The new rhetoric*. (J. Wilkinson & P. Weaver, Trans.). Notre Dame, Ind.: Notre Dame University Press.

Riches, S. V., and Sillars, M. O. (1980). The status of movement criticism. *Western Journal of Speech Communication, 44*, 275–87.

Rieff, D. (1993, August). Multiculturalism's silent partner. *Harper's, 285*, 62–72.

Riesman, D., Denney, R., & Glazer, N. (1961). *The lonely crowd*. New Haven, Conn.: Yale University Press.

Simons, H. W., Mechling, E. W., & Schreier, H. N. (1980). On terms, definitions and theoretical distinctiveness: Comments on papers by McGee and Zarefsky. *Central States Speech Journal, 31*, 306–15.

Simons, H. W., Mechling, E. W., & Schreier, H. N. (1984). The functions of human communication in mobilizing for action from the bottom up: The rhetoric of social movements. In C. C. Arnold & J. W. Bowers (Eds.), *Handbook of rhetorical and communication theory* (pp. 792–867). Boston: Allyn & Bacon.

Simons, H. W., Mechling, E. W., & Schreier, H. N. (1991). On the rhetoric of social movements, historical movements, and "top-down" movements: A commentary. *Communication Studies, 42*, 94–101.

Taylor, C. (1971). Interpretation and the science of man. *Review of Metaphysics, 25*, 3– 51.

Taylor, V., & Whittier, N. (1992). Collective identity in social movement communities: Lesbian feminist mobilization. In A. D. Morris & C. Mc-Clurg Mueller (Eds.), *Frontiers in social movement theory* (pp. 104–29). New Haven, Conn.: Yale University Press.

Touraine, A. (1981). *The voice and the eye: An analysis of social movements.* New York: Cambridge University Press.

Touraine, A. (1988). *Return of the actor: Social theory in postindustrial society.* Minneapolis: University of Minnesota Press.

Vico, G. (1990). On the study methods of our time. In P. Bizzell & B. Herzberg (Eds.), *The rhetorical tradition* (pp. 888–96). Boston: Bedford Books of St. Martin's Press.

Zarefsky, D. (1980). A skeptical view of movement studies. *Central States Speech Journal, 31*, 245–54.

7. MANAGING GOVERNMENT COMPETITIVENESS

Cullen, R. B. (1995). Public sector performance and private sector management. In D. Cushman & S. King (Eds.), *Communicating organizational change: A management perspective* (pp. 147–59). Albany: State University of New York Press.

Ohmae, K. (1994). *The boarderless world: Power and strategy in the interlinked economy.* London: HarperCollins.

Osborne, D., & Gaebler, T. (1993). *Reinventing government: How the entrepreneurial spirit is transforming the public sector.* Harmondsworth, England: Penguin Books.

Peters, T. (1993). *Liberation management: Necessary disorganization for the nanosecond nineties.* London: Pan Books.

World Economic Forum. (1994). *The World Competiveness Report 1994* (14th ed.). Geneva, Switzerland: World Economic Forum.

8. A PLURALISTIC VIEW OF THE EMERGING
THEORIES OF HUMAN COMMUNICATION

Alexander, J. C. (1987). *Twenty lectures: Sociological theory since World War II.* New York: Columbia University Press.

Brown, R. B. (1992). *Society as text: Essays on rhetoric, reason, and reality.* Chicago: University of Chicago Press.

Cushman, D. P., & Kovacic, B. (1994). Human communication: A rules perspective. In F. L. Casmir (Ed.), *Building communication theories: A socio/cutural approach* (pp. 269–95). Hillsdale, N.J.: Lawrence Erlbaum.

Cushman, D. P., & Kovačić, B. (Eds.). (1995). *Watershed research traditions in human communication theory.* Albany: State University of New York Press.

Deetz, S. (1992). *Democracy in an age of corporate colonization: Developments in communication and the politics of everyday life.* Albany: State University of New York Press.

Fitch, F. B. (1966). Natural deduction rules for obligation. *American Philosophical Quarterly, 3,* 27–38.

Kovačić, B. (1994). New perspectives on organizational communication. In B. Kovačić (Ed.), *New approaches to organizational communication* (pp. 1–37). Albany: State University of New York Press.

Kripke, S. A. (1959). A completeness theorem in modal logic. *Journal of Symbolic Logic, 24,* 1–14.

Lewis, D. (1983). *Philosophical papers* (vol. 1). Oxford: Oxford University Press.

Lewis, D. (1985). *On the plurality of worlds.* Oxford: Blackwell.

Lewis, D. (1986). *Philosophical papers* (vol. 2). Oxford: Oxford University Press.

Lyotard, J. F. (1984). *The postmodern condition: A report on knowledge.* Minneapolis: University of Minnesota Press.

Mead, G. H. (1932). *The philosophy of the present* (A. E. Murphy, Ed.). Chicago: Open Court.

Nolt, J. E. (1984). *Informal logic: Possible worlds and imagination.* New York: McGraw-Hill.

Rescher, N. (1966). Practical reasoning and values. *Philosophical Quarterly, 16,* 38 – 49.

Seidman, S. (1994). The end of sociological theory. In S. Seidman (Ed.), *The postmodern turn: New perspectives on sociological theory* (pp. 119–39). New York: Cambridge University Press.

Sigman, S. J. (Ed.). (1995) *The consequentiality of communication.* Hillsdale, N.J.: Lawrence Erlbaum.

Stinchcombe, A. L. (1968). *Constructing social theories.* New York: Harcourt, Brace & World.

von Wright, G. H. (1951). Deontic logic. *Mind, 60,* 1–15.

von Wright, G. H. (1963). *The logic of preference.* Edinburgh: Edinburgh University press.

von Wright, G. H. (1971). *Explanation and understanding.* Ithaca, N.Y.: Cornell University Press.

About the Contributors

Deborah Blood, has a Ph.D. in communication sciences from the University of Connecticut. She wrote a dissertation on "Economic news headlines, consumer confidence, the state of the economy, and Presidential popularity."

Dudley D. Cahn is professor of communications at the State University of New York at New Paltz. A Fulbright scholar, he has published six books and numerous journal articles on interpersonal communication and conflict. He edits the SUNY Press series in speech communication.

Donal Carbaugh is professor of communication and faculty affiliate in American studies at the University of Massachusetts, Amherst. His primary research is devoted to creating a communication theory of meaning and culture. His work has appeared in more than twenty journals and in several languages. His books include *Situating Selves* (SUNY Press), *Cultural Communication and Intercultural Contact,* and *Talking American.*

Ron B. Cullen is CEO of Performance Management Solutions, a consulting firm based in Australia. He has served as director of finance for Australia Telecommunications, has headed the public service and higher education coordination agencies in Victoria, and has been a consultant or manager for many public sector change projects. He has published articles on public administration and has led government reviews of programs and agencies.

Donald P. Cushman is professor emeritus of communication at the University at Albany, State University of New York. He has authored or co-authored more than 120 book chapters or journal articles and has written, co-written, or edited ten books, including *High-Speed Management: Organizational Communication in the Twenty-first Century* (with Sarah S. King, SUNY Press, 1995). He is co-editor of the SUNY Press series on human communication processes.

WILLIAM A. DONOHUE is professor of communication at Michigan State University. He has published three books on conflict, communication, and negotiation and mediation, including *Interpersonal Conflict* (1992) and *Communication, Marital Dispute, and Divorce Mediation* (1992), a research-based guide for mediators.

TIMOTHY A. GIBSON is a doctoral student in communication at Simon Fraser University, Canada. His interests include cultural studies of verbal and visual media in particular social settings.

GERARD A. HAUSER is professor of communication and of comparative literature at the University of Colorado at Boulder. He has published numerous articles and reviews on rhetorical theory and criticism, and is the author of *Introduction to Rhetorical Theory* (1986). His research focuses on political rhetoric with respect to theoretical features of the public sphere. He has served on the editorial boards of several scholarly journals, and has co-edited *Philosophy and Rhetoric*. He has been on the faculty at Penn State University, as well as an Eastern Communication Association visiting scholar and an Excellence visiting professor at Temple University.

BRANISLAV KOVAČIĆ is associate professor of communication at the University of Hartford, Connecticut. A former journalist and magazine editor in Yugoslavia, he edited and contributed to *New Approaches to Organizational Communication* (SUNY Press, 1994), and co-edited and contributed to *Watershed Research Traditions in Human Communication Theory* (with Donald P. Cushman, SUNY Press, 1995). His current projects include books on benchmarking and organizational communication, communication and transformations in the public sector, and communication crisis management (with Thomas Florence).

TRUDY MILBURN is a doctoral candidate in communication at the University of Massachusetts, Amherst. Her interests include explorations of identity as a communicative accomplishment, with special attention to cross-cultural analyses.

HIROSHI OTA is a graduate student in communication at the University of California, Santa Barbara. His research focuses on international students' adaptation, intercultural communication competence, and intergroup communication. For the past three years he has conducted research across nations in the Pacific Rim on the communication effects of young adults' perceptions of the elderly.

JIRO TAKAI is associate professor of psychology at Nagoya City University in Japan, and a doctoral student in communication at the University of California, Santa Barbara. His research centers on the cultural implications of interpersonal competence. His work has been published in *The International Journal of Intercultural Relations, Japanese Journal of Experimental Social Psychology,* and *Japanese Journal of Interpersonal Behavior.*

Susan Whalen is oral historian in residence at the Archives, University of Colorado at Boulder. She has co-authored book chapters and journal articles on rhetoric, social theory, and the contemporary labor movement. She is currently managing an extensive oral history project on Soviet Jewish prisoners-of-conscience and *refuseniks,* with respect to freedom of movement and expression.

John M. Wiemann is vice chancellor for institutional advancement, and professor of communication and Asian American studies, at the University of California, Santa Barbara. He has co-edited the Sage *Annual Reviews of Communication Research,* as well as special issues of *Communication Research* and *American Behavioral Scientist.* His most recent book is *Competent Communication* (with D. O'Hair, G. Friedrich, and M. Wiemann). He has been a W. K. Kellog Foundation national fellow and a Fulbright-Hays senior research scholar at the University of Bristol, England.

Mary O. Wiemann is assistant professor and chairperson of the Department of Communication at Santa Barbara City College, in California. She is co-author of *Competent Communication* (with D. O'Hair, G. Friedrich, and J. Wiemann) and author of several student and instructor manuals on interpersonal and nonverbal communication.

Jian-Hua Zhu is associate professor of communication sciences at the University of Connecticut. His research focuses on mass media and public opinion, journalistic professionalism, and political participation in socialist societies. His work has been published in *Journal of Communication, Human Communication Research, International Journal of Communication, Journalism Monographs, Journalism Quarterly, Gazette,* and *Asian Journal of Communication.*

Index